DAVID M. KENNEDY
Stanford University

LIZABETH COHEN
Harvard University

THOMAS A. BAILEY

MEL PIEHL
Valparaiso University

The Brief
American Pageant

FIFTH EDITION

Guidebook

A Manual for Students

MEL PIEHL
Valparaiso University

HOUGHTON MIFFLIN COMPANY
Boston   New York

Sponsoring Editor: Colleen Shanley Kyle
Editorial Assistant: Michael Kerns
Senior Manufacturing Coordinator: Marie Barnes
Senior Marketing Manager: Sandra McGuire

Printed in the U.S.A.

ISBN: 0-395-97869-6

3 4 5 6 7 8 9 - CRS - 03 02

Contents

To the Student

This Guidebook is intended to assist you in comprehending American history as presented in *The Brief American Pageant,* Fifth Edition, by Thomas A. Bailey, David M. Kennedy, Lizabeth Cohen, and Mel Piehl. The *Guidebook* focuses attention on the central themes and major historical developments of each chapter, while presenting a variety of exercises and other material designed to reinforce your comprehension of the text. Factual knowledge of history is important, and some of the exercises will help you to review facts and recall their significance. but the *Guidebook* attempts to demonstrate that facts are best learned when they are understood in relation to key historical events and issues.

The forty-two chapters of the *Guidebook* correspond with those of *The Brief American Pageant* and are best used in close association with the text. Each chapter of the *Guidebook* contains the same sequence of material and exercises, though sometimes of varying length.

The **Checklist of Learning Objectives** in Part I ("Reviewing the Chapter") of each *Guidebook* chapter provides a summary of the essential chapter themes and underscores the major historical developments to be learned. The **Glossary** defines basic social science terms and shows their usage in the text. Learning this vocabulary will not only reinforce your understanding of *The Brief American Pageant* but also familiarize you with terms often encountered in the study of politics, economics, geography, military science, and law, as well as history.

The various exercises in Part II ("Checking Your Progress") will assist in your careful reading of the text as well as foster your comprehension and spotlight the essential facts and concepts. **True-False, Multiple Choice,** and **Identification** exercises stress reading for understanding of important ideas and terms. **Matching People, Places, and Events** checks your knowledge of key historical figures, locations, and events. **Putting Things in Order** (which is specifically tied to the Chronology section at the end of each chapter of *The Brief American Pageant*) develops an essential principle of historical understanding: chronological sequence.

Completion of the exercises in Part II should enable you to handle successfully the crucial questions in Part III ("Applying What You Have Learned"). Your instructor may suggest that you use these questions as guides to study and review or may assign them as essay questions to be answered following your reading of the chapter. The last question, number 5, is an especially challenging one that often draws on earlier chapters of *The Brief American Pageant* and asks you to make historical comparisons, draw conclusions, or consider broad historical issues.

Hence you and your instructor may utilize the *Guidebook* in a variety of ways, to suit a variety of needs. It can be used for class preparation and assignments, for guidance in your reading of the text, or for independent review of course content. The answers to all the exercises, except the questions in Part III, may be found in the back of this *Guidebook* or by carefully rereading the pertinent sections of *The Brief American Pageant*. May your exploration of American history be stimulating and enriching.

M.P.

1

★★★★★★★★★

New World Beginnings,

33,000 B.C.–A.D. 1769

PART I: Reviewing the Chapter

A. Checklist of Learning Objectives

After mastering this chapter, you should be able to

1. describe the basic geological and geographical conditions that set the stage for North American history.
2. describe the origins and development of the major Native American cultures of the Americas.
3. explain the social and cultural developments that made possible Columbus's voyage to America.
4. explain the changes and conflicts that happened when the diverse worlds of Europe, Africa, and the Americas encountered one another after 1492.
5. describe the Spanish conquest of Mexico and South America, and indicate the major features of Spanish colonization and expansion in North America.

B. Glossary

To build your social science vocabulary, familiarize yourself with the following terms.

1. **nation-state** The modern form of political society that combines centralized government with a high degree of ethnic and cultural unity. ". . . the closest North American approximation to the great nation-states of Mexico and Peru." (p. 8)
2. **matrilinear** The form of society in which power, possessions, and family descent are passed primarily through the female side. ". . . many North American native peoples, including the Iroquois, developed matrilinear cultures. . . ." (p. 9)
3. **primeval** Having to do with the earliest origins of things. ". . . the whispering, primeval forests . . . (p. 9)
4. **saga** A lengthy story or poem recounting the great deeds and adventures of a people and its heroes. ". . . their discovery was forgotten, except in Scandinavian saga and song." (p. 9)
5. **middlemen** In trading systems, those dealers who stand between original buyers and retail sellers to consumers. ". . . for which Muslim and Italian middlemen charged dearly. . . ." (p. 10)
6. **plantation** A large-scale agricultural enterprise, growing commercial crops and usually employing coerced or slave labor. ". . . contained the origins of the modern plantation. . . ." (p. 10)

7. **ecosystem** A naturally evolved network of relations among organisms in a stable environment. "Two ecosystems . . . commingled and clashed when Columbus waded ashore." (p. 11)

8. **demographic** Concerning the large characteristics of an entire population, including such factors as numbers, age, gender, birthrates, death rates, and so on. ". . . a demographic catastrophe without parallel in human history." (p. 13)

9. **conquistador** A Spanish conqueror or adventurer in the Americas. "Spanish *conquistadores* . . . fanned out across the Caribbean. . . ." (p. 14)

10. **capitalism** An economic system characterized by private property, generally free trade, and open markets. ". . . the fuel that fed the growth of the economic system known as capitalism." (p. 14)

11. **mestizo** A person of mixed Native American and European ancestry. "He intermarried with the surviving Mexicans, creating a distinctive culture of mestizos. . . ." (p. 15)

12. **province** A medium-sized subunit of territory and governmental administration within a larger nation or empire. "The Spaniards proclaimed the area to be the province of New Mexico. . . ." (p. 16)

PART II: Checking Your Progress

A. True-False

Where the statement is true, mark **T**. Where it is false, mark **F**, and correct it in the space immediately below.

T
1. The geography of the North American continent was fundamentally shaped by the glaciers of the Great Ice Age.

____
2. North America was first settled by people who came by boat across the waters of the Bering Strait from Siberia to Alaska.

____
3. The early Indian civilizations of Mexico and Peru were built on the economic foundations of cattle and wheat growing.

____
4. The most "urban" Indian societies of North America were in the Southwest and the Mississippi and Ohio River valleys.

____
5. The Iroquois culture passed power and possessions through the female line.

____
6. No Europeans had ever set foot on the American continents prior to Columbus's arrival in 1492.

____
7. A primary motive for the European voyages of discovery was the desire to find a less expensive route to Asian goods and markets.

____
8. The beginnings of African slavery developed in response to the Spanish conquest of the Americas.

____
9. Columbus immediately recognized in 1492 that he had come across new continents previously unknown to Europeans.

____
10. The greatest effect on the Indians of the European intrusion was to increase their population through intermarriage with the whites.

____
11. Cortés exploited unrest within the Aztec empire to achieve his conquest of Tenochtitlan.

____ 12. The Spanish completely annihilated the Indians of Mexico and Central America and replaced them with African slave labor.

____ 13. The province of New Mexico was first settled by French colonizers from the North.

____ 14. The original motive for the Spanish colonization of California was conversion of the Indians to Christianity.

____ 15. The Spanish empire in the New World was larger, richer, and longer lasting than that of the English.

B. Multiple Choice

Select the best answer and put the proper letter in the space provided.

____ 1. The geologically oldest mountains in North America are
   a. the Appalachians.
   b. the Rockies.
   c. the Cascades.
   d. the Sierra Nevada.

____ 2. The Native American peoples of the New World
   a. developed no advanced forms of civilization.
   b. were divided into many diverse cultures speaking over 2,000 different languages.
   c. were all organized into the two large empires of the Incas and the Aztecs.
   d. relied primarily on nomadic herding of domesticated animals for their sustenance.

____ 3. The most politically powerful Indian nation of North America was
   a. the Creek.
   b. the Pueblo.
   c. the Cherokee.
   d. the Iroquois.

____ 4. One important influence that first stimulated European interest in trade and discovery was
   a. the Christian crusaders who brought back a taste for the silks and spices of Asia.
   b. the Arab slave traders on the east coast of Africa.
   c. the Scandinavian sailors who had maintained continuing trade contacts with North America.
   d. the division of Spain into small kingdoms competing for wealth and power.

____ 5. The most important Native American products to spread to the Old World were
   a. animals such as buffalo and horses.
   b. technologies such as the compass and the wheel.
   c. economic systems such as plantation agriculture.
   d. foodstuffs such as maize, beans, and tomatoes.

6. A crucial political development that paved the way for the European colonization of America was

    a. the rise of Italian city-states like Venice and Genoa.
    b. the feudal nobles' political domination of the merchant class.
    c. the rise of centralized national monarchies such as that of Spain.
    d. the political alliance between the papacy and Muslim traders.

7. The primary reason for the drastic decline in the Native American population after the encounter with the Europeans was

    a. the rise of intertribal warfare.
    b. the Native Americans' lack of resistance to European diseases such as smallpox and malaria.
    c. the sharp decline in the Native Americans' birthrate.
    d. the sudden introduction of the deadly disease syphilis to the New World.

8. Cortés and his men were able to conquer the Aztec capital Tenochtitlan partly because

    a. they had larger forces than the Aztecs.
    b. the Aztec ruler Montezuma believed that Cortés was a god whose return had been predicted.
    c. the Aztecs were peace-loving people who did not believe in war or conquest.
    d. the city of Tenochtitlan had already been devastated by a disease epidemic.

9. The primary centers of Spain's New World empire were

    a. Cuba and Puerto Rico.
    b. Mexico and Peru.
    c. Florida and Panama.
    d. New Mexico and California.

10. The myth that the Spanish only killed, tortured, and stole while doing no good is called

    a. the *malinchista.*
    b. the mission of civilization.
    c. the Black Legend.
    d. the Evil Empire.

C. Identification

Supply the correct identification for each numbered description.

Great Ice Age   1. The extended period when glaciers covered most of the North American continent

Cahokia   2. Site of the large Mississippian culture settlement near East St. Louis, Illinois

Newfoundland   3. Probable location of brief Norse visitation to North America about A.D. 1000

Portugal   4. The first European nation to send explorers around the west coast of Africa

Mali   5. The West African kingdom that developed a flourishing Islamic university at Timbuktu

Indies   6. The mistaken term European explorers gave to American lands in the belief that they were "islands" off the coast of Asia

horse   7. The animal introduced to the Americas by Europeans that transformed the Indian way of life on the Great Plains

syphilis   8. The sexually transmitted disease originating in America that was given to Europeans after 1492

Treaty of Tordesillas   9. The treaty that secured Spanish title to lands in America by dividing them with Portugal

Tenochtitlan   10. The wealthy capital of the Aztec empire

mestiozo   11. A person of mixed European and Indian ancestry

Dia de la Raza   12. Mexican holiday honoring the "birthday" of the nation's unique people

_____   13. An Indian uprising in New Mexico caused by Spanish efforts to suppress Indian religion

Pueblos   14. The Native American people of the Rio Grande Valley who were cruelly oppressed by the Spanish conquerors

Franciscans   15. The Roman Catholic religious order of friars that organized a chain of missions in California

D. Matching People, Places, and Events

Match the person, place, or event in the left column with the proper description in the right column by inserting the correct letter on the blank line.

_D_   1. Ferdinand and Isabella

___   2. Cortés and Pizarro

___   3. Lake Bonneville

___   4. Diaz and da Gama

___   5. Columbus

___   6. Malinche

___   7. Montezuma

___   8. Hiawatha

___   9. Tenochtitlan

___   10. St. Augustine

A. Female Indian slave who served as interpreter for Cortés
B. Legendary founder of the Iroquois Confederacy
C. Wealthy capital of the Aztec empire
D. Financiers and beneficiaries of Columbus's voyages to the New World
E. Portuguese navigators who sailed around the African coast
F. The oldest continually inhabited European settlement in United States territory, founded in 1565
G. Italian-born navigator sent by English king to explore North American coast in 1498
H. Italian-born explorer who reached unknown continents but thought he had arrived off the coast of Asia
I. Powerful Aztec emperor who fell to Spanish conquerors
J. Spanish conquerors of great Indian civilizations
K. Franciscan missionary who settled California
L. Inland sea, left by melting glaciers, whose remnant is the Great Salt Lake

___ 11. John Cabot

___ 12. Junipero Serra

E. Putting Things in Order

Put the following events in correct order by numbering them from 1 to 5.

___ The wealthy Aztec civilization falls to Cortés.

___ Portuguese navigators sail down the west coast of Africa.

___ The first human inhabitants cross into North America from Siberia across a temporary land bridge.

___ Spanish Franciscan missionaries colonize California.

___ The Spanish conquerors move into the Rio Grande Valley of New Mexico.

PART III: Applying What You Have Learned*

1. How did the geographic setting of North America—including its relation to Asia, Europe, and Africa—affect its subsequent history?
2. What were the characteristics common to all Indian cultures in the New World, and what were the important differences between them?
3. What were the fundamental factors that drew the Europeans to their exploration, conquest, and settlement?
4. What was the impact on the Indians, Europeans, and Africans when their previously separate worlds "collided" with one another?
5. In what ways did Columbus's encounter with the New World lay the foundation for the future civilizations of Latin America?

---

*Space is provided at the end of each chapter for answering the essay questions. Students needing more room should answer on separate sheets of paper.

2

★★★★★★★★

The Planting of English America,

1500–1755

PART I: Reviewing the Chapter

A. Checklist of Learning Objectives

After mastering this chapter, you should be able to
1. list the factors that led the English into their late start on colonization.
2. describe the development of the Jamestown colony from its disastrous beginnings to its later prosperity.
3. describe the role of Indians and African slaves in the early history of England's southern colonies.
4. describe the similarities and differences among the southern colonies of Virginia, Maryland, the Carolinas, and Georgia.

B. Glossary

To build your social science vocabulary, familiarize yourself with the following terms.
1. **nationalism** Fervent belief in and loyalty toward the political unit of the nation-state. ". . . a vibrant sense of nationalism. . . ." (p. 21)
2. **primogeniture** The legal principle that the oldest son inherits all property or land. ". . . laws of primogeniture decreed that only eldest sons were eligible to inherit landed estates." (p. 21)
3. **joint-stock companies** An economic arrangement for a number of investors to pool investment capital. "Joint-stock companies provided the financial means." (p. 21)
4. **charter** A legal document granted by a government to some group or agency for a specific purpose that spells out the attending rights and obligations. "The Virginia Company of London received a charter from King James I of England. . . ." (p. 21)
5. **feudal** Concerning the decentralized medieval social system of personal obligation between ruler and ruled. ". . . would be the vanguard of a vast new feudal domain." (p. 24)
6. **indentured servant** A poor person obligated to a fixed term of labor. ". . . it depended for labor in its early years mainly on white indentured servants. . . ." (p. 24)
7. **toleration** Originally, religious freedom granted by an established church to a religious minority. "This statute guaranteed toleration to all Christians. . . . " (p. 24)
8. **slave code** The laws defining slavery and governing its practice. "The notorious Barbados slave code of 1661. . . ." (p. 25)

9. **squatte** A frontier farmer who illegally occupied land owned by others or not yet officially opened for settlement. "These small farmers, who were often 'squatters'. . . ." (p. 25)
10. **melting pot** A term for an ethnically diverse population, which is presumed to be "melting" toward some eventual unity. "The hamlet of Savannah, like Charleston, was a melting-pot community. . . . (p. 28)

PART II: Checking Your Progress

A. True-False

Where the statement is true, mark **T.** Where it is false, mark **F,** and correct it in the space immediately below.

____ 1. Protestant England's early colonial ambitions were fueled by its rivalry with Catholic Spain.

____ 2. The earliest English colonization efforts experienced surprising success.

____ 3. The defeat of the Spanish Armada was important to North American colonization because it enabled England to conquer Spain's New World empire.

____ 4. Among the English citizens most attracted to the colonies were unemployed yeomen and the younger sons of the gentry.

____ 5. The defeat of Powhatan's Indian forces in Virginia was achieved partly by Lord de la Warr's use of brutal "Irish tactics."

____ 6. Originally, the primary purpose of the joint-stock Virginia Company was to provide for the well-being of the freeborn English settlers in the colony.

____ 7. John Rolfe enabled the Virginia colony to survive by introducing African slave labor in 1619.

____ 8. The Maryland colony was founded in part to establish religious freedom for Quakers.

____ 9. From the time of its founding, South Carolina had close economic ties with the British West Indies.

____ 10. Sugar was considered a "poor man's crop" that could be grown by individual farmers on smaller plots of land.

____ 11. By about 1720, the Indians of the Carolina coast had been defeated and nearly annihilated.

____ 12. In their early years, neither North Carolina nor Georgia relied very much on slave labor.

____ 13. Compared with its neighbors Virginia and South Carolina, North Carolina was more democratic and independent-minded.

____ 14. England valued the Georgia colony primarily as a rich source of gold and timber.

____ 15. All the southern colonies relied on staple-crop plantation agriculture for their economic well-being.

B. Multiple Choice

Select the best answer and put the proper letter in the space provided.

___   1. The pattern for England's treatment of "natives" in the New World was largely established by its experience of war and conquest in

   a. Germany.
   b. Ireland.
   c. Scotland.
   d. Africa.

___   2. At the time of the first colonization efforts, England

   a. was struggling under the political domination of Spain.
   b. was enjoying a period of social and economic stability.
   c. was undergoing rapid economic and social transformations.
   d. was undergoing sharp political conflicts between the "sea dogs" and the monarchy of Elizabeth I.

___   3. England's first colony at Jamestown

   a. was an immediate economic success.
   b. was saved from failure by the political leadership of John Smith and the agricultural efforts of John Rolfe.
   c. enjoyed the strong and continual support of King James I.
   d. depended on the introduction of African slave labor for its survival.

___   4. Representative government was first introduced to America in the colony of

   a. Virginia.
   b. Maryland.
   c. North Carolina.
   d. Georgia.

___   5. One important difference between the founding of the Virginia and Maryland colonies was that

   a. Virginia colonists were willing to come only if they could acquire their own land, while Maryland colonists labored for their landlords.
   b. Virginia depended primarily on its tobacco economy, while Maryland turned to rice cultivation.
   c. Virginia depended on African slave labor, while Maryland relied mainly on white indentured servitude.
   d. Virginia was founded mainly as an economic venture, while Maryland was intended partly to secure religious freedom for persecuted Roman Catholics.

___   6. Maryland's Act of Toleration in 1649 provided religious freedom for

   a. people of any religious belief.
   b. atheists.
   c. Christians but not those of other faiths.
   d. indentured servants.

7. The primary reason that no new colonies were founded between 1634 and 1670 was

    a. the severe economic conditions in Virginia and Maryland, which discouraged colonizers.
    b. the civil war in England.
    c. the continual naval conflicts between Spain and England that disrupted sea lanes.
    d. the English kings' increasing hostility to colonial ventures.

8. All of England's southern colonies

    a. practiced slavery from their first beginnings.
    b. relied on staple-crop plantation agriculture.
    c. strongly persecuted religious dissenters.
    d. quickly established fine churches and schools.

9. The early conflicts between the English settlers and the Indians near Jamestown laid the basis for

    a. the intermarriage of white settlers and Indians.
    b. the incorporation of Indians into the "melting pot" of American culture.
    c. the forced movement of Indians into the separate territory of the "reservation system."
    d. the use of Indians as a slave labor force on white plantations.

10. The labor system of the West Indies sugar plantations relied almost entirely on

    a. the importation of African slaves.
    b. indentured white servants.
    c. the *encomienda* system.
    d. temporary hired workers from the mainland colonies.

11. After the defeat of the coastal Tuscarora and Yamasee Indians by North and South Carolinians from 1711 to 1715

    a. there were very few Indians left east of the Mississippi River.
    b. the remaining southeastern Indian tribes united to wage continual warfare against the whites.
    c. the powerful Creek, Cherokee, and Iroquois remained in the Appalachian Mountains as a barrier against white settlement.
    d. the numerous coastal Indians were confined on reservations in North Carolina and Georgia.

C. Identification

Supply the correct identification for each numbered description.

Ireland 1. Catholic nation whose rivalry with Protestant England fueled colonial ambitions

Roanoke 2. Colony founded by Sir Walter Raleigh that mysteriously disappeared in the 1580s

wool 3. Primary product of the eastern and western English areas that supplied most early immigrants to North America

Joint-stock co 4. Forerunner of the modern corporation that enabled investors to pool financial capital for colonial ventures

Anglo-Powhatan wars 5. Term for two wars, fought in 1614 and 1644 between the English in Jamestown and the nearby Indian leader

Barbados-slave code 6. The harsh system of Barbados laws governing African labor, officially adopted by South Carolina in 1696

Royal Charter 7. Royal document granting a specified group the right to form a colony and guaranteeing settlers their rights as English citizens

Indentured servants 8. Penniless people obligated to work for a fixed number of years, often in exchange for passage to the New World

Act of toleration 9. Maryland statute of 1649 that granted religious freedom to all Christians, but not to Jews and atheists

Squatters 10. Poor farmers in North Carolina and elsewhere who occupied land and raised crops without gaining title to the soil

Royal colony 11. A colony under direct control of the English crown

Tobacco 12. The primary staple crop of early Virginia, Maryland, and North Carolina

Georgia 13. The southern colony not settled until the eighteenth century

D. Matching People, Places, and Events

Match the person, place, or event in the left column with the proper description in the right column by inserting the correct letter on the blank line.

B 1. Powhatan

M 2. Walter Raleigh and Humphrey Gilbert

I 3. Roanoke

L 4. John Smith and John Rolfe

K 5. Virginia

A 6. Maryland

C 7. Lord de la Warr

D 8. Jamaica and Barbados

A. Colony founded as a haven for Roman Catholics
B. Indian leader who ruled tribes in the James River area of Virginia
C. Harsh military governor of Virginia who employed "Irish tactics" against the Indians
D. British West Indian sugar colonies where large-scale plantations developed and slavery took root
E. Colony founded as a refuge for debtors and a military buffer
F. Colony called "a vale of humility between two mountains of conceit"
G. The unmarried ruler who led England to national glory
H. The Catholic aristocrat who sought to build a sanctuary for his fellow believers
I. The failed "lost colony" founded by Sir Walter Raleigh
J. Riverbank site where Virginia Company settlers planted the first permanent English colony

K 9. Lord Baltimore

O 10. South Carolina

F 11. North Carolina

E 12. Georgia

N 13. James Oglethorpe

G 14. Elizabeth I

J 15. Jamestown

K. Tobacco colony where wealthy planters and poor whites clashed during Bacon's Rebellion

L. Leaders who rescued Jamestown colonists from the "starving time"

M. Elizabethan courtiers who failed in their attempts to found New World colonies

N. Philanthropic soldier-statesman who founded the Georgia colony

O. Colony that turned to disease-resistant African slaves for labor in its extensive rice plantations

E. Putting Things in Order

Put the following events in correct order by numbering them from 1 to 5.

1 A surprising naval victory by the English inspires a burst of national pride and paves the way for colonization.

3 A Catholic aristocrat founds a colony as a haven for his fellow believers.

4 Settlers from the West Indies found a colony on the North American mainland.

5 An English colony is founded by philanthropists as a haven for imprisoned debtors.

2 A company of investors launches a disaster-stricken but permanent English colony along a mosquito-infested river.

PART III: Applying What You Have Learned

1. What factors contributed to England's establishment of its first successful North American colonies?
2. What problems did the English have to overcome before their North American colonies could be established on a permanent and successful basis?
3. What features were common to all of England's southern colonies, and what characteristics were peculiar to each one?
4. Discuss similarities and differences in the colonizing experiences of Spain and England, including differences in their relations with Indian peoples.
5. What were the original goals of English colonization in North America? In what ways did they succeed or fail? How did the colonies develop quite differently than expected?

3
★★★★★★★★

Settling the Northern Colonies,

1619–1700

PART I: Reviewing the Chapter

A. Checklist of Learning Objectives

After mastering this chapter, you should be able to

1. describe the Puritans and their beliefs and explain why they left England for the New World.
2. explain the basic governmental and religious practices of the Massachusetts Bay Colony.
3. explain how conflict with religious dissenters, among other forces, led to the expansion of New England.
4. describe the various attempts to create greater unity and tighter political control of England's northern colonies and explain why these attempts failed.
5. explain why New York, Pennsylvania, and the other middle colonies became so ethnically, religiously, and politically diverse.
6. describe the central features of the middle colonies and explain how they differed from New England.

B. Glossary

To build your social science vocabulary, familiarize yourself with the following terms.

1. **predestination** The Calvinist doctrine that God has foreordained some people to be saved and some to be damned. "Good works could not save those whom *predestination* had marked for the infernal fires." (p. 31)
2. **elect** In Calvinist doctrine, those who have been chosen by God for salvation. "But neither could the elect count on their determined salvation. . . ." (p. 31)
3. **conversion** A religious turn to God, thought by Calvinists to involve an intense, identifiable personal experience. "Those who had the intense personal experience of conversion. . . ." (p. 31)
4. **visible saints** In Calvinism, those who publicly proclaimed their experience of conversion and were expected to lead godly lives. "All Puritans agreed that only 'visible saints' should be admitted to church membership." (p. 31)
5. **calling** In Protestantism, the belief that saved individuals have a religious obligation to engage in worldly work. "Like John Winthrop, [the Puritans] believed in the doctrine of a 'calling' to do God's work on this earth." (p. 33)
6. **heresy** Departure from correct or officially defined belief. ". . . she eventually boasted that she had come by her beliefs through a direct revelation from God. This was even higher heresy." (p. 33)

7. **seditious** Concerning resistance to or rebellion against the government. "[His was] a seditious blow at the Puritan idea of government's very purpose." (p. 35)

8. **commonwealth** An organized civil government or social order. "They were allowed the colonies, in effect, to become semiautonomous commonwealths." (p. 37)

9. **despotic** Tyrannical or dictatorial rule. ". . . the able but despotic director-general. . . ." (p. 39)

10. **passive resistance** Nonviolent action or opposition to authority in accord with religious or moral beliefs. "As advocates of passive resistance, [the Quakers] would . . . rebuild their meetinghouse on the site where their enemies had torn it down." (p. 39)

11. **asylum** A place of refuge and security, especially for the persecuted or unfortunate. "Eager to establish an asylum for his people. . . ." (p. 39)

12. **naturalization** The granting of citizenship to foreigners or immigrants. "No restrictions were placed on immigration, and naturalization was made easy." (p. 40)

13. **ethnic** Concerning diverse peoples or cultures, specifically those of non-Anglo Saxon background. ". . . Pennsylvania attracted a rich mix of ethnic groups." (p. 40)

14. **blue laws** Laws designed to restrict personal behavior in accord with a strict code of morality. "Even so, there were some 'blue laws' aimed at 'ungodly revelers.' . . ." (p. 40)

15. **proprietor** A person to whom a colonial legal charter was granted. "One of the proprietors sold West New Jersey in 1674. . . ." (p. 41)

PART II: Checking Your Progress

A. True-False

Where the statement is true, mark **T**. Where it is false, mark **F**, and correct it in the space immediately below.

___ 1. The Puritans believed that the Church of England was corrupt because it did not restrict its membership to "visible saints" who had experienced conversion.

___ 2. All Puritans wanted to break away from the Church of England and establish a new "purified" church.

___ 3. The larger, more powerful Plymouth colony strongly influenced Puritan Massachusetts Bay.

___ 4. Massachusetts Bay restricted the vote for elections to the General Court to adult male members of the Congregational church—the "visible saints."

___ 5. Both Roger Williams and Anne Hutchinson were banished for organizing rebellions against the Massachusetts Bay authorities.

___ 6. Rhode Island was the most religiously and politically tolerant of the New England colonies.

___ 7. King Philip's War represented the last attempt of New England's Indians to halt the white advance on their lands.

___ 8. Edmund Andros's autocratic Dominion of New England was overthrown in connection with the Glorious Revolution in England.

9. England maintained tight political and economic control of the colonies throughout the seventeenth century.

0. New York became the most democratic and economically equal of the middle colonies.

!. Although politically authoritarian, New Netherland contained a population of diverse ethnic groups.

. William Penn intended his Pennsylvania colony to be an exclusive refuge for his fellow Quakers.

The middle colonies' broad, fertile river valleys enabled them to develop a richer agricultural economy than that of New England.

The middle colonies were more uniformly English in ethnic composition than either the southern colonies or the New England colonies.

The middle colonies were characterized by tightly knit communities and were dominated by a shared ense of religious purpose.

B. Mul   Choice

Select   st answer and put the proper letter in the space provided.

___   ιe Puritans all believed strongly that

    they should separate completely from the Church of England.
    only the elect of "visible saints" should be members of the church.
    ιuman beings were fundamentally good and capable of working out their own salvation.
    Ϗing Henry VIII and King James I had sufficiently reformed the Church of England.

___   ιpared with the Plymouth colony, the Massachusetts Bay colony was

    ιedicated to complete separation from the Church of England.
    'flicted with corrupt and incompetent leaders.
    ss focused on religious questions.
    'ger and more prosperous.

___   3.   ·eason that the Massachusetts Bay Colony was not a true democracy is that

    ly church members could vote for the governor and the General Court.
    ιtical offices could be held only by the clergy.
    ple were not permitted to discuss issues freely in their own towns.
    governor and his assistants were appointed rather than elected.

___   4. 1   ·st distinctive feature of the Rhode Island colony was that

    a.   ·oyed the most complete religious freedom of all the English colonies.
    b.   ·ured an official charter from England.
    c.   ·tained a high proportion of well-educated and well-off colonists.
    d.   a strong sense of unity because the colonists had a common sense of religious purpose.

_____ 5. The primary value of the New England Confederation lay in

    a. restoring harmony between Rhode Island and the other New England colonies.
    b. promoting better relations between New England colonists and their Indian neighbors.
    c. providing the first small step on the road to intercolonial cooperation.
    d. defending the colonial rights against increasing pressure from the English kings.

_____ 6. The event that sparked the collapse of the Dominion of New England was

    a. King Philip's War.
    b. the revocation of the Massachusetts Bay Colony's charter.
    c. Andros's harsh attacks on colonial liberties.
    d. the Glorious Revolution in England.

_____ 7. The Dutch colony of New Netherland

    a. was harshly and undemocratically governed.
    b. contained little ethnic diversity.
    c. was eventually conquered by neighboring New Sweden.
    d. had grown wealthy and powerful under the policies of the Dutch West India Company.

_____ 8. William Penn's colony of Pennsylvania

    a. sought settlers primarily from England and Scotland.
    b. experienced continuing warfare with neighboring Indian tribes.
    c. made no provisions for military defense against enemies.
    d. set up the Quaker religion as its tax-supported established church.

_____ 9. Besides Pennsylvania, Quakers were also involved in the early settlement of both

    a. New Jersey and New York.
    b. New Jersey and Delaware.
    c. New Netherland and New York.
    d. New York and Delaware.

_____ 10. The middle colonies of New York, New Jersey, Pennsylvania, and Delaware

    a. depended almost entirely on industry rather than agriculture for their prosperity.
    b. had powerful established churches that suppressed religious dissenters.
    c. relied heavily on slave labor in agriculture.
    d. had more ethnic diversity than either New England or the southern colonies.

C. Identification

Supply the correct identification for each numbered description.

_____ 1. Sixteenth-century religious movement begun by Martin Luther

_____ 2. English Calvinists who sought a thorough reformation of the Church of England

_____ 3. Radical Calvinists who considered the Church of England so corrupt that they broke with it and formed their own independent churches

_____ 4. The shipboard agreement by the Pilgrim Fathers to establish a body politic and submit to majority rule

_____ 5. Puritans' term for their belief that Massachusetts Bay had contracted an agreement with God to become a holy society

_____ 6. Charles I's political action of 1629 that led to persecution of the Puritans and the formation of the Massachusetts Bay Company

_____ 7. Term for the Puritan belief that hard work and engagement with the world constituted doing God's work on earth

_____ 8. Anne Hutchinson's heretical belief that the truly saved need not obey human or divine law

_____ 9. Common fate of Roger Williams and Anne Hutchinson after they were convicted of heresy in Massachusetts Bay

_____ 10. Primary Indian tribe whom the Puritans encountered in Massachusetts

_____ 11. English revolt that also led to the overthrow of the Dominion of New England in America

_____ 12. Small colony in present-day Delaware conquered by the Dutch of New Netherland in 1655

_____ 13. River valley where vast estates created an aristocratic landholding elite in New Netherland and later New York

_____ 14. Required, sworn statements of loyalty or religious belief resisted by Quakers

_____ 15. The other middle colony besides Pennsylvania settled by Quakers (not Delaware)

D. Matching People, Places, and Events

Match the person, place, or event in the left column with the proper description in the right column by inserting the correct letter on the blank line.

____ 1. Martin Luther

____ 2. John Calvin

____ 3. Pilgrims

____ 4. New York

A. Dominant religious organization in Massachusetts Bay

B. Founder of the most tolerant and democratic of the middle colonies

C. Wampanoag chieftain who aided Pilgrims and helped them celebrate the first Thanksgiving in 1621

D. Colony originally founded by Dutch, conquered by England

E. Religious dissenter convicted of the heresy of antinomianism

___	5. Massachusetts Bay	**F.**	Native American leader who waged unsuccessful war against New England
___	6. John Winthrop	**G.**	German monk who began the Protestant Reformation
___	7. Massasoit	**H.**	Religious group persecuted in Massachusetts and New York but not in Pennsylvania
___	8. General Court	**I.**	Representative assembly of Massachusetts Bay
___	9. Congregational church	**J.**	Promoter of Massachusetts Bay as a holy "city upon a hill"
___	10. Quakers	**K.**	Conqueror of New Sweden who lost New Netherland
		L.	Person whose religious ideas inspired English Puritans, Scotch Presbyterians, French Huguenots, and the Dutch Reformed Church
___	11. Anne Hutchinson	**M.**	Separatist Calvinists who founded the Plymouth colony
___	12. Roger Williams	**N.**	Colony whose government sought to enforce God's law on believers and nonbelievers alike
___	13. King Philip	**O.**	Radical founder of the most tolerant New England colony
___	14. Peter Stuyvesant		
___	15. William Penn		

E. Putting Things in Order

Put the following events in correct order by numbering them from 1 to 10.

___ New England Confederation achieves a notable military success.

___ English separatists migrate from Holland to America.

___ Swedish colony on Delaware River is conquered.

___ Manhattan Island is acquired by non-English settlers.

___ Protestant Reformation begins in Europe and England.

___ Quaker son of an English admiral obtains a royal charter for a colony.

___ Puritans bring a thousand immigrants and a charter to America.

___ England conquers a colony on the Hudson River.

___ Convicted Massachusetts Bay heretic founds a colony as a haven for dissenters.

___ James II is overthrown in England, and Edmund Andros is overthrown in America.

PART III: Applying What You Have Learned

1. Compare and contrast the New England and middle colonies in terms of motives for founding, religious and social composition, and political development.
2. How did the Puritans' religious outlook affect the development of all the New England colonies?
3. What efforts were made to strengthen English control over the colonies in the seventeenth century, and why did they generally fail?
4. Discuss the development of religious and political freedom in Massachusetts, Rhode Island, New York, and Pennsylvania. How did the greater degree of such freedoms enjoyed by Rhode Island and Pennsylvania affect life in those colonies?
5. What economic, social, and ethnic conditions typical of the early southern colonies (Chapter 2) were generally absent in the New England and middle colonies? What characteristics did these northern colonies have that were not generally present in the South?

4

★★★★★★★★

American Life in the Seventeenth Century,

1607–1692

PART I: Reviewing the Chapter

A. Checklist of Learning Objectives

After mastering this chapter, you should be able to

1. describe the basic population structure and social life of the seventeenth-century colonies.
2. compare and contrast the different populations and ways of life of the southern colonies and New England.
3. explain how the problems of indentured servitude led to political trouble and the growth of African slavery.
4. describe the slave trade and the character of early African-American slavery.
5. explain how the New England way of life centered on family, town, and church and describe the changes that affected this way of life.
6. describe the various conditions affecting women and family life in the seventeenth-century colonies.

B. Glossary

To build your social science vocabulary, familiarize yourself with the following terms.

1. **headright** The right to acquire a certain amount of land granted to the person who financed the passage of a laborer. "Both Virginia and Maryland employed the 'headright' system. . . ." (p. 46)
2. **disenfranchise** To take away the right to vote. ". . . the Virginia Assembly in 1670 disenfranchised most of the landless knockabouts. . . ." (p. 46)
3. **civil war** A conflict between the citizens or inhabitants of the same country. "As this civil war in Virginia-ground on. . . ." (p. 47)
4. **tidewater** The territory adjoining water affected by tides—that is, near the seacoast or coastal rivers. "[Bacon] had pitted the hardscrabble backcountry frontiersmen against the haughty gentry of the tidewater plantations." (p. 47)
5. **middle passage** The ocean voyage in which slaves were carried from Africa to the Americas aboard slave ships. ". . . the captives were herded aboard sweltering ships for the gruesome 'middle passage.' . . ." (p. 49)

6. **fertility** The ability to mate and produce young. "The captive black population soon began to grow not only through new imports but also through its own fertility. . . ." (p. 49)
7. **menial** Humble or ordinary. ". . . they performed the sweaty toil of clearing swamps, grubbing out trees, and other menial tasks." (p. 49)
8. **hierarchy** A social group arranged in ranks or classes. ". . . rough equality . . . was giving way to a hierarchy of wealth and status. . . ." (p. 50)
9. **jeremiad** A sermon or prophecy warning of doom and calling for repentance; the term is derived from the biblical prophet Jeremiah. " . . . a new form of sermon—the 'jeremiad.' "(p. 52)
10. **social structure** The basic pattern of the distribution of status and wealth in a society. ". . . many settlers . . . tried to re-create on a modified scale the social structure they had known in the Old World." (p. 53)

PART II: Checking Your Progress

A. True-False

Where the statement is true, mark **T**. Where it is false, mark **F**, and correct it in the space immediately below.

____ 1. Life expectancy among the seventeenth-century settlers of Maryland and Virginia was about seventy years.

____ 2. Because men greatly outnumbered women in the Chesapeake region, fierce competition arose among men for scarce females.

____ 3. The more stable family life of New England led to fewer pregnancies among unmarried women than occurred in the more unstable family environment of the Chesapeake.

____ 4. The flourishing tobacco production of the Chesapeake region was based on steady prices and a stable supply of satisfied laborers.

____ 5. The "headright" system of land grants to those who brought laborers to America benefited wealthy planters rather than poor indentured servants.

____ 6. Most of the white Europeans who came to Virginia and Maryland in the seventeenth century were indentured servants.

____ 7. Bacon's Rebellion involved an alliance of white indentured servants and Native Americans against wealthy whites.

____ 8. African slaves existed only in small numbers until the 1680s, when they began to replace white indentured servants as the primary labor supply in the plantation colonies.

____ 9. Slaves brought to North America developed a culture that mixed African and American elements.

____ 10. Directly beneath the wealthy slaveowning planters in the southern social structure were the white indentured servants.

____ 11. On average, married women in colonial New England gave birth to 8–10 children.

___ 12. New England expansion was carried out primarily by land speculators who bought up large plots and then sold them to individual farmers.

___ 13. The Half-Way Covenant allowed those who had not experienced conversion to become partial members of the Congregational church.

___ 14. New England's commercial wealth was based on overseas shipment of the agricultural products of its rich soil.

___ 15. Seventeenth-century American life was generally simple and lacking in displays of wealth or elaborate class distinctions.

B. Multiple Choice

Select the best answer and put the proper letter in the space provided.

___ 1. For most of their early history, the colonies of Maryland and Virginia

a. represented a healthy environment for child rearing.
b. contained far more men than women.
c. had harsh laws punishing premarital sexual relations.
d. encouraged the formation of stable and long-lasting marriages.

___ 2. The primary beneficiaries of the "headright" system were

a. landowners who paid the passage for indentured servants.
b. widows who acquired new husbands from England.
c. indentured servants who were able to acquire their own land.
d. English shipowners who transported new laborers across the Atlantic.

___ 3. The primary cause of Bacon's Rebellion was

a. Governor Berkeley's harsh treatment of the Indians.
b. the refusal of landlords to grant indentured servants their freedom.
c. the poverty and discontent of many single young men unable to acquire land.
d. the persecution of the colonists by King Charles 11.

___ 4. African slavery became the prevalent form of labor in the 1680s when

a. planters were no longer able to rely on white indentured servants as a labor force.
b. the first captives were brought from Africa to the New World.
c. blacks could be brought to the New World in safer and healthier condition.
d. the once-clear legal difference between a servant and a slave began to be blurred.

____ 5. The culture that developed among slaves in the English colonies of North America was

    a. derived primarily from that of the white masters.
    b. based mainly on the traditions of southern Africa.
    c. a combination of several African and American cultures.
    d. originally developed in the West Indies and spread northward.

____ 6. Political and economic power in the southern colonies was dominated by

    a. urban professional classes such as lawyers and bankers.
    b. small landowners.
    c. a small number of wealthy planters.
    d. the English royal governors.

____ 7. In contrast to the Chesapeake Bay colonists, those in New England

    a. had fewer women and more men in their population.
    b. had shorter life expectancies.
    c. practiced birth control as a means of preventing overpopulation.
    d. enjoyed longer lives and more stable families.

____ 8. The focus of much of New England's politics, religion, and education was the institution of

    a. the colonial legislature.
    b. the town.
    c. the militia company.
    d. the college.

____ 9. The Half-Way Covenant provided

    a. partial church membership to people not converted.
    b. partial participation in politics to people who were not church members.
    c. partial church membership to women.
    d. partial participation in colonial affairs to new immigrants from England.

____ 10. Compared with those of the southern and middle colonies, the economy of New England relied less on

    a. fishing.
    b. agriculture.
    c. free labor.
    d. trading and commerce.

C. Identification

Supply the correct identification for each numbered description.

_____ 1. The social institution that early Maryland and Virginia settlers found difficult to sustain

_____ 2. Primary cause of death among tobacco-growing settlers

_____ 3. Small payment of goods or land given to indentured servants at the end of their term

_____ 4. Maryland's and Virginia's system of granting land to anyone who would pay transatlantic passage for laborers

_____ 5. Fate of many of Nathaniel Bacon's followers, though not of Bacon himself

_____ 6. Term for the slave journey by ship from Africa to the Americas

_____ 7. The cruel business engaged in by Africans and some Rhode Islanders and other Americans

_____ 8. African-American dialect that blended English with several African languages

_____ 9. Violent events that occurred in New York City in 1712 and in South Carolina in 1739

_____ 10. Staple crop that formed basis of South Carolina's plantation economy

_____ 11. The "town fathers" who were granted charters to found the New England towns

_____ 12. The basic local political institution of New England, in which all freemen gathered to elect officials and debate local affairs

_____ 13. Formula devised by Puritan ministers in 1662 to offer partial church membership to people who had not experienced conversion

_____ 14. Outburst of fanaticism in New England that inflamed popular feelings, led to the deaths of twenty people, and weakened the Puritan clergy's prestige

_____ 15. Primary occupation of most seventeenth-century Americans

D. Matching People, Places, and Events

Match the person, place, or event in the left column with the proper description in the right column by inserting the correct letter on the blank line.

____ 1. Chesapeake

____ 2. Indentured servants

____ 3. Nathaniel Bacon

____ 4. Governor Berkeley

____ 5. Royal African Company

____ 6. Middle passage

A. Middle colonies' racial rebellion
B. Helped erase the earlier Puritan distinction between the converted "elect" and other members of society
C. Small New York revolt of 1689–1691 that reflected class antagonism between landlords and merchants
D. Primary source of labor in early southern colonies until the 1680s
E. Experience for which human beings were branded and chained, and in which only 80 percent survived
F. One of the key economic foundations of New England

___   7. Ringshout

___   8. New York City slave revolt of 1712

___   9. Codfish

___   10. Gullah

___   11. Harvard

___   12. William and Mary

___   13. Half-Way Covenant

___   14. Salem witch trials

___   15. Leisler's Rebellion

G. West African religious rite, retained by African-Americans, in which participants "danced" in a circle

H. Phenomenon started by adolescent girls' accusations that ended with the deaths of twenty people

I. Virginia-Maryland bay area, site of the earliest colonial settlements

J. Carolina coastal language that blended African and English speech

K. Individual driven from Jamestown who eventually crushed those responsible and wreaked cruel revenge

L. Founded in 1693, the oldest college in the South

M. Organization whose loss of the slave trade monopoly in 1698 led to free-enterprise expansion of the business

N. Person who led poor former indentured servants and frontiersmen on a rampage against Indians and colonial government

O. The oldest college in America, which reflected Puritan commitment to an educated ministry

E. Putting Things in Order

Put the following events in correct order by numbering them from 1 to 5.

___   Execution of twenty accused "witches" occurs.

___   First colonial college is founded.

___   Partial church membership is opened to the unconverted.

___   Poor Virginia whites revolt against governor and rich planters.

___   First Africans arrive in Virginia.

PART III: Applying What You Have Learned

1. How did the factors of population, economics, disease, and climate shape the basic social conditions and ways of life of early Americans in both the South and New England?
2. Why did the initially successful indentured-servant system of labor undergo a crisis, and why was it increasingly replaced by African slavery?
3. How did the numbers and condition of women affect family life and society in New England, among southern whites, and among African-American slaves? Compare and contrast the typical family conditions and ways of life among various members of these three groups.
4. How did the harsh climate and soil, stern religion, and tightly knit New England town shape the "Yankee character"?
5. Would seventeenth century colonial society best be described as "democratic," "aritsocratic," or neither? Why?

5
★★★★★★★★★

Colonial Society on the Eve of Revolution,

1700–1775

PART I: Reviewing the Chapter

A. Checklist of Learning Objectives

After mastering this chapter, you should be able to

1. describe the basic population and social structure of the eighteenth-century colonies and indicate how they had changed since the seventeenth century.
2. explain how the economic life of the colonies was related to the changing patterns of social prestige and wealth.
3. explain the causes and effects of the religious changes of the early eighteenth century, especially the Great Awakening.
4. describe the origins and development of education, culture, and the learned professions in the colonies.
5. describe the basic features of colonial politics, including the role of various official and informal political institutions.

B. Glossary

To build your social science vocabulary, familiarize yourself with the following terms.

1. **stratification** The visible arrangement of society into a hierarchical pattern, with distinct social groups layere one on top of the other. "... colonial society ... was beginning to show signs of stratification. ..." (p. 5!
2. **mobility** The capacity to pass readily from one social or economic condition to another. "... barriers mobility ... raised worries about the 'Europeanization' of America." (p. 59)
3. **almshouse** A home for the poor, supported by charity or public funds. "Both Philadelphia and New Yc built almshouses in the 1730s. ..." (p. 59)
4. **gentry** People of substantial property, social standing, and leisure, but not titled nobility. "Wealth was cc centrated in the hands of the largest slaveowners, widening the gap between the prosperous gentry and 'poor whites.' ..." (p. 59)

5. **veto** The executive power to prevent acts passed by the legislature from becoming law. "Thomas Jefferson ... assailed such vetoes. . . ." (p. 59)
6. **apprentice** A person who works under a master in order to receive instruction in a trade or profession. "Aspiring young doctors served for a while as apprentices to older practitioners. . . ." (p. 60)
7. **revival** In religion, a movement of renewed enthusiasm and commitment, often accompanied by special meetings or evangelical activity. "The stage was thus set for a rousing religious revival." (p. 63)

PART II: Checking Your Progress

A. True-False

Where the statement is true, mark **T**. Where it is false, mark **F,** and correct it in the space immediately below.

___ 1. Most of the spectacular growth of the colonial population came from immigration rather than natural increase.

___ 2. The largest white ethnic groups in the colonies were the Germans and the Scots-Irish.

___ 3. Compared with those of the seventeenth century, the eighteenth-century colonies were becoming more socially equal and democratic.

___ 4. The lowest class of whites in the colonies consisted of the convicted criminals shipped to America by British authorities.

___ 5. Attempts by some colonial legislatures to halt the importation of slaves were vetoed by Britain.

___ 6. Doctors and lawyers were more highly regarded in the colonies than clergymen.

___ 7. Besides agriculture, the most important colonial economic activities were related to the sea.

___ 8. Colonial merchants were generally satisfied to trade in protected British markets and accepted British restrictions on trade with other countries.

___ 9. The established Anglican church in the South was generally more influential than the established Congregational church of New England.

___ 10. The Great Awakening came after a period of religious decline caused by clerical overintellectualism and lay liberalism.

___ 11. Great Awakening revivalists like Edwards and Whitefield tried to replace the older Puritan ideas of conversion and salvation with more rational and less emotional beliefs.

___ 12. The Great Awakening tended to break down denominational and sectional barriers, creating a greater sense of common American identity and unity.

___ 13. Most early colonial education, including that at the college level, was closely linked with religion.

____ 14. The greatest colonial cultural achievements came in art and imaginative literature rather than in theology and political theory.

____ 15. The central point of conflict in colonial politics was the relation between the democratically elected lower house of the assembly and the governors appointed by the king or colonial proprietor.

B. Multiple Choice

Select the best answer and put the proper letter in the space provided.

____ 1. The primary reason for the spectacular growth of America's population in the eighteenth century was

   a. the conquering of new territories.
   b. the natural fertility of the population.
   c. the increased importation of white indentured servants and black slaves.
   d. new immigration from Europe.

____ 2. German settlement in the colonies was especially heavy in

   a. Massachusetts.
   b. Maryland.
   c. New York.
   d. Pennsylvania.

____ 3. The Scots-Irish eventually became concentrated especially in

   a. the seacoast settlements.
   b. the New England colonies.
   c. the frontier areas.
   d. the cities.

____ 4. Compared with the seventeenth century, American colonial society in the eighteenth century showed

   a. greater domination by small farmers and artisans.
   b. greater equality of wealth and status.
   c. greater gaps in wealth and status between rich and poor.
   d. greater opportunity for convicts and indentured servants to climb to the top.

____ 5. The most honored professional in colonial America was the

   a. lawyer.
   b. clergyman.
   c. doctor.
   d. journalist.

____ 6. The primary source of livelihood for most colonial Americans was

   a. manufacturing.
   b. agriculture.
   c. lumbering.
   d. commerce and trade.

_____ 7. The passage of British restrictions on trade encouraged colonial merchants to
    a. organize political resistance in the British Parliament.
    b. turn to smuggling and other illegal forms of trade.
    c. turn to domestic trade within the colonies.
    d. turn from trading to such other enterprises as fishing and manufacturing.

_____ 8. The two denominations that were officially "established" in some colonies were the

    a. Quakers and Lutherans.
    b. Dutch Reformed and Anglicans.
    c. Anglicans and Congregationalists.
    d. Roman Catholics and Presbyterians.

_____ 9. Among the many important results of the Great Awakening was that it

    a. broke down sectional boundaries and created a greater sense of common American identity.
    b. contributed to greater religious liberalism and toleration in the churches.
    c. caused a decline in colonial concern for education.
    d. moved Americans closer to a single religious outlook.

_____ 10. A primary weapon used by colonial legislatures in their conflicts with royal governors was

    a. extending the franchise to include almost all adult white citizens.
    b. passing laws prohibiting the governors from owning land or industries.
    c. voting them out of office.
    d. using their power of taxation to withhold the governors' salaries.

C. Identification

Supply the correct identification for each numbered description.

_____ 1. Corruption of a German word used to designate German immigrants in Pennsylvania

_____ 2. Section of the colonies where most Scots-Irish settlers were located

_____ 3. Activity in which many colonial merchant princes made fortunes that aroused fears of "Europeanization"

_____ 4. Popular term for convicted criminals dumped on colonies by British authorities

_____ 5. Dreaded epidemics of disease, especially smallpox and diphtheria

_____ 6. A once-despised profession that rose in prestige after 1750 because its practitioners defended colonial rights

_____ 7. Small but profitable trade route that linked New England, Africa, and the West Indies

_____ 8. Popular colonial centers of recreation, gossip, and political debate

_____ 9. Term for tax-supported condition of Congregational and Anglican churches, but not of Baptists, Quakers, and Roman Catholics

_____ 10. Spectacular, emotional religious revival of the 1730s and 1740s

_____ 11. Ministers who supported religious revivals against the "old light" clergy who rejected them

_____ 12. The first nondenominational American college, founded by Benjamin Franklin

_____ 13. The charge of which printer John Peter Zenger was acquitted, setting an important precedent for freedom of the press

_____ 14. The upper house of a colonial legislature, appointed by the crown or the proprietor

_____ 15. Commodity that a person had to own a certain amount of in order to be eligible to vote

D. Matching People, Places, and Events

Match the person, place, or event in the left column with the proper description in the right column by inserting the correct letter on the blank line.

___ 1. Philadelphia

___ 2. African-Americans

___ 3. Scots-Irish

___ 4. Paxton Boys and Regulators

___ 5. James Otis and Patrick Henry

___ 6. Molasses Act

___ 7. Anglican church

___ 8. Jonathan Edwards

___ 9. George Whitefield

___ 10. Phyllis Wheatley

___ 11. Benjamin Franklin

___ 12. John Peter Zenger

A. Itinerant English evangelist who spread Great Awakening throughout the colonies

B. Colonial printer whose case helped establish freedom of the press

C. Colonial painters who studied and worked in England

D. Leading city of the colonies; home of Benjamin Franklin

E. Largest non-English group in the colonies

F. Worst example of a corrupt and incompetent royal governor

G. Former slave who became a poet at an early age

H. Scots-Irish frontiersmen who protested against colonial elites of Pennsylvania and North Carolina

I. Attempt by British authorities to squelch colonial trade with French West Indies

J. Brilliant New England theologian who instigated the Great Awakening

K. Ethnic group that settled the frontier, made whiskey, and hated the British and other governmental authorities

L. Nonestablished religious group that benefited from the Great Awakening

M. Author, scientist, printer; "the first civilized American"

N. Eloquent lawyer-orators who argued in defense of colonial rights

O. Established in southern colonies and New York; weakened by lackadaisical clergy and too-close ties with British crown

___ 13. Lord Cornbury

___ 14. Baptists

___ 15. John Singleton Copley and Benjamin West

E. Putting Things in Order

Put the following events in correct order by numbering them from 1 to 10.

___ Epochal freedom of the press case is settled.

___ First southern college to train Anglican clergy is founded.

___ Britain vetoes colonial effort to halt slave importation.

___ Scots-Irish protestors stage armed marches.

___ First medical attempts are made to prevent dreaded epidemics.

___ Parliament attempts to restrict colonial trade with French West Indies.

___ Princeton College is founded to train "new light" ministers.

___ An eloquent English clergyman preaches in America.

___ Benjamin Franklin starts printing his most famous publication.

___ A fiery, learned New England preacher sets off a powerful religious revival that spreads through the colonies.

PART III: Applying What You Have Learned

1. What factors contributed to the growing numbers and wealth of the American colonists in the eighteenth century?
2. What were the causes and consequences of the Great Awakening?
3. What were the features of colonial politics that contributed to the development of popular democracy, and what were those that kept it from being more truly democratic?
4. How did the various churches, established and nonestablished, affect colonial life, including education and politics, in the eighteenth century?
5. How did social, religious, and political developments contribute to a growing sense of British North Americans' shared identity in the eighteenth century?

6
★★★★★★★★★

The Duel for North America,

1608–1763

PART I: Reviewing the Chapter

A. Checklist of Learning Objectives

After mastering this chapter, you should be able to

1. explain how France and Britain came to engage in a great contest for North America and why Britain won.
2. explain how the contest affected Britain's American subjects and helped pave the way for their later rebellion.
3. describe France's North American empire and compare it with Britain's colonies.
4. explain how North American political and military events were affected by developments on the larger European stage.

B. Glossary

To build your social science vocabulary, familiarize yourself with the following terms.

1. **domestic** Concerning the internal affairs of a country. "It was convulsed . . . by foreign wars and domestic strife. . . ." (p. 70)
2. **autocratic** Authoritarian and arbitrary rule. "The royal regime was almost completely autocratic." (p. 71)
3. **peasant** A farmer or agricultural laborer, sometimes legally tied to the land. "Land-owning French peasants . . . had little economic motive to move." (p. 71)
4. **coureurs des bois** French-Canadian fur trappers; literally, "runners of the woods. "These colorful *coureurs des bois* . . . were also runners of risk. . . ." (p. 71)
5. **voyageurs** French-Canadian fur traders and adventurers. "Singing, paddle-swinging French *voyageurs* also recruited Indians. . . ." (p. 71)
6. **ecological** Concerning the relations between biological organisms and their environment. " . . . they extinguished the beaver population . . ., inflicting incalculable ecological damage." (p. 71)
7. **mutinous** Concerning the revolt by subordinate soldiers or seamen against their commanding officers. "He . . . was murdered by his mutinous men." (p. 71)
8. **strategic** Concerning the placement and planned movement of large-scale military forces so as to gain advantage, usually prior to actual engagement with the enemy. "Commanding the mouth of the Mississippi River, this strategic semitropical outpost also tapped the fur trade. . . ." (pp. 71–72)

9. **guerrilla warfare** Unconventional combat waged by small military units using hit-and-run tactics. ". . . so a kind of primitive guerrilla war prevailed." (p. 72)
10. **seige** A military operation of surrounding and attacking a fortified place, often over a sustained period. "After a ten-hour siege he was forced to surrender. . . ." (p. 73)
11. **regulars** Trained professional soldiers, as distinct from militia or conscripts. ". . . they had fought bravely beside the crack British regulars. . . ." (p. 75)
12. **commission** An official certification granting a commanding rank in the armed forces. " . . . the British refused to recognize any American militia commission. . . ." (p. 75)

PART II: Checking Your Progress

A. True-False

Where the statement is true, mark **T.** Where it is false, mark **F,** and correct it in the space immediately below.

____ 1. French Canada was tightly controlled from above under the autocratic rule of the French kings.

____ 2. The French empire in North America rested on an economic foundation of forestry and sugar production.

____ 3. Early imperial conflicts in North America often saw the French and their Indian allies engaging in guerrilla warfare against British frontier outposts.

____ 4. Britain's North American colonists managed to avoid direct involvement in most of Britain's "world wars" until the French and Indian War.

____ 5. The conflict between British colonists and the French arose because French colonists and fur traders were encroaching into New England and Virginia.

____ 6. George Washington's battle at Fort Necessity substantially resolved the issue of control of the Ohio Valley.

____ 7. The Albany Congress demonstrated a strong desire among some English colonists to join together and control their own affairs.

____ 8. William Pitt's successful strategy in the French and Indian War was to concentrate British forces and try to capture the strongholds of Louisbourg, Quebec, and Montreal.

____ 9. British regular troops under Braddock succeeded in capturing the key French forts in the Ohio Valley.

____ 10. The French and Indian War left France with only Louisiana as a remnant of its once-mighty North American empire.

____ 11. American soldiers gained new respect for British military men after the British success against the French.

____ 12. The American colonists enthusiastically united in patriotic support of the British cause against the French.

____ 13. The removal of the French threat made American colonists more secure and therefore less reliant on the mother country for protection.

____ 14. The British suppressed Pontiac's Indian uprising in the Ohio Valley and Great Lakes region.

____ 15. The British government's attempt to prohibit colonial expansion across the Appalachian Mountains aroused colonial anger and defiance of the law.

B. Multiple Choice

Select the best answer and put the proper letter in the space provided.

____ 1. Compared with the English colonies, New France was

    a. wealthier and more successful.
    b. able to maintain consistently friendly relations with the Indians.
    c. more heavily populated.
    d. more autocratically governed.

____ 2. The expansion of New France occurred especially

    a. in the interior mountain areas.
    b. along the paths of lakes and rivers.
    c. in areas already occupied by English settlers.
    d. to the north of the original St. Lawrence settlement.

____ 3. Colonial Americans were unhappy after the peace treaty following the "War of Jenkins' Ear" because

    a. it failed to settle the issue that had caused the war.
    b. it gave the Louisbourg fortress they had captured back to France.
    c. it created further conflicts with Spain.
    d. it failed to deal with the issue of Indian attacks on the frontier.

____ 4. The original cause of the French and Indian War was

    a. conflict in Europe between Britain and France.
    b. British removal of the "Acadian" French settlers from Nova Scotia.
    c. competition between French and English colonists for land in the Ohio River valley.
    d. the French attack on George Washington at Fort Necessity.

____ 5. The French and Indian War eventually became part of the larger world conflict known as

    a. the Seven Years' War.
    b. the War of Jenkins' Ear.
    c. the War of the Austrian Succession.
    d. King George's War.

___ 6. The result of Benjamin Franklin's attempt to create intercolonial unity at the Albany Congress was

    a. a permanent cooperative organization of the colonies.
    b. rejection by London and by the individual colonies of the congress's proposal for colonial home rule.
    c. a sharp increase in Indian attacks on colonial settlements.
    d. a growing colonial sympathy with France in the war against Britain.

___ 7. William Pitt's strategy in the assault on New France finally succeeded because

    a. he was able to arouse more support for the war effort from the colonists.
    b. he gave full support to General Braddock as commander of the British forces.
    c. he concentrated British forces on attacking the vital strong points of Quebec and Montreal.
    d. he was able to gain the support of the British aristocracy for the war effort.

___ 8. The decisive event in the French-British contest for North America was

    a. the British capture of Fort Duquesne.
    b. the British victory in the Battle of Quebec.
    c. the British capture of the Louisbourg fortress.
    d. the British attack on the West Indies.

___ 9. The French and Indian War created conflict between the British and the American military because

    a. the American soldiers had failed to support the British military effort.
    b. the British regulars had carried the brunt of the fighting.
    c. British officers treated the American colonial militia with contempt.
    d. American soldiers refused to accept orders from British officers.

___ 10. The effect on the colonists of the French removal from North America was

    a. to increase their gratitude to Britain for defending them in the war.
    b. to create new threats to colonial expansion from Spain and the Indians.
    c. to reduce the colonies' reliance on Britain and increase their sense of independence.
    d. to focus colonial energies on trade.

C. Identification

Supply the correct identification for each numbered description.

_____ 1. French Protestants who were granted toleration by the Edict of Nantes in 1598 but not permitted to settle in New France

_____ 2. First settled by Samuel de Champlain, governed directly by King Louis XIV

_____ 3. Animal whose skin profited the French empire and enhanced European fashion at enormous ecological cost

_____ 4. French Catholic missionary order that explored the North American interior and sought to protect and convert the Indians

_____ 5. Far-traveling, high-living French fur trappers

_____ 6. A portion of a certain British naval officer's anatomy that set off an imperial war with Spain

_____ 7. Strategic French fortress conquered by New England settlers, handed back to the French, and finally conquered again by the British in 1759

_____ 8. Inland river territory, scene of fierce competition between the French and land-speculating English colonists

_____ 9. Bloodiest European theater of the Seven Years' War, where British money and Frederick the Great's troops drained French strength away from North America

_____ 10. Attempt at colonial unity that Benjamin Franklin nearly inspired to success by eloquent leadership and cartoon artistry

_____ 11. Military aide of British General Braddock and defender of the frontier after Braddock's defeat

_____ 12. Fortress boldly conquered by General Wolfe, spelling doom for New France

_____ 13. The "buckskin" colonial soldiers whose military success did nothing to alter British officers' contempt for them

_____ 14. Allies of the French against the British, who continued to fight under Pontiac even after the peace settlement in 1763

_____ 15. Name for the larger European struggle of which the French and Indian War was part

D. Matching People, Places, and Events

Match the person, place, or event in the left column with the proper description in the right column by inserting the correct letter on the blank line.

____ 1. Samuel de Champlain

____ 2. Robert de la Salle

____ 3. Treaty of Utrecht

____ 4. War of Austrian Succession

____ 5. Fort Duquesne

____ 6. George Washington

A. Advocate of colonial unity at the unsuccessful Albany Congress
B. Document that aroused colonial anger but failed to stop frontier expansion
C. One-time French territory, renamed Nova Scotia, whose citizens were removed to Louisiana by the British in 1755
D. Conflict that started with War of Jenkins' Ear (called King George's War in North America) and ended with return of Louisbourg to France
E. Strategic French outpost at the mouth of the Mississippi
F. Indian leader whose frontier uprising caused the British to attempt to limit colonial frontier expansion

___	7. Benjamin Franklin	**G.**	Blundering British officer defeated in the first battles of the French and Indian War
___	8. General Braddock	**H.**	The Father of New France
		I.	Site of the death of Generals Wolfe and Montcalm
___	9. William Pitt	**J.**	Strategic French stronghold, later renamed after a great British statesman
___	10. Plains of Abraham	**K.**	Militia commander whose frontier skirmish touched off a world war
___	11. Seven Years' War	**L.**	Document that ended the War of the Spanish Succession (Queen Anne's War) and awarded Acadia to Britain
___	12. Pontiac	**M.**	Conflict that, in Europe, pitted France against Britain's ally Frederick the Great of Prussia
___	13. Proclamation of 1763	**N.**	French empire builder who explored the Mississippi basin and named it after his monarch
___	14. New Orleans	**O.**	Splendid British orator and organizer of the winning strategy against the French in North America
___	15. Acadia		

E. Putting Things in Order

Put the following events in correct order by numbering them from 1 to 10.

___ A Virginia militia commander attempts an unsuccessful invasion of the Ohio Valley.

___ The "Great Commoner" takes command of the British government and its war effort.

___ Toleration of French Huguenots brings religious peace to France.

___ New France is founded, one year after Jamestown.

___ Britain issues a proclamation to prohibit colonial expansion and thereby prevent another Indian war.

___ The second "world war" between France and Britain ends in British victory and the acquisition of Acadia.

___ British victory on the Plains of Abraham seals the fate of New France.

___ Return of Louisbourg fortress at the end of King George's War angers colonial New Englanders.

___ War begins badly for British when Braddock fails to take Fort Duquesne.

___ A great empire builder explores Louisiana and claims it for the French king.

PART III: Applying What You Have Learned

1. How were the British and their American colonial subjects able to win the contest with the French for control of North America?

2. In what ways were the American colonists involved in the mother country's struggle with France?

3. How did the development and final outcome of the imperial struggle affect relations between the colonists and Britain and alter relations among the colonies themselves?

4. How did events in France, Britain, and elsewhere in Europe affect the history of North America in this period?

5. Compare France's colonizing efforts in the New World with those of Spain and England (see Chapters I and 2). What factors might explain France's relatively weak impact on the New World compared with that of England and Spain?

7
★★★★★★★★★

The Road to Revolution,

1763–1775

PART I: Reviewing the Chapter

A. Checklist of Learning Objectives

After mastering this chapter, you should be able to

1. explain the long-term historical factors that moved America toward independence from Britain.
2. describe the theory and practice of mercantilism and explain why Americans resented it.
3. explain why Britain attempted tighter control and taxation of Americans after 1763 and why Americans resisted these efforts.
4. describe the major British efforts to impose taxes and tighten control of the colonies.
5. describe the methods of colonial resistance that forced repeal of all taxes except the tax on tea.
6. explain how sustained agitation and resistance to the tea tax led to the Intolerable Acts and the outbreak of war.
7. assess the balance of forces between the British and the American Patriots as the two sides prepared for war.

B. Glossary

To build your social science vocabulary, familiarize yourself with the following terms.

1. **insurrection** Rebellion against political authority. "Insurrection of thought usually precedes insurrection of deed." (p. 80)
2. **mercantilism** The economic theory that all parts of an economy should be coordinated for the good of the whole state; hence, that colonial economics should be subordinated for the benefit of an empire. "The British authorities nevertheless embraced a theory, called 'mercantilism,'...." (p. 81)
3. **depreciate** To decrease in value, as in the decline of the purchasing power of money. "... dire need finally forced many of the colonies to issue paper money, which unfortunately depreciated." (p. 81)
4. **mortgage** To pledge property to a creditor as security for a loan or debt. "Virginia planters ... were forced to buy their necessities in England by mortgaging future crops." (p. 83)
5. **admiralty courts** In British law, special administrative courts designed to handle maritime cases without a jury. "Both [acts] provided for trying offenders in the hated admiralty courts...." (p. 83)

6. **virtual representation** The political theory that a class of persons is represented in a lawmaking body without direct vote. "Elaborating the theory of 'virtual representation,' Grenville claimed that every member of Parliament represented all British subjects, even . . . Americans. . . ." (p. 83)

7. **nonimportation agreement** Pledges to boycott, or decline to purchase, certain goods from abroad. "More effective than the congress was the widespread adoption of nonimportation agreements. . . ." (p. 84)

8. **mulatto** A person of mixed African and European ancestry. ". . . Crispus Attucks [was] described . . . as a 'mulatto.' . . ." (p. 86)

9. **duty** A customs tax on the export or import of goods. ". . . Parliament . . . repeal[ed] the Townshend revenue duties." (p. 86)

10. **propaganda** A systematic program or particular materials designed to spread certain ideas; sometimes but not always the term implies the use of manipulative or deceptive means. "Their chief function was to spread propaganda. . . ." (p. 86)

11. **boycott** An organized refusal to deal with some person, organization, or product. ". . . this one called for a *complete* boycott of British goods. . . ." (p. 88)

PART II: Checking Your Progress

A. True-False

Where the statement is true, mark **T**. Where it is false, mark **F**, and correct it in the space immediately below.

_____ 1. By the mid–eighteenth century, Americans had developed a considerable degree of freedom from British political control.

_____ 2. The theory of mercantilism was based on the idea that colonies existed primarily for the economic benefit of the mother country.

_____ 3. British mercantilism forbade the importation of any non-British goods into the colonies.

_____ 4. In practice, British mercantilism provided the colonies with the substantial benefits of economic subsidies, military protection, and guaranteed markets.

_____ 5. The purpose of Grenville's Sugar Act, Quartering Act, and Stamp Act was to make the colonists pay part of the high costs of maintaining British troops in America.

_____ 6. Americans generally accepted the right of Parliament to tax colonies to provide for defense, but denied its right to legislate colonial affairs.

_____ 7. When Americans first cried "no taxation without representation," what they wanted was to be represented in the British Parliament.

_____ 8. The colonies finally forced repeal of the Stamp Act by organizing protests and enforcing nonimportation agreements against British goods.

_____ 9. Colonial resistance to the Townshend Acts' import taxes was even more violent and effective than resistance to the Stamp Act.

____ 10. After the Boston Massacre, the British government pursued even harsher enforcement of the Townshend Acts.

____ 11. Weakening resistance to the tea tax was revived by the agitation of the Committees of Correspondence and the British authorities' decision to support the import of large amounts of tea by the British East India monopoly.

____ 12. The colonists considered the Quebec Act especially oppressive because it appeared to threaten the liberties of all the colonies and extend the domain of Roman Catholicism.

____ 13. The First Continental Congress proclaimed that the colonies would declare independence from Britain unless their grievances were redressed.

____ 14. One fundamental American asset in the impending war with Britain was its military force of volunteers.

____ 15. A British advantage was that they did not have to defeat all the American forces but only fight to a draw in order to crush the Revolution.

B. Multiple Choice

Select the best answer and put the proper letter in the space provided.

____ 1. The theory of mercantilism, by which the colonies were governed, held that

   a. the economy should be shaped by market forces, without government interference.
   b. the colonies should develop by becoming as economically self-sufficient as possible
   c. the colonial economy should be carefully controlled to serve the mother country's
   d. colonists should promote economic growth by free trade with other countries.

____ 2. One of the ways in which mercantilism harmed the colonial economy was

   a. by prohibiting colonial merchants from owning and operating their own ships
   b. by inhibiting the development of banking and paper currency in the colonies
   c. by forcing the colonists to fall into debt through the purchase of goods on c
   d. by forcing Virginia tobacco planters to sell their product only in Britain.

____ 3. In protesting against the Sugar Act and the Stamp Act, the colonists argued

   a. Britain had a right to regulate colonial trade but not to impose taxes or
   b. Britain had no right to regulate or tax colonial trade.
   c. Britain had a right to tax colonial trade, but not to try violators in ad   y courts.
   d. Britain had no right to impose taxes unless the colonists could be r   ited in the British Parliament.

_____ 4. The British troops killed in the Boston Massacre had been sent to the city as a result of

    a. colonial protests against the Stamp Act.
    b. the illegal activities of the Committees of Correspondence.
    c. colonial resistance to the Quartering Act of 1767.
    d. disruptive colonial resistance to the Townshend Act tax on tea and other products.

_____ 5. The British reacted to the Boston Tea Party by

    a. shipping the colonial protestors to Britain for trial.
    b. closing the port of Boston until damages were paid and order restored.
    c. passing the Quebec Act, prohibiting trial by jury, and permitting the practice of Catholicism.
    d. lifting the tax on tea but granting a monopoly on its sale to the British East India Company.

_____ 6. The most important action the First Continental Congress took to protest the Intolerable Acts was

    a. the formation of The Association to impose a complete boycott of all British goods.
    b. the organization of a colonial militia to prepare for military resistance.
    c. the formation of Committees of Correspondence to unite all the colonies in political opposition to British rule.
    d. the sending of petitions to the British Parliament demanding repeal of the laws.

_____ 7. The event that precipitated the first shooting between the British and the colonists was

    a. colonial resistance to the Stamp Act.
    b. the British attempt to seize colonial supplies and leaders at Lexington and Concord.
    c. the Boston Tea Party.
    d. the Boston Massacre.

_____ 8. One of the advantages the British enjoyed in the impending conflict with the colonies was

    a. a determined and politically effective government.
    b. the ability to enlist foreign soldiers, Loyalists, and Native Americans in their military forces.
    c. a highly motivated and efficiently run military force in America.
    d. the concentration of colonial resistance in a few urban nerve centers.

_____ 9. One of the advantages the colonists enjoyed in the impending conflict with Britain was

    a. fighting defensively on a large, agriculturally self-sufficient continent.
    b. a well-organized and effective political leadership.
    c. a strong sense of unity among the various colonies.
    d. the ability to provide substantial financial support for the war effort.

_____ 10. The American military forces benefited greatly from

    a. the leadership and training of foreign officers like Lafayette and von Steuben.
    b. the wealth of military supplies provided by the colonists.
    c. the effective tactics and high morale of the colonial militia.
    d. the united patriotic support of merchants and other citizens.

C. Identification

Supply the correct identification for each numbered description.

_____ 1. The basic economic and political theory by which seventeenth- and eighteenth-century European powers governed their overseas colonies

_____ 2. The set of Parliamentary laws, first passed in 1650, that restricted colonial trade and directed it to the benefit of Britain

_____ 3. The term for products, such as tobacco, that could be shipped only to Britain and not to foreign markets

_____ 4. Hated British courts in which juries were not allowed and defendants were assumed guilty until proved innocent

_____ 5. British governmental theory that Parliament spoke for all British subjects, including Americans, even if they did not vote for its members

_____ 6. The effective form of organized colonial resistance against the Stamp Act that made homespun clothing fashionable

_____ 7. The item taxed under the Townshend Acts that generated the greatest colonia resistance

_____ 8. Underground networks of communication and propaganda, established by Sam Adams, that sustained colonial resistance

_____ 9. Religion that was granted toleration in the trans-Allegheny West by the Quebe arousing deep colonial hostility

_____ 10. British political party opposed to Lord North's Tories and generally more   a-thetic to the colonial cause

_____ 11. German mercenaries hired by George III to fight the American revolutior

_____ 12. Currency that was authorized by Congress to finance the Revolution and   ciated to near worthlessness

_____ 13. Effective organization created by the First Continental Congress to   e a total, unified boycott of all British goods

_____ 14. Rapidly mobilized colonial militiamen whose refusal to disperse   ed the first battle of the Revolution

_____ 15. Term for British regular troops, scorned as "lobster backs" and   dy backs" by Bostonians and other colonials

D. Matching People, Places, and Events

Match the person, place, or event in the left column with the proper description in the right column by inserting the correct letter on the blank line.

___ 1. John Hancock

___ 2. George Grenville

___ 3. Stamp Act

___ 4. Sons and Daughters of Liberty

___ 5. "Champagne Charley" Townshend

___ 6. Crispus Attucks

___ 7. George III

___ 8. Samuel Adams

___ 9. Boston Tea Party

___ 10. Intolerable Acts

___ 11. Quebec Act

___ 12. First Continental Congress

___ 13. Marquis de Lafayette

___ 14. Baron von Steuben

___ 15. Quartering Act

A. British minister who raised a storm of protest by passing the Stamp Act

B. Legislation passed in 1765 but repealed the next year, after colonial resistance made it impossible to enforce

C. Body that issued a Declaration of Rights and organized The Association to boycott all British goods

D. Legislation that required colonists to feed and shelter British troops

E. Nineteen-year-old major general in the Revolutionary army

F. Wealthy president of the Continental Congress and "King of Smugglers"

G. Minister whose clever attempt to impose import taxes nearly succeeded but eventually brewed trouble for Britain

H. Zealous defender of the common people's rights and organizer of underground propaganda committees

I. Harsh measures of retaliation for a tea party, including the Boston Port Act

J. Stubborn ruler, lustful for power; served by compliant ministers like Lord North

K. Alleged leader of radical protesters killed in Boston Massacre

L. Military organizational genius who turned raw colonial recruits into tough professional soldiers

M. Organized women and men who enforced the nonimportation agreements, sometimes by coercive means

N. Actually a sensible piece of colonial legislation, linked by colonists to Intolerable Acts and seen as a sign of British repression

O. Drastic protest organized by disguised "Indians" to sabotage British support of British East India Company monopoly

E. Putting Things in Order

Put the following events in correct order by numbering them from 1 to 10.

___ Britain attempts to gain revenue by a stamp tax on papers and documents.

___ Britain closes the port of Boston and opens the western frontier to Catholicism.

___ Crispus Attucks leads a Boston crowd in an attack on British troops, and eleven people are killed.

___ Colonial Minute Men fire "the shot heard round the world" in the first battle of the Revolution.

___ A British minister cleverly attempts to gain revenue and dampen colonial protest by imposing an import tax only on certain specialized products.

___ A British agency is established with broad but generally ineffective power over colonial commerce.

___ Samuel Adams and others organize revolutionary cells of communication and agitation across the colonies.

___ Parliament repeals a direct tax in response to colonial protest but declares that it has the right to tax colonies.

___ A band of "Indians" dumps the rich cargo of the British East India Company into Boston Harbor.

___ First Navigation Acts are passed by Parliament to regulate colonial trade based on mercantilist principles.

PART III: Applying What You Have Learned

1. How did the American colonies move from loyalty to protest to rebellion in the twelve years following the end of the French and Indian War?
2. How and why did the Americans and the British differ in their views of taxation and of the relationship of colonies to the empire?
3. What was the theory and practice of mercantilism? What were its actual effects on the colonies, and why did they resent it so much?
4. What methods did the colonists use in their struggle with British authorities, and how did the British try to counteract them?
5. Was the American Revolution inevitable? Or could the thirteen colonies have remained attached to Britain for many years and then gained independence peacefully, as Canada and Australia eventually did?

8
★★★★★★★★

America Secedes from the Empire,
1775–1783

PART I: Reviewing the Chapter

A. Checklist of Learning Objectives

After mastering this chapter, you should be able to

1. describe how America passed from military hostilities with Britain to declaring its independence.
2. explain the specific reasons and general principles used in the Declaration of Independence to justify America's separation.
3. explain why some Americans remained loyal to Britain and what happened to them during and after the Revolution.
4. describe how the British attempt to crush the Revolution quickly was foiled, especially by the Battle of Saratoga.
5. describe the role of the French alliance in the Revolution.
6. describe the military and political obstacles Washington and his generals had to overcome before the final victory at Yorktown.
7. describe the terms of the Treaty of Paris and explain how America was able to achieve such a stunning diplomatic victory.

B. Glossary

To build your social science vocabulary, familiarize yourself with the following terms.

1. **indictment** A formal written accusation charging someone with a crime. "The overdrawn bill of indictment included imposing taxes without consent. . . ." (p. 97)
2. **dictatorship** A form of government characterized by absolute state power and the unlimited authority of the ruler. "The [charges] included . . . establishing a military dictatorship. . . ." (p. 97)
3. **civilian** A citizen not in military service. "The opposing forces contended . . . for the allegiance of the civilian population." (p. 97)
4. **confiscate** To seize private property for public use, often as a penalty. ". . . their estates were confiscated. . . ." (p. 98)

5. **envoy** A messenger or agent sent by a government on official business. "Benjamin Franklin, recently sent to Paris as an envoy, truthfully jested [about] Howe. . . ." (p. 99)
6. **rabble** A mass of disorderly and crude common people. "This rabble was nevertheless whipped into a professional army. . . ." (p. 99)
7. **arsenal** A place for making or storing weapons and ammunition. "About 90 percent of all the gunpowder . . . came from French arsenals." (p. 100)
8. **privateer** A private vessel temporarily authorized to capture or plunder enemy ships in wartime. "More numerous and damaging than ships of the regular American navy were swift privateers." (p. 102)
9. **blockade** The isolation of a place by hostile ships or troops. ". . . de Grasse blockaded them by sea. . . ." (p. 102)

PART II: Checking Your Progress

A. True-False

Where the statement is true, mark **T.** Where it is false, mark **F,** and correct it in the space immediately below.

____ 1. George Washington was chosen commander of the American army more for his military abilities than for his personal and political attributes.

____ 2. Following the Battle of Bunker Hill, King George and the Continental Congress made one last attempt at reconciliation.

____ 3. The American army invaded Canada before the Declaration of Independence.

____ 4. Some American Patriots favored independence but rejected Tom Paine's arguments against social hierarchy in *Common Sense*.

____ 5. The Declaration of Independence was especially important because it enabled the Americans to appeal for direct aid from France.

____ 6. American militiamen proved politically very effective in pushing their apathetic or neutral fellow citizens into supporting the Patriot cause.

____ 7. About 20 percent of the American colonists were Loyalists.

____ 8. The Patriots were strongest in New York, New Jersey, Pennsylvania, and the South outside Virginia.

____ 9. Most Loyalists were executed or driven from the country after the Patriot victory.

____ 10. General Burgoyne's defeat at Saratoga in 1777 was critical for the American cause because it led to the alliance with France.

____ 11. French entry into the war turned the American Revolutionary War into a world war.

____ 12. During much of the Revolutionary War, the British controlled cities like New York, Boston, Philadelphia, and Charleston.

____ 13. At Yorktown, the Americans finally showed that they could win an important battle without French assistance.

____ 14. American diplomats were successful in guaranteeing American political independence but failed to gain the territorial concessions they wanted.

____ 15. American success in the Revolutionary War and the peace treaty was due in significant measure to developments in Europe.

B. Multiple Choice

Select the best answer and put the proper letter in the space provided.

____ 1. During the period of fighting between April 1775 and July 1776, the colonists claimed to want

    a. the removal of all British troops from America.
    b. to restore their rights within the British Empire.
    c. complete independence from Britain.
    d. to end the power of King George III to rule them.

____ 2. Tom Paine's *Common Sense* startled the colonists by arguing boldly for

    a. direct military resistance to British rule.
    b. an alliance with the French king against Britain.
    c. the invasion and conquest of Canada.
    d. an independent and republican America separate from Britain.

____ 3. The Loyalists were particularly strong among

    a. conservative and well-off Americans.
    b. the younger generation.
    c. Presbyterians and Congregationalists.
    d. citizens of New England.

____ 4. Besides George Washington, the most militarily effective American officer in the early campaigns of 1776 and 1777 was

    a. General Johnny Burgoyne.
    b. General Freidrich von Steuben.
    c. General Benedict Arnold.
    d. General William Howe.

____ 5. The Battle of Saratoga was a key turning point of the War for Independence because

    a. it prevented the British from keeping control of the key port of New York City.
    b. it brought about crucial French assistance to the Revolutionary cause.
    c. it ended the possibility of a peaceful settlement with Britain.
    d. it effectively destroyed British military power in the middle colonies.

6. The primary French motive in aiding the American cause was

    a. to weaken the British Empire.
    b. to promote republican government and the principles of the Declaration of Independence.
    c. to test new forms of military weaponry and tactics.
    d. to gain the economic advantage of trade with the former British colonies.

7. The British especially relied on numerous Loyalists to aid them in fighting the Patriots

    a. in Rhode Island and the rest of New England.
    b. in the western Illinois country.
    c. in the naval battles at sea.
    d. in the Carolinas.

8. In addition to Washington's army, the British defeat at Yorktown was brought about by

    a. the French navy under Admiral de Grasse.
    b. the American navy under John Paul Jones.
    c. the American militia under George Rogers Clark.
    d. the Armed Neutrality under Catherine the Great.

9. In the peace negotiations at Paris, the French wanted the Americans

    a. to stop short of demanding full independence.
    b. to negotiate a separate peace with Britain.
    c. to acquire only the territory east of the Appalachian Mountains.
    d. to achieve political and military domination of North America.

10. The British yielded the Americans a generous peace treaty that included the western territories primarily because of

    a. the desire of the new Whig ministry in London for friendly future relations with the United States.
    b. the threat of further war with France.
    c. the military power of the United States.
    d. the willingness of the Americans to yield on other issues like trade and fishing rights.

C. Identification

Supply the correct identification for each numbered description.

_____ 1. The body that chose George Washington commander of the Continental Army

_____ 2. The British colony that Americans invaded in hopes of adding it to the rebellious thirteen

_____ 3. The inflammatory pamphlet that demanded independence and heaped scorn on "the Royal Brute of Great Britain"

_____ 4. The document that provided a lengthy explanation and justification of Richard Henry Lee's resolution, approved by Congress on July 2, 1776

_____ 5. The term by which the American rebels were commonly known, to distinguish them from the American "Tories"

_____ 6. Another name for the American Tories

_____ 7. The church body most closely linked with Tory sentiment, except in Virginia

_____ 8. The river valley that was the focus of Britain's early military strategy and the scene of Burgoyne's surrender at Saratoga in 1777

_____ 9. Term for the alliance of Catherine the Great of Russia and other European powers who did not declare war but assumed a hostile neutrality toward Britain

_____ 10. The region that saw some of the Revolution's most bitter fighting, from 1780 to 1782, between the American General Greene and the British General Cornwallis

_____ 11. "Legalized pirates," more than a thousand strong, who inflicted heavy damage on British shipping

_____ 12. British political party that replaced Lord North's Tories in 1782 and made a generous treaty with the United States

_____ 13. The western boundary of the United States established by the Treaty of Paris

_____ 14. The irregular American troops who played a crucial role in swaying the neutral civilian population toward the Patriot cause

_____ 15. The other European nation besides France and Spain that supported the American Revolution by declaring war on Britain

D. Matching People, Places, and Events

Match the person, place, or event in the left column with the proper description in the right column by inserting the correct letter on the blank line.

____ 1. George Washington

____ 2. Bunker Hill

____ 3. Benedict Arnold

____ 4. Thomas Paine

____ 5. Richard Henry Lee

____ 6. Thomas Jefferson

____ 7. Loyalists

____ 8. General John Burgoyne

A. British general who chose to relax in New York and Philadelphia rather than march up the Hudson to battle

B. Brilliant American general who invaded Canada, foiled Burgoyne's invasion, and in 1780 betrayed his country

C. American naval commander who harassed British shipping

D. Author of an explanatory indictment, signed on July 4, 1776, that accused George III of establishing a military dictatorship and maintaining standing armies in peacetime

E. Shrewd American diplomat who established the French alliance and worked with Jay and Adams to win a generous peace treaty

F. American diplomat whose clever secret negotiations with the British paved the way for a peace more in America's interests and less in France's interests

___	9. General William Howe	**G.**	The decisive early battle of the American Revolution that led to the alliance with France
___	10. Benjamin Franklin	**H.**	Military engagement that, although technically a British victory, cost the redcoats heavily and led the king to declare the colonists in revolt
___	11. George Rogers Clark	**I.**	Those who, despite their American birth, fought for King George and earned the contempt of Patriots
___	12. John Paul Jones	**J.**	A wealthy Virginian of great character and leadership abilities who served his country without pay
___	13. Saratoga	**K.**	The British defeat that led to the fall of North's government and the end of the war
___	14. Yorktown	**L.**	Leader whose small force conquered British forts in the West
___	15. John Jay	**M.**	A radical British immigrant who put an end to American toasts to King George
		N.	Fiery Virginian and author of the official resolution of July 2, 1776, formally authorizing the colonies' independence
		O.	Blundering British general whose slow progress down from Canada ended in disaster at Saratoga

E. Putting Things in Order

Put the following events in correct order by numbering them from 1 to 6.

___ Lord North's military collapses, and Whigs take power ready to make peace.

___ Thomas Jefferson writes an eloquent justification of Richard Henry Lee's resolution.

___ Burgoyne and Howe are defeated both by the generalship of Washington and Arnold and by their own blundering.

___ The Treaty of Paris is signed, guaranteeing American independence.

___ The British launch a frontal attack on entrenched American forces near Boston and suffer drastic losses in their "victory."

___ Washington's army and the French navy trap General Cornwallis, spelling the end for the British.

PART III: Applying What You Have Learned

1. Why was the Battle of Saratoga such a key to American success in the Revolutionary War?
2. What were the causes and consequences of the American Declaration of Independence in 1776?
3. What role did Washington, Paine, Jefferson, Arnold, Franklin, and Jay each play in bringing about the success of the American cause?
4. Who were the Loyalists, what role did they play during the Revolution, and what happened to them afterward?
5. How did Americans move from defending their "rights of Englishmen" to declaring their independenceon the basis of "self-evident truths" and universal human rights?

9

★★★★★★★★★

The Confederation and the Constitution,

1776–1790

PART I: Reviewing the Chapter

A. Checklist of Learning Objectives

After mastering this chapter, you should be able to

1. explain how and why the United States replaced the Articles of Confederation with the Constitution.
2. describe the basic intentions of the founding fathers and how they incorporated their principles into the Constitution.
3. describe the process of ratification of the Constitution.
4. explain the effects of the Revolution on American society and politics at the state and national levels.
5. describe the government of the Articles of Confederation and indicate its achievements and failures.
6. explain the crucial role of Shays's Rebellion in sparking the movement for a new Constitution.
7. describe the antifederalists and their social, economic, and political differences with the federalists.

B. Glossary

To build your social science vocabulary, familiarize yourself with the following terms.

1. **disestablish** To separate an official state church from its connection with the government. ". . . the Protestant Episcopal church . . . was everywhere disestablished." (p. 109)
2. **emancipation** Setting free from servitude or slavery. "Several northern states . . . provided for the gradual emancipation of blacks." (p. 109)
3. **chattel** An article of personal or movable property; hence a term applied to slaves, since they were considered the personal property of their owners. ". . . a few idealistic masters freed their human chattels." (p. 109)
4. **abolitionist** Favoring the end of slavery. "In this . . . were to be found the first frail sprouts of the later abolitionist movement." (p. 109)
5. **ratification** The confirmation or validation of an act (such as a constitution) by authoritative approval. "Massachusetts . . . submitted the final draft directly to the people for ratification." (p. 109)

6. **bill of rights** A list of fundamental freedoms assumed to be central to society. "Most of these documents included bills of rights. . . ." (p. 110)

7. **speculators** Those who buy land, goods, or financial instruments not for their intrinsic value, but to hold them for sale after an expected rise in price. ". . . rich speculators had their day. . . ." (p. 110)

8. **township** In America, a surveyed territory six miles square; the term also refers to a unit of local government, smaller than a county, that is often based on these survey units. "The sixteenth section of each township was set aside to be sold for the benefit of the public schools. . . ." (p. 113)

9. **territory** In American government, an organized political entity not yet enjoying the full and equal status of a state. ". . . when a territory could boast sixty thousand inhabitants, it might be admitted by Congress as a state. . . ." (p. 113)

10. **annex** To make a smaller territory or political unit part of a large one. ". . . to annex Vermont to Canada." (p. 113)

11. **foreclosure** Depriving someone of the right to redeem mortgaged property because the legal payments on the loan have not been kept up. ". . . these desperate debtors demanded . . . a suspension of mortgage foreclosures." (p. 114)

12. **quorum** The minimum number of persons who must be present in a group before it can conduct valid business. "A quorum of the fifty-five emissaries . . . finally convened at Philadelphia. . . ." (p. 115)

13. **anarchy** The theory that formal government is unnecessary and wrong in principle; the term is also used generally for lawlessness or antigovernmental disorder. "Delegates were determined to preserve the union [and] forestall anarchy. . . ." (p. 116)

PART II: Checking Your Progress

A. True-False

Where the statement is true, mark **T**. Where it is false, mark **F**, and correct it in the space immediately below.

_____ 1. The American Revolution created a substantial though not radical push in the direction of social and political equality.

_____ 2. The movement toward the separation of church and state was greatly accelerated by the disestablishment of the Anglican church in Virginia.

_____ 3. After the Revolution, Americans made a strong effort to abolish slavery in both the North and the South.

_____ 4. The special constitutional convention and ratification of constitutions by the people was an important new idea of the Revolutionary period.

_____ 5. The state governments after the Revolution stayed mostly under the tight political control of the eastern seaboard elite.

_____ 6. The United States experienced hard economic times and some social discontent during the years of the Confederation (1781–1787).

_____ 7. The greatest failure of the national government under the Articles of Confederation was its inability to deal with the issue of western lands.

___   8. The Articles of Confederation were weak because they authorized neither an executive nor a power to tax or regulate commerce.

___   9. The Northwest Ordinance originally attempted to make the western territories permanent colonial possessions of the United States.

___   10. Shays's Rebellion raised the fear of anarchy among conservatives and significantly strengthened the movement for a stronger central government.

___   11. The states sent their delegates to Philadelphia in 1787 for the clear purpose of writing a new Constitution with a strong central government.

___   12. The delegates to the Constitutional Convention were a good cross section of American society at that time.

___   13. The "Great Compromise" at the convention resulted in a bicameral legislature, with different principles of representation in the House and the Senate.

___   14. The antifederalists opposed the Constitution partly because they thought it gave too much power to the states and not enough to Congress.

___   15. The federalists used tough political maneuvering and the promise of a bill of rights to win a narrow ratification of the Constitution in key states.

B. Multiple Choice

Select the best answer and put the proper letter in the space provided.

___   1. Among the important changes brought about by the American Revolution was

    a. the abolition of slavery in all the states.
    b. a strong movement toward equality of property rights.
    c. the increasing separation of church and state.
    d. full equality and voting rights for women.

___   2. A major new political innovation that emerged in the Revolutionary era was

    a. the election of legislative representatives capable of voting on taxation.
    b. the shifting of power from the legislative to the executive branch of government.
    c. the idea of a written constitution drafted by a convention and ratified by direct vote of the people.
    d. the regulation of land sales by the courts.

___   3. The primary obstacle to the formation of the first American government under the Articles of Confederation was

    a. disputes among the jealous states over control of western lands.
    b. disagreement over the relative power of Congress and the executive branch.
    c. conflict over the right of Congress to regulate trade and manufacturing.
    d. conflict over slavery between northern and southern states.

greatest weakness of the government under the Articles of Confederation was that

    it was unable to deal with the issue of western lands.

b. it had no power to regulate commerce or collect taxes from the sovereign states.

c. it had no power to establish relations with foreign governments.

d. the legislative branch was unable to cope with the powerful executive branch.

5. The Northwest Ordinance of 1787 provided that

    a. the states should retain permanent control of their western lands.

    b. money from the sale of western lands should be used to promote manufacturing.

    c. after sufficient population growth, western territories could be organized and then join the union as states.

    d. the settlers in the northwest could vote on whether or not they should have slavery.

6. Shays's Rebellion contributed to the movement for a new constitution by

    a. demonstrating the desire of western farmers for a strong government to assist them.

    b. raising the fear of anarchy and disorder, especially among wealthy conservatives.

    c. raising the prospect of British or French interference in American domestic affairs.

    d. demonstrating that the Northwest Ordinance had failed to resolve western land issues.

7. In addition to George Washington, the most influential figures in the Constitutional Convention included

    a. Alexander Hamilton, Daniel Shays, and John Hancock.

    b. Thomas Jefferson, Patrick Henry, and Thomas Paine.

    c. John Adams, Abigail Adams, and Gouverneur Morris.

    d. Benjamin Franklin, James Madison, and Alexander Hamilton.

8. The "Great Compromise" in the Constitutional Convention provided that

    a. the House of Representatives would be elected by the people and the Senate by the state legislatures.

    b. the large states would be taxed on the basis of population and the small states on the basis of territory.

    c. there would be separation of powers between the executive and legislative branches of government.

    d. there would be representation by population in the House of Representatives but equal representation of all states in the Senate.

9. Antifederalists generally found their greatest support among

    a. small states like Delaware and New Jersey.

    b. the commercial areas of the eastern seaboard.

    c. the poorer debtors and farmers.

    d. the wealthy and well educated.

10. The crucial federalist successes in the fight for ratification occurred in

    a. Georgia, Maryland, and Delaware.

    b. Massachusetts, Virginia, and New York.

    c. Pennsylvania, North Carolina, and Rhode Island.

    d. Connecticut, South Carolina, and New Hampshire.

Name _____ Section _____ Date _____

C. Identification

Supply the correct identification for each numbered description.

_____   1. New name for the Anglican church after it was disestablished in Virginia and elsewhere

_____   2. State that temporarily gave women the right to vote after the American Revolution

_____   3. A type of special assembly, originally developed in Massachusetts, for drawing up a fundamental law that would be superior to ordinary law

_____   4. The framework under which the first constitutional government of the United States was set up

_____   5. The territory north of the Ohio and east of the Mississippi governed by the acts of 1785 and 1787

_____   6. One-square-mile areas, thirty-six of which comprised a township, with one set aside for the support of schools

_____   7. The status of a western area under the Northwest Ordinance after it established an organized government but before it became a state

_____   8. A failed revolt in 1786 by poor debtor farmers that raised fears of "mobocracy"

_____   9. The plan proposed by Virginia at the Constitutional Convention for a legislature with representation based on population

_____   10. The plan proposed by New Jersey for a legislature with equal representation of states regardless of size and population

_____   11. The compromise between North and South that resulted in each slave being counted as 60 percent of a free person for purposes of representation

_____   12. The opponents of the Constitution who argued against creating a strong central government

_____   13. A masterly series of pro-Constitution articles printed in New York by Jay, Madison, and Hamilton

_____   14. The official of the new Constitution who would be commander in chief of the armed forces, appoint judges and other officials, and have the power to veto legislation

_____   15. A list of guaranteed liberties that federalists promised to add to the Constitution after it was ratified

Matching People, Places, and Events

Match the person, place, or event in the left column with the proper description in the right column by inserting the correct letter on the blank line.

___ 1. Society of the Cincinnati

___ 2. Virginia Statute for Religious Freedom

___ 3. Articles of Confederation

___ 4. Northwest Ordinance of 1787

___ 5. Dey of Algiers

___ 6. Daniel Shays

___ 7. George Washington

___ 8. James Madison

___ 9. Federalists

___ 10. Antifederalists

___ 11. Patrick Henry

___ 12. Alexander Hamilton

___ 13. John Jay

___ 14. Massachusetts

___ 15. New York

A. Group that opposed the Constitution and forced the promise of a bill of rights

B. Father of the Constitution and author of *Federalist #10*

C. An exclusive order of military officers that aroused strong democratic opposition

D. Wealthy conservatives who advocated passage of the Constitution

E. Legislation passed by an alliance of Jefferson and the Baptists that disestablished the Anglican church

F. War veteran who led poor farmers in a revolt that failed but had far-reaching consequences

G. North African leader who preyed on American shipping and took advantage of the weakness of the Articles of Confederation

H. State that narrowly ratified the Constitution after persuasive efforts of Alexander Hamilton

I. Frustrated foreign affairs secretary under the Articles; one of the three authors of *The Federalist*

J. Legislation that provided for the orderly transformation of western territories into states

K. First of key states where federalists won by a narrow margin, overcoming the opposition of antifederalist Sam Adams

L. Virginia antifederalist leader who thought the Constitution spelled the end of liberty and equality

M. Unanimously elected chairman of the secret convention of "demi-gods"

N. Young New Yorker who argued eloquently for the Constitution even though he favored a still stronger central government

O. Document that was put into effect in 1781, then put out of business by the Constitution

E. Putting Things in Order

Put the following events in correct order by numbering them from 1 to 5.

___ Fifty-five "demi-gods" meet secretly in Philadelphia to draft a new charter of government.

___ The first American national government, more a league of states than a real government, goes into effect.

___ At the request of Congress, the states draft new constitutions based on the authority of the people.

___ The Constitution is ratified by the nine states necessary to put it into effect.

____   Debtor farmers fail in a rebellion, sett[...]ff conservative fears and demands for a stronger government to control anarchy.

PART III: Applying [...]t You Have Learned

1. What problems of the post-Revolutionary perio[...] weaknesses of the Articles of Confederation led to the adoption of a new Constitution?
2. What were the basic features of the new Constit[...], and how did they differ from the government under the Articles of Confederation?
3. Who were the federalists and the antifederalists, [...] were the issues that divided them, and why did the federalists win?
4. What changes in American politics and society we[...] used by the Revolution, and how did those changes arouse conservative fears of anarchy?
5. The text declares that the Constitution was a victory [...] conservatives that effectively preserved the principles of popular, democratic government. What featu[...] the new Constitution were plainly "conservative," and what features reflected the founders' adherence [...] ic ideals of the American Revolution?

10
★★★★★★★★★

Launching the New Ship of State,
1789–1800

PART I: Reviewing the Chapter

A. Checklist of Learning Objectives

After mastering this chapter, you should be able to

1. describe how the new federal government was put into place and began functioning
2. describe the various means Alexander Hamilton used to put the federal govern____ ____und financial footing.
3. explain how the conflict over Hamilton's policies led to the emergence of the ____ ____cal parties.
4. describe the polarizing effects of the French Revolution on American foreig____ ____and politics from 1790 to 1800.
5. explain why Washington negotiated the conciliatory Jay's Treaty with the ____ ____sh and why it provoked Jeffersonian outrage.
6. describe the causes of the undeclared war with France and analyze Ada____ decision to move toward peace rather than declare war.
7. describe the poisonous political atmosphere that produced the Alien ____ ____edition Acts and the Kentucky and Virginia resolutions in response.
8. describe the contrasting membership and principles of the Ham____ ____ian Federalists and the Jeffersonian Republicans.

B. Glossary

To build your social science vocabulary, familiarize yourself wi____ ____following terms.

1. **census** An official count of population; in the United Sta____ ____he federal census occurs every ten years. ". . . the first official census of 1790 recorded almost 4 milli____ ____ple." (p. 125)
2. **public debt** The debt of a government or nation to i____ ____ual creditors, also called the national debt. ". . . the public debt . . . was mountainous." (p. 126)
3. **cabinet** The body of official advisers to the head ____ ____overnment; in the United States, it consists of the heads of the major executive departments. "The C____ ____ution does not mention a cabinet. . . ." (p. 126)

4. **circuit court** A court of appeals that hears cases in several designated locations rather than a single place. "The act organized . . . federal district and circuit courts. . . ." (p. 127)

5. **fiscal** Concerning public finances—expenditures and revenues. "His plan was to shape the fiscal policies of the administration. . . ." (p. 128)

6. **assumption** The appropriation or taking on of obligations not originally one's own. "The secretary made a convincing case for 'assumption.'" (p. 128)

7. **excise** A tax on the manufacture, sale, or consumption of certain products. "Hamilton . . . secured from Congress an excise tax on a few domestic items, notably whiskey." (p. 129)

8. **medium of exchange** Any item, paper or otherwise, used as money. "They regarded [whiskey] as a . . . medium of exchange." (p. 130)

9. **impress** To force people or property into public service without choice. "They . . . impressed scores of seamen into service on English vessels. . . ." (p. 132)

10. **assimilation** The merging of diverse cultures or peoples into one. "This drastic new law violated the traditional American policy of . . . speedy assimilation." (p. 135)

11. **witch hunt** An investigation carried on with much publicity, supposedly to uncover dangerous activity but actually intended to weaken the political opposition. "Anti-French hysteria played directly into the hands of witch-hunting conservatives." (p. 136)

12. **compact** An agreement or covenant between states to perform some legal act. "Both Jefferson and Madison stressed the compact theory. . . ." (p. 136)

13. **nullification** In American politics, the assertion that a state may legally invalidate a federal act deemed inconsistent with its rights or sovereignty. ". . . 'nullification' was the 'rightful remedy.'" (p. 136)

PART II: Checking Your Progress

A. True-False

Where the statement is true, mark **T.** Where it is false, mark **F,** and correct it in the space immediately below.

_____ 1. Two important political institutions not mentioned in the Constitution that became established in the first Washington administration were the cabinet and political parties.

_____ 2. The passage of the first ten amendments to the Constitution demonstrated the federalist determination to develop a powerful central government.

_____ 3. Hamilton's basic purpose in all his financial measures was to strengthen the federal government.

_____ 4. Both "funding at par" of the federal debt and assumption of state debts were designed to give wealthier interests a strong stake in the success of the federal government.

_____ 5. Hamilton financed his large national debt by revenues from tariffs and taxes on products such as whiskey.

_____ 6. In the battle over the Bank of the United States, Jefferson favored a "loose construction" of the Constitution and Hamilton favored a "strict construction."

_____ 7. The first American political parties grew mainly out of states'-rights resistance to Hamilton's centralizing policies.

____ 8. The French Revolution, in both its moderate and its radical phases, was greeted with great approval by both Jeffersonian Republicans and Federalists.

____ 9. The founders welcomed political parties as an effective way to link politics and government.

____ 10. The British showed their respect for George Washington's military ability by carefully refraining from any acts that would violate American neutrality.

____ 11. George Washington supported Jay's unpopular treaty because he feared a disastrous war with Britain if it were rejected.

____ 12. Adams decided to negotiate peace with France in order to enhance his own popularity with the public.

____ 13. The Alien Laws were partly a conservative Federalist attempt to prevent radical French immigrants and spies from supporting the Jeffersonians.

____ 14. Jeffersonian Republicans believed that the common people were not to be trusted and had to be led by those who were better educated.

____ 15. The Jeffersonian Republicans generally sympathized with Britain in foreign policy, while the Hamiltonian Federalists sympathized with France.

B. Multiple Choice

Select the best answer and put the proper letter in the space provided.

____ 1. A key addition to the new federal government that had been demanded by many of the ratifying states was
   a. the organization of a cabinet to aid the president.
   b. a written bill of rights to guarantee liberty.
   c. the establishment of a supreme court.
   d. federal assumption of state debts.

____ 2. Hamilton's first financial policies were intended

   a. to finance the new government through the sale of western lands.
   b. to fund the entire national debt and to have the federal government assume the debts owed by the states.
   c. to repudiate the debts accumulated by the government of the Articles of Confederation.
   d. to issue sound federal currency backed by gold.

____ 3. The essential disagreement between Hamilton and Jefferson over the proposed Bank of the United States was

   a. whether or not the Constitution should be loosely constructed to permit the federal government to establish such a bank.
   b. whether or not it would be economically wise to create a single national currency.
   c. whether the bank should be under the control of the federal government or the states.
   d. whether or not such a bank would plunge the federal government into excessive debt.

4. The first American political parties developed out of

    a. the disagreement of Jefferson and his states'-rights followers with Hamilton's economic policies.
    b. the belief of the founding fathers that organized political opposition was a necessary part of good government.
    c. the continuing hostility of the antifederalists to the legitimacy of the new federal Constitution.
    d. patriotic opposition to foreign intervention in American domestic affairs.

5. Regarding the French Revolution, most Jeffersonian Democratic-Republicans believed that

    a. the violence was regrettable but necessary, and America ought to back the Revolution.
    b. the overthrow of the king was necessary, but the Reign of Terror went much too far.
    c. the Revolution was good, but America ought to stay strictly neutral in relation to European conflicts.
    d. the Revolution represented a complete distortion of American ideals of liberty.

6. George Washington's foreign policy rested on the basic belief that

    a. it was in America's interest to aid the British against revolutionary France.
    b. it was in America's interest to stay neutral in European wars.
    c. America was morally obligated to adhere to the alliance with France.
    d. America ought to enter the French-British war only if republican ideals were at stake.

7. The United States became involved in undeclared hostilities with France in 1797 because of

    a. fierce American opposition to the concessions of Jay's Treaty.
    b. American anger at attempted French bribery in the XYZ Affair.
    c. French interference with American shipping and freedom of the seas.
    d. President Adams's sympathy with Britain and hostility to revolutionary France.

8. The Alien and Sedition Acts were aimed primarily at

    a. the Jeffersonians and their allegedly pro-French activities and ideas.
    b. the opponents of President Adams's peace settlement with France.
    c. Napoleon's French agents who were infiltrating the country.
    d. the Hamiltonian Federalists and their pro-British activities and ideas.

9. Jefferson's Kentucky resolutions argued that

    a. the Alien and Sedition Acts were constitutional.
    b. the states ought to secede from the federal government.
    c. the states had the right to nullify unconstitutional federal laws.
    d. the Supreme Court had the right to declare legislation unconstitutional.

10. The Federalists essentially believed that

    a. most governmental power should be retained by the states.
    b. government should provide no special aid to any private enterprise.
    c. the common people could, if educated, participate in government affairs.
    d. there should be a strong central government controlled by the wealthy and well educated.

C. Identification

Supply the correct identification for each numbered description.

_____ 1. The official body of voters, chosen by the states under the new Constitution, who in 1789 unanimously elected George Washington as president

_____ 2. The constitutional office into which John Adams was sworn on April 30, 1789

_____ 3. The cabinet office in George Washington's administration headed by a brilliant young West Indian immigrant who distrusted the people

_____ 4. Alexander Hamilton's policy of paying off all federal bonds at face value, with interest, in order to strengthen the national credit

_____ 5. Hamilton's policy of having the federal government take over and pay the financial obligations of the states

_____ 6. The first ten amendments to the Constitution

_____ 7. Political organizations not envisioned in the Constitution and considered dangerous to national unity by most of the founding fathers

_____ 8. Political and social upheaval supported by most Americans during its moderate beginnings in 1789 but the cause of bitter division among Americans after it took a radical turn in 1792

_____ 9. Agreement signed between two anti-British countries in 1778 that increasingly plagued American foreign policy in the 1790s

_____ 10. Message issued by George Washington in 1793 that urged Americans to stay impartial in the French Revolutionary wars with the British

_____ 11. Document signed in 1794 whose terms favoring Britain outraged Jeffersonian Republicans

_____ 12. The nation with which the United States fought an undeclared war from 1798 to 1800

_____ 13. The political theory of American federalism on which Jefferson and Madison based their Virginia and Kentucky resolutions

_____ 14. The doctrine, proclaimed in the Virginia and Kentucky resolutions, that a state can block a federal law it considers unconstitutional

_____ 15. The nation to which most Hamiltonian Federalists were sentimentally attached and that they favored in foreign policy

D. Matching People, Places, and Events

Match the person, place, or event in the left column with the proper description in the right column by inserting the correct letter on the blank line.

___ 1. Census of 1790

___ 2. Alexander Hamilton

___ 3. Thomas Jefferson

___ 4. James Madison

___ 5. Supreme Court

___ 6. Funding and assumption

___ 7. Bank of the United States

___ 8. Whiskey Rebellion

___ 9. Federalists

___ 10. Republicans

___ 11. XYZ

___ 12. Talleyrand

___ 13. Alien and Sedition Acts

___ 14. Bill of Rights

___ 15. Washington's Farewell Address

A. A protest by poor western farmers that was firmly suppressed by George Washington and Hamilton's army

B. Body organized by the Judiciary Act of 1789 and first headed by John Jay

C. Brilliant administrator and financial wizard whose career was plagued by doubts about his character and loyalty

D. Political party that believed in the common people, no government aid for business, and a pro-French foreign policy

E. Effort that showed the 4 million Americans to be 90 percent rural and 95 percent east of the Appalachians

F. Skillful politician-scholar who drafted the Bill of Rights and moved it through the First Congress

G. Institution established by Hamilton to create a stable currency and bitterly opposed by states'-rights advocates

H. Hamilton's aggressive financial policies of paying off all federal bonds and taking on all state debts

I. Harsh and probably unconstitutional laws aimed at radical immigrants and Jeffersonian writers

J. Crafty French foreign minister who was first hostile and then friendly to Americans during a crisis

K. Message telling America that it should avoid unnecessary foreign entanglements

L. Code names for three French agents who attempted to bribe American diplomats in 1797

M. George Washington's secretary of state and organizer of a political party opposed to Hamilton's policies

N. Ten Constitutional amendments designed to protect liberties

O. Political party that believed in a strong government run by the wealthy, government aid to business, and a pro-British foreign policy

E. Putting Things in Order

Put the following events in correct order by numbering them from 1 to 5.

___ Revolutionary turmoil in France causes the U.S. president to urge Americans to stay out of foreign quarrels.

___ Envoys sent to make peace in France are insulted by bribe demands from three mysterious French agents.

___ First ten amendments to the Constitution are adopted.

___ Western farmers revolt against a Hamiltonian tax and are harshly suppressed.

___ Jefferson organizes a political party in opposition to Hamilton's financial policies.

PART III: Applying What You Have Learned

1. What were the most important issues facing the new federal government, and how were they addressed?
2. What were Hamilton's basic economic and political goals, and how did he attempt to achieve them?
3. What were the basic goals of George Washington's and John Adams's foreign policies, and how successful were they in achieving them?
4. How did the divisions over domestic and foreign policy create the first American political parties? Are political parties an asset or a liability in governing a democratic society? Defend your answer, using the first party system as an example.
5. Were the deep conflicts over domestic policy and relations with France ever really a threat to the stability of the new American government? What factors or leaders worked to overcome the most dangerous conflicts?

11

★★★★★★★★

The Triumphs and Travails of Jeffersonian Democracy,

1800–1812

PART I: Reviewing the Chapter

A. Checklist of Learning Objectives

After mastering this chapter, you should be able to

1. indicate how Jefferson's moderation and compromises turned the "Revolution of 1800" into a relatively smooth transition of party control from Federalists to Republicans.
2. describe the conflicts between Federalists and Republicans over the judiciary and the important legal precedents that developed from these conflicts.
3. analyze the causes and effects of the Louisiana Purchase.
4. describe how America became entangled against its will in the turbulent international crisis of the Napoleonic Wars.
5. describe the original intentions and actual results of Jefferson's embargo, and explain why it failed.
6. explain the causes of the War of 1812.

B. Glossary

To build your social science vocabulary, familiarize yourself with the following terms.

1. **writ** A formal legal document ordering or prohibiting some act. ". . . his Jeffersonian rivals . . . would hardly . . . enforce a writ to deliver the commission. . . ." (p. 144)
2. **cede** To yield or grant something, often upon request or under pressure. (Anything ceded is a *cession*.) "Napoleon Bonaparte induced the king of Spain to cede to France . . . the immense trans-Mississippi region. . . ." (p. 145)
3. **precedent** In law and government, a decision or action that establishes a sanctioned rule for determining similar cases in the future. ". . . the transfer established a precedent that was to be followed repeatedly. . . ." (p. 146)
4. **conscription** Compulsory enrollment into the armed forces. "Impressment . . . was a crude form of conscription. . . ." (p. 147)

5. **frigate** A fast, medium-sized sailing ship carrying twenty-eight to sixty guns. "... fired on a U.S. frigate, the Chesapeake. ..." (p. 148)

6. **embargo** A government order prohibiting commerce in or out of a port. "Irate citizens cynically transported the letters of 'embargo'. ..." (p. 148)

7. **inquisitorial** Concerning an excessively strict or aggressive official inquiry based on a presumption of guilt. "[The enforcing legislation] was so inquisitorial and tyrannical. ..." (p. 148)

8. **belligerent** A group or nation engaged in fighting. "... the United States would bribe the belligerents. ..." (p. 150)

9. **expansionist** Person who supports extending a nation's territory or sphere of influence, often at the expense of other nations. "Less vocal southern expansionists also cast a covetous eye on Florida. ..." (p. 151)

10. **treason** The criminal act of betraying one's country through providing material or assistance to an enemy, "The bitterness of New Englanders ... led them to treason and near-treason." (p. 152)

PART II: Checking Your Progress

A. True-False

Where the statement is true, mark **T.** Where it is false, mark **F,** and correct it in the space immediately below.

___ 1. Upon taking office, Jefferson dismissed most Federalist appointees and replaced them with his own Republican supporters.

___ 2. Two Federalist laws that Jefferson repealed were the fourteen-year naturalization requirement and the excise tax.

___ 3. Jefferson and his treasury secretary, Gallatin, kept most Federalist financial policies—such as funding, assumption, and the Bank of the United States—in place.

___ 4. The Jeffersonian Republicans showed their hostility to the Federalist Supreme Court by impeaching Chief Justice John Marshall.

___ 5. The case of *Marbury* v. *Madison* established the principle that the president could appoint but not remove Supreme Court justices.

___ 6. Jefferson cut the United States Army to 2,500 men because he believed that a large standing military was a threat to liberty and an economically frugal government.

___ 7. Jefferson's envoys to Paris initially intended to buy only New Orleans and the immediate vicinity.

___ 8. Jefferson's deepest concern about the Louisiana Purchase was that the price of $15 million was too high.

___ 9. The Federalists' opposition to the Louisiana Purchase made them more of a narrow New England party.

___ 10. After the *Chesapeake* affair, Jefferson could have declared war on Britain with the enthusiastic support of both Federalists and Republicans.

____ 11. Jefferson's embargo badly hurt Federalist New England but did little damage to the Republican South and West.

____ 12. New Englanders tried to overcome the effects of the embargo by trading illicitly with Canada and developing more domestic manufacturing.

____ 13. The large western delegation in Congress was not concerned about foreign-policy issues such as Canada and maritime rights.

____ 14. A good deal of western hostility to Britain arose because the war hawks believed that the British were supplying the Indians for war.

____ 15. New Englanders opposed the War of 1812 partly because they believed that Canada could be acquired by peaceful negotiation rather than war.

B. Multiple Choice

Select the best answer and put the proper letter in the space provided.

____ 1. The most "revolutionary" development in the critical election of 1800 was

a. the nasty campaign smears against Jefferson.
b. Jefferson's radical proposals for overturning the existing political system.
c. the peaceful transition of power from one political party to its opponent.
d. the electoral stalemate between Jefferson and his running mate, Burr.

____ 2. One Federalist policy that Jefferson quickly overturned was

a. funding and assumption.
b. the excise tax.
c. the Bank of the United States.
d. the protective tariff.

____ 3. The case of *Marbury* v. *Madison* established the principle that

a. the Supreme Court has the right to determine the constitutionality of legislation.
b. federal laws take precedence over state legislation.
c. the president has the right to appoint the federal judiciary.
d. federal judges cannot be impeached.

____ 4. Jefferson was forced to reverse his strong opposition to substantial military forces because of

a. growing French intervention in Santo Domingo and Louisiana.
b. the plunder and blackmailing of American shipping by North African states.
c. the threat to America posed by the British-French wars.
d. the political attacks by his Federalist opponents.

_____ 5. Jefferson's greatest concern in purchasing Louisiana was

    a. whether it was in America's interest to acquire the territory.
    b. whether the cost was excessive for his small-government philosophy.
    c. whether the purchase was permissible under the Constitution.
    d. how to defend and govern the territory once it was part of the United States.

_____ 6. The greatest political beneficiary of the Louisiana Purchase was

    a. Thomas Jefferson.
    b. Aaron Burr.
    c. the Federalist party.
    d. Napoleon.

_____ 7. _Impressment_ was the British practice of

    a. forcibly seizing American sailors for the British navy.
    b. stopping American ships to search for deserters.
    c. prohibiting American ships from entering European ports.
    d. demanding that American ships pay blackmail for protection against attack.

_____ 8. Jefferson's Embargo Act provided that

    a. America would not trade with Britain until it ended impressment.
    b. American goods could be carried only in American ships.
    c. America would sell no military supplies to either warring nation, Britain or France.
    d. America would prohibit all foreign trade.

_____ 9. One unintended effect of the embargo was

    a. to induce Britain and France to respect American neutral rights.
    b. to increase Jefferson's popularity in New England.
    c. to encourage domestic manufacturing in New England.
    d. to strengthen the American navy.

_____ 10. The embargo was replaced in 1809 by

    a. the Non-Intercourse Act prohibiting trade with Britain and France only.
    b. free and open trade with all nations.
    c. the Navigation Acts permitting trade in all nonmilitary goods.
    d. an undeclared naval war with Britain.

_____ 11. A crucial goal for many "war hawks" in the War of 1812 was

    a. the restoration of trade with Britain.
    b. the capture and annexation of Canada.
    c. the military protection of Louisiana.
    d. the destruction of the British navy.

___ 12. The War of 1812 was bitterly opposed by

    a. the military leaders of the army and navy.
    b. New England Federalists.
    c. Jeffersonians in the South.
    d. frontiersmen threatened by Indian attack.

C. Identification

Supply the correct identification for each numbered description.

_____ 1. Hamiltonian economic measure repealed by Jefferson and Gallatin

_____ 2. Action Jefferson took toward Republican "martyrs" convicted under the Federalist Sedition Law

_____ 3. Derogatory Republican term for Federalist judges appointed at the last minute by President Adams

_____ 4. Precedent-setting Supreme Court case in which Chief Justice Marshall dismissed a Federalist judge's suit but also declared part of the Judiciary Act of 1789 unconstitutional

_____ 5. The principle, established by Chief Justice Marshall in a famous case, that the Supreme Court can declare laws unconstitutional

_____ 6. Action voted by the House of Representatives against Supreme Court Justice Samuel Chase and feared by Chief Justice Marshall

_____ 7. Branch of military service that Jefferson considered least threatening to liberty and most necessary to suppressing the Barbary states

_____ 8. Sugar-rich island where Toussaint L'Ouverture's slave rebellion disrupted Napoleon's dreams of a vast New World empire

_____ 9. Territory beyond Louisiana, along the Columbia River, explored by Lewis and Clark

_____ 10. Harsh British orders closing all French-controlled ports to American shipping

_____ 11. Price paid by the United States for the Louisiana Purchase

_____ 12. American ship fired on by British in 1807, nearly leading to war between the two countries

_____ 13. Jefferson's policy of forbidding the shipment of any goods in or out of the United States

_____ 14. British policy of seizing American sailors and forcing them to serve on British ships

_____ 15. More moderate trade-restriction law that replaced the embargo in 1809 and opened trade with all nations except Britain and France

D. Matching People, Places, and Events

Match the person, place, or event in the left column with the proper description in the right column by inserting the correct letter on the blank line.

____ 1. Thomas Jefferson

____ 2. Albert Gallatin

____ 3. John Marshall

____ 4. *Marbury* v. *Madison*

____ 5. Samuel Chase

____ 6. Pasha of Tripoli

____ 7. Napoleon Bonaparte

____ 8. Robert Livingston

____ 9. Toussaint L'Ouverture

____ 10. Lewis and Clark

____ 11. Aaron Burr

____ 12. *Chesapeake* affair

____ 13. Embargo Act of 1807

____ 14. Non-Intercourse Act

____ 15. Orders in Council

A. Jefferson's vice president, the killer of Alexander Hamilton, and a plotter of mysterious secessionist schemes

B. Milder substitute for embargo that prohibited trade only with Britain and France

C. Swiss-born treasury secretary who disliked national debt but kept most Hamiltonian economic measures in effect

D. American minister to Paris who joined James Monroe in making a magnificent real estate deal

E. Strong believer in strict construction, weak government, and antimilitarism who was forced to modify some of his principles in office

F. Strict British prohibitions on any American trade with French-controlled Europe

G. Federalist Supreme Court justice impeached by the House in 1804 but acquitted by the Senate

H. British attack on American sailors that aroused angry demands for war

I. Explorers who crossed the Louisiana Purchase territory and went on to Oregon and the Pacific coast

J. Restrictive trade policy that hurt Britain but hurt American shippers and farmers even more

K. Ruling based on a "midnight judge" case that established the right of the Supreme Court to declare laws unconstitutional

L. North African leader who fought an undeclared war with the United States from 1801 to 1805

M. Gifted black revolutionary whose successful slave revolution indirectly led to Napoleon's sale of Louisiana

N. French ruler who acquired Louisiana from Spain only to sell it to the United States

O. Federalist Supreme Court justice whose rulings established the principle of judicial review

E. Putting Things in Order

Put the following events in correct order by numbering them from 1 to 5.

____   Rather than declare war after a British attack on an American ship, Jefferson imposes a ban on all American trade.

____   President Adams appoints a host of "midnight judges" just before leaving office, outraging Republicans.

____   The foreign difficulties of a French dictator lead him to offer a fabulous real estate bargain to the United States.

____   After four years of naval war, the Barbary state of Tripoli signs a peace treaty with the United States.

____   Western "War Hawks" push a divided America into a war against Britain.

PART III: Applying What You Have Learned

1. How were the two major events of Jefferson's presidency—the Louisiana Purchase and the embargo—related to events in Europe?
2. How did Jefferson end up modifying some of his Republican beliefs in strict constructionism, limited federal government, and militarism in the face of events during his presidency?
3. How did the conflict between Federalists and Republicans over the judiciary lead to a balance of power among political interests and different branches of government?
4. What were the causes of the War of 1812?
5. Americans sometimes refer to their system of government as "Jeffersonian democracy." How valid is this description in light of Jefferson's principles and practices as president from 1801 to 1809? Which of Jefferson's ideas have endured, and which have not?

12
★★★★★★★★★

The Second War for Independence and the Upsurge of Nationalism,

1812–1824

PART I: Reviewing the Chapter

A. Checklist of Learning Objectives

After mastering this chapter, you should be able to

1. describe the crucial military developments of the War of 1812.
2. explain the outcome of the war and its long-term effects.
3. describe and explain the burst of American nationalism that came in the wake of the War of 1812.
4. describe the major economic developments of the period, particularly the tariff, finances, and the Panic of 1819.
5. describe the conflict over slavery that arose in 1819 and the terms of the Missouri Compromise that temporarily resolved it.
6. indicate how John Marshall's Supreme Court promoted the spirit of nationalism through its rulings in favor of federal power.
7. describe the Monroe Doctrine and explain its real and symbolic significance for American foreign policy.

B. Glossary

To build your social science vocabulary, familiarize yourself with the following terms.

1. **protection (protective)** In economics, the policy of stimulating or preserving domestic producers by placing barriers against imported goods, often through high tariffs. "The infant industries bawled lustily for protection." (p. 159)
2. **raw materials** Products in their natural, unmanufactured state. "Through these new arteries of transportation would flow foodstuffs and raw materials. . . ." (p. 159)
3. **internal improvements** The basic public works, such as roads and canals, that create the structure for economic development. "Persistent and eloquent demands . . . for internal improvements struck a responsive chord with the public." (p. 160)

4. **intrastate** Existing wholly within a state of the United States. "Jeffersonian Republicans . . . choked on the idea of direct federal support of intrastate internal improvements." (p. 160)

5. **depression** In economics, a severe and often prolonged period of declining economic activity, rising unemployment, and falling wages and prices. "It brought deflation, depression, [and] bankruptcies. . . ." (p. 161)

6. **boom** In economics, a period of sudden, spectacular expansion of business activity or prices. "The western boom was stimulated by additional developments." (p. 161)

7. **peculiar institution** The institution of American black slavery. "If Congress could abolish the 'peculiar institution' in Missouri, might it not do likewise in the older states of the South?" (p. 162)

8. **manhood suffrage** The right of all men to vote, without regard to property or other qualifications. "In an age when white manhood suffrage was flowering. . . ." (p. 164)

9. **demagogic (demagogue)** Concerning a leader who stirs up the common people by appeals to emotion and prejudice, often for selfish or irrational ends. ". . . Marshall's decisions bolstered judicial barriers against democratic or demagogic attacks on property rights." (p. 164)

10. **contract** In law, an agreement in which each of two or more parties agrees to perform some act in exchange for what the other party promises to do. "But the Supreme Court . . . decreed that the legislative grant was a contract. . . ." (p. 164)

PART II: Checking Your Progress

A. True-False

Where the statement is true, mark **T**. Where it is false, mark **F**, and correct it in the space immediately below.

___ 1. The American strategy for conquering Canada was brilliant but failed because of a lack of equipment and troops.

___ 2. American naval forces under Perry and Macdonough thwarted British-Canadian invasion threats to Detroit and upstate New York.

___ 3. By 1814, British forces were nearly exhausted and eager to make peace.

___ 4. Andrew Jackson's victory at the Battle of New Orleans was morale-boosting but meaningless, since the peace treaty had already been signed.

___ 5. The Treaty of Ghent was essentially an armistice that did not settle the original issues of the war.

___ 6. The Hartford Convention passed resolutions in favor of nullification and possible secession from the Union.

___ 7. South Carolina's John C. Calhoun attempted to block Daniel Webster's nationalistic Tariff of 1816 in order to defend southern agricultural interests.

___ 8. Clay's and Calhoun's plans for an extensive system of federally funded roads and canals were blocked by the western states.

___ 9. The "Era of Good Feelings" under President Monroe was a period of sustained economic prosperity.

Name _____ Section _____ Date _____

____ 10. Because of its wildcat banking practices and land speculation, the West was hit especially hard in the Panic of 1819.

____ 11. The Missouri Compromise admitted Missouri to the Union as a free state in exchange for the admission of Louisiana as a slave state.

____ 12. John Marshall's Supreme Court rulings generally defended the power of the federal government against the power of the states.

____ 13. Andrew Jackson's military actions in Florida forced Spain to yield Florida to the United States.

____ 14. Secretary of State John Quincy Adams initially proposed to Britain that the two countries issue a joint declaration against further European interference in the Western Hemisphere.

____ 15. The Monroe Doctrine effectively prevented Britain and other European monarchies from threatening the new Latin American republics.

B. Multiple Choice

Select the best answer and put the proper letter in the space provided.

____ 1. The greatest American military successes of the War of 1812 came

    a. in the land invasions of Canada.
    b. in the campaign fought around Washington.
    c. in the naval battles on the Great Lakes and elsewhere.
    d. in the defense of Fort Michilimackinac.

____ 2. The American victory in the Battle of New Orleans proved essentially meaningless because

    a. General Jackson was unable to pursue the British any farther.
    b. the British continued their attacks on the Mississippi Valley region.
    c. the peace treaty had been signed several weeks before.
    d. the British navy retained control of the shipping lanes around New Orleans.

____ 3. The terms of the Treaty of Ghent ending the War of 1812 provided that

    a. there would be a buffer Indian state between the United States and Canada.
    b. Britain would stop impressment of American sailors.
    c. the United States would acquire western Florida in exchange for guaranteeing British control of Canada.
    d. the two sides would stop fighting and return to the status quo before the war.

____ 4. The Hartford Convention proposed that

    a. President Madison be impeached.
    b. America abandon its claims to Canada.
    c. new constitutional amendments be passed to protect Federalist influence.
    d. the peace negotiations at Ghent be pursued more vigorously.

5. One significant consequence of the War of 1812 was

    a. a weakening of respect for American naval forces.
    b. an increased threat from Indians in the West.
    c. an increase in domestic manufacturing and economic independence.
    d. the growth of sectionalism.

6. The so-called Era of Good Feelings was sharply disrupted by

    a. the bitter political battle over the Tariff of 1816.
    b. the rise of international tensions with Britain.
    c. the Panic of 1819 and subsequent economic hard times.
    d. the nasty presidential campaign of 1820.

7. Besides admitting both Missouri and Maine to the Union, the Missouri Compromise provided that

    a. no more slavery would be permitted in the Louisiana Purchase territory north of the southern boundary of Missouri.
    b. the number of proslavery and antislavery members of the House of Representatives would be kept equal.
    c. the slave trade would be permanently ended.
    d. slavery would be ended in the District of Columbia.

8. In the case of *McCulloch v. Maryland*, Chief Justice John Marshall held that

    a. the states had the right to regulate commerce within their boundaries.
    b. the federal Bank of the United States was constitutional, and no state had a right to tax it.
    c. the Supreme Court had the right to review the decisions of state supreme courts.
    d. the Supreme Court had the power to determine the constitutionality of federal laws.

9. The most prominent political figure who joined Marshall in expanding the power of the federal government at the expense of the states was

    a. James Monroe.
    b. John Calhoun.
    c. Daniel Webster.
    d. Andrew Jackson.

10. Andrew Jackson's invasion of Florida led to permanent acquisition of the territory after

    a. President Monroe ordered him to seize all Spanish military posts in the area.
    b. the United States declared its rights under the Monroe Doctrine.
    c. Monroe's cabinet endorsed Jackson's action.
    d. Secretary of State Adams further pressured Spain to cede the area to the United States.

11. As proclaimed by Monroe in his message of 1823, the Monroe Doctrine asserted that

    a. only the United States had a right to intervene in Latin America.
    b. the British and Americans would act together to prevent further Russian expansion on the Pacific coast.
    c. the United States would not tolerate further European intervention or colonization in the Americas.
    d. the United States would support the Greeks in their fight for independence against Turkey.

Name _____ Section _____ Date _____

____ 12. The immediate effect of the Monroe Doctrine at the time it was issued was

    a. a rise in tension between the United States and the major European powers.
    b. very minor.
    c. a close alliance between the United States and the Latin American republics.
    d. a series of clashes between the American and British navies.

C. Identification

Supply the correct identification for each numbered description.

_____ 1. One of the Great Lakes where Oliver H. Perry captured a large British fleet

_____ 2. Stirring patriotic song written by Francis Scott Key after naval battle at Baltimore

_____ 3. One of the specially designed American "superfrigates"

_____ 4. Gathering of prominent New England Federalists who debated secession

_____ 5. Intellectual magazine that reflected the post-1815 spirit of American nationalism

_____ 6. Hamiltonian financial institution, allowed to expire in 1811 and revived by Jeffersonian Republicans in 1816

_____ 7. Henry Clay's ambitious nationalistic plans for tariffs, internal improvements, and expanded manufacturing

_____ 8. General term for the roads and canals favored by Clay and others who wanted government-funded transportation systems for the West

_____ 9. Somewhat inappropriate term applied to the Monroe administrations suggesting they lacked major conflicts

_____ 10. Once-prominent political party that effectively died by 1820

_____ 11. Speculative western financial institutions that collapsed in the Panic of 1819

_____ 12. Major water transportation route financed and built by New York State

_____ 13. Line designated as the future boundary between free and slave territories under the Missouri Compromise

_____ 14. Territory occupied jointly by Britain and the United States under the Treaty of 1818

_____ 15. A presidential foreign-policy proclamation warning European powers not to seek new colonies in the Americas

D. Matching People, Places, and Events

Match the person, place, or event in the left column with the proper description in the right column by inserting the correct letter on the blank line.

___ 1. Stephen Decatur

___ 2. John C. Calhoun

___ 3. Daniel Webster

___ 4. Henry Clay

___ 5. James Monroe

___ 6. Hartford Convention

___ 7. Treaty of Ghent

___ 8. Missouri Compromise

___ 9. John Marshall

___ 10. John Quincy Adams

___ 11. Florida

___ 12. Andrew Jackson

___ 13. George Canning

___ 14. Alaska

___ 15. Latin America

A. Measure that admitted both Maine and Missouri to the Union and fixed the boundary between slave and free territories

B. Military commander who exceeded his government's instructions but eventually won its support for his actions

C. Eloquent spokesman for the "American System" and key architect of the Missouri Compromise

D. Russian territory in North America whose boundary was fixed in the Russo-American Treaty of 1824

E. Nationalistic secretary of state who promoted American interests against Spain and Britain

F. Area where the vulnerability of former Spanish colonies tempted European monarchies and aroused American concern

G. American naval hero of the War of 1812 who said, ". . . our country, right or wrong!"

H. Gathering of New Englanders opposed to the War of 1812 who were accused of treason

I. Territory ceded by Spain after Americans invaded and applied diplomatic pressure

J. British foreign secretary who tried to get Americans to join him in a declaration warning other European nations out of Latin America

K. Compromise agreement that ended the War of 1812

L. Aristocratic Federalist jurist whose rulings bolstered national power against the states

M. Young southern congressman who began as a nationalistic defender of protective tariffs and internal improvements

N. Uninspiring but effective president, reelected almost unanimously in 1820

O. Bushy-browed congressman who defended Dartmouth College and New England economic interests

E. Putting Things in Order

Put the following events in correct order by numbering them from 1 to 8.

___ American naval commanders win victories of the Great Lakes.

___ A battle over extending slavery finally results in two new states and an agreement on how to handle slavery in the territories.

___ A major water route is completed across New York State.

___ Infant American manufacturers successfully press Congress to raise barriers against foreign imports.

___ Rather than follow a British diplomatic lead, President Monroe and Secretary Adams announce a bold new policy for the Western Hemisphere.

___ Spain cedes Florida to the United States.

___ Britain and the United States settle a number of difficult diplomatic issues, including the status of Oregon.

___ Andrew Jackson wins the greatest American victory of the War of 1812

PART III: Applying What You Have Learned

1. How were Americans able to emerge with positive outlooks after the War of 1812, despite the military setbacks they experienced?
2. What were the most important signs of the new American nationalism that developed in the period 1815–1824?
3. How did the forces of nationalism compete with sectional interests in the economic and judicial struggles of the period?
4. Why did the issue of admitting Missouri to the Union precipitate a major national crisis? Why did the North and South each agree to the terms of the Missouri Compromise?
5. Why had the Jeffersonian Republicans, by 1815–1824, adopted many of the principles of "loose construction" once held by Hamiltonian Federalists? (See Chapters 6 and 10.) What kinds of strong federal power did the Democratic-Republicans use, and what kinds were they still reluctant to employ?

13
★★★★★★★★★

The Rise of
Jacksonian Democracy,

1824–1830

PART I: Reviewing the Chapter

A. Checklist of Learning Objectives

After mastering this chapter, you should be able to

1. describe and explain the growth of the New Democracy in the 1820s.
2. indicate how the "corrupt bargain" of 1824 weakened Adams and set the stage for Jackson's election in 1828.
3. describe the "Tariff of Abominations" and explain why it aroused such furor in the South.
4. analyze the significance of Jackson's victory in 1828 as a triumph of the "New Democracy."
5. describe the "spoils system" and indicate its consequences for American politics.
6. trace the increasing sectionalism that appeared in the 1820s and show how it was reflected in the Hayne-Webster debate.

B. Glossary

To build your social science vocabulary, familiarize yourself with the following terms.

1. **divine right** The belief that government or rulers are directly established by God. ". . . America was now bowing to the divine right of the people." (p. 170)
2. **hard money** Coins, as distinguished from paper money. "They sought . . . to substitute hard money for bank notes. . . ." (p. 170)
3. **deference** The yielding of opinion to the judgment of someone else. "The deference, apathy, and virtually nonexistent party organizations gave way to . . . boisterous democracy. . . ." (p. 171)
4. **subversive** Tending to corrupt, overthrow, or destroy something established. "Presidential nominations by a congressional caucus were . . . condemned as . . . subversive of democracy." (p. 171)
5. **clique** A small, exclusive, and snobbish circle of people. "The voters . . . turned against the candidate . . . who had been selected by the congressional clique." (p. 171)

6. **puritanical** Extremely or excessively strict in matters of morals or religion. "The only candidate left was the puritanical Adams. . . ." (p. 172)

7. **usurpation** The act of seizing, occupying, or enjoying the place, power, or functions of someone without right. ". . . Adams [was] . . . smarting under charges of . . . 'usurpation.'" (p. 173)

8. **mudslinging** Malicious, unscrupulous attacks against an opponent. "Mudslinging reached a disgraceful level. . . ." (p. 175)

9. **bare-knuckle** Hard, unrestrained, brutal. ". . . the taste of the new mass electorate for bare-knuckle politics." (p. 175)

10. **machine** A political organization, often controlled through patronage or spoils. ". . . [in] New York and Pennsylvania, . . . well-greased machines were run by professional politicians. . . ." (p. 178)

11. **spoils** Public offices given as a reward for political support. "Finally, the spoils system built up a potent, personalized political machine." (p. 178)

PART II: Checking Your Progress

A. True-False

Where the statement is true, mark **T.** Where it is false, mark **F,** and correct it in the space immediately below.

_____ 1. The New Democracy was based on the ending of property qualifications for the ballot in most states.

_____ 2. One sign of the New Democracy was that presidents were now chosen by democratically elected state legislatures rather than by the Electoral College.

_____ 3. The congressional caucus increasingly replaced the national political convention as the method for nominating a party's presidential candidates.

_____ 4. Because the voters failed to give an electoral majority to any candidate in 1824, the House of Representatives had to choose the president from among the top three candidates.

_____ 5. Henry Clay disproved the charge of a "corrupt bargain" between himself and President Adams by refusing to accept any favors from the Adams administration.

_____ 6. President Adams attempted to uphold strong nationalistic principles in a time of growing sectionalism.

_____ 7. The South and its leading spokesman, John C. Calhoun, opposed a strong tariff in 1816 but reversed their position and favored a strong tariff in 1828.

_____ 8. The election campaign of 1828 was notable for its focus on the issues of the tariff and popular democracy.

_____ 9. The election of 1828 was in some ways a "revolution" of the common people of the West and South against the older, entrenched governing classes of the East.

_____ 10. Jackson believed in using the federal government as a powerful instrument of economic activism on behalf of the common people.

___ 11. The Jacksonians practiced their belief that the ordinary citizen was capable of holding almost any public office without particular qualifications.

___ 12. One consequence of the spoils system was the building of powerful political machines based on favors and rewards distributed to political supporters.

___ 13. Jackson relied heavily on his strong official cabinet for policy decisions and political advice.

___ 14. Both President Jackson and Vice President Calhoun fought to maintain a strong nationalism in the face of growing sectionalism.

___ 15. In the Hayne-Webster debate, Daniel Webster attacked the doctrine of nullification as contrary to a union formed by the whole American people rather than by the states.

B. Multiple Choice

Select the best answer and put the proper letter in the space provided.

___ 1. An essential cause of the New Democracy was

    a. the corruptions and scandals among the wealthy who had previously controlled politics.
    b. the increased stake in politics felt by ordinary citizens after the Panic of 1819 and the Missouri Compromise.
    c. the rise of the common school and better education among the citizenry.
    d. the growing threat of war felt by ordinary citizens who might be drafted.

___ 2. A new, seemingly more democratic method of nominating presidential candidates was

    a. the direct primary.
    b. the national nominating convention.
    c. the congressional caucus.
    d. the petition system.

___ 3. The Jacksonian charge of a "corrupt bargain" to gain John Quincy Adams the presidency arose partly because

    a. William Crawford threw his electoral votes to Adams in exchange for a seat in the Senate.
    b. Adams was charged with having bribed members of the House to vote for him.
    c. Adams ended his previous opposition to Clay's American System.
    d. Clay was named secretary of state after throwing his support to Adams.

___ 4. In the battle over the "Tariff of Abominations,"

    a. New England backed high tariffs while the South demanded lower duties.
    b. both New England and the South opposed the higher tariff rates.
    c. the South fought for higher tariffs while the West sought lower rates.
    d. the South backed higher tariffs while New England sought to lower the rates.

5. The concept of a political "Revolution of 1828" rests on

    a. the radical Jacksonian call for a redistribution of wealth and an end to slavery.
    b. the weakening of elite control of politics and the growing involvement of ordinary voters in the political process.
    c. the riots and political violence that accompanied Jackson's rise to power.
    d. the weakening of the power of party machines to control the political process.

6. One of the central beliefs of the new Jacksonian democracy was that

    a. the presidency should be weakened and Congress strengthened.
    b. officeholding should be open to as many ordinary citizens as possible.
    c. the federal government should take an active role in shaping the economy.
    d. public offices should be distributed on the basis of merit rather than political affiliation.

7. One unfortunate consequence of the spoils system was

    a. the weakening of political parties.
    b. a growing lack of interest in politics.
    c. a growing conflict between the executive and legislative branches of government.
    d. an increase in incompetence and corruption in government.

8. The Eaton affair contributed to the bitter, personal, and political conflict between

    a. Andrew Jackson and John C. Calhoun.
    b. John C. Calhoun and Henry Clay.
    c. Andrew Jackson and Martin Van Buren.
    d. Martin Van Buren and John Quincy Adams.

9. Jackson's Maysville Road veto signaled his opposition to

    a. the principle of states' rights.
    b. Henry Clay's American System.
    c. the replacement of canals by roads as a primary means of transportation.
    d. the use of tariff revenue to finance internal improvements.

10. In his debate with Hayne, Daniel Webster argued that

    a. the federal government had been formed by the people, and the states had no right to nullify federal law.
    b. the federal government had been created by the states.
    c. the states and the Supreme Court had an equal right to rule on the constitutionality of laws.
    d. only a majority of states could interfere with federal legislation.

C. Identification

Supply the correct identification for each numbered description.

_____ 1. New form of Jacksonian government that created boisterous political parties and wide popular involvement in politics

_____ 2. Requirements inhibiting the common people's involvement in politics that were first eliminated in Vermont and then gradually fell away in most other states as well

_____ 3. Older method by which a party's representatives in Congress nominated its presidential candidate

_____ 4. New, circuslike method of nominating presidential candidates that involved wider participation but usually left effective control in the hands of party bosses

_____ 5. Small, short-lived third political party that originated a new method of nominating presidential candidates in 1831

_____ 6. Body that chose the president in 1824 after no candidate received an electoral majority

_____ 7. Contemptuous Jacksonian term for the alleged political deal by which Clay threw his support to Adams in exchange for a high cabinet office

_____ 8. Office to which President Adams appointed Henry Clay, raising Jacksonian charges of unfair dealings

_____ 9. Scornful southern term for the high Tariff of 1828

_____ 10. Action led by Denmark Vesey in 1822, raising southern fears of federal power

_____ 11. Pamphlet secretly written by John C. Calhoun that bluntly called on the states to nullify the federal tariff law

_____ 12. Description of Jackson's victory over Adams that defined it as a victory of the poorer masses over the entrenched wealthy classes

_____ 13. The popular idea, widely practiced by the New Democracy, that public offices should be handed out on the basis of political support rather than special qualifications

_____ 14. Highly developed professional political organizations that were "greased" by the offices and favors handed out by winning candidates

_____ 15. President Jackson's informal political advisers, who kept him well informed on public opinion

D. Matching People, Places, and Events

Match the person, place, or event in the left column with the proper description in the right column by inserting the correct letter on the blank line.

____ 1. Davy Crockett

____ 2. Election of 1824

____ 3. Henry Clay

____ 4. John Quincy Adams

____ 5. Tariff of 1828

____ 6. Denmark Vesey

____ 7. John C. Calhoun

____ 8. Rachel Robards Jackson

____ 9. "Revolution of 1828"

____ 10. Andrew Jackson

____ 11. Samuel Swartwout

____ 12. Martin Van Buren

____ 13. Peggy Eaton

____ 14. Robert Y. Hayne

____ 15. Daniel Webster

A. Election that witnessed the triumph of the New Democracy's homespun masses and their political hero

B. Silver-tongued South Carolina senator who defended nullification in a famous debate of 1830

C. Presidential candidate who threw vital support to Adams and then became his secretary of state

D. Sky-high protectionist measure backed by New Englanders and hated by the South

E. Once an ardent nationalist and vice president of the United States, who became a spokesman for purely southern interests

F. Semiliterate, bear-killing Tennessee congressman whose rough popular appeal exemplified the New Democracy

G. Free South Carolina black whose 1822 rebellion raised southern fears about slavery

H. Washington figure whose supposedly scandalous social life caused a cabinet crisis and the resignation of Vice President Calhoun

I. Majestic New England statesman who defended "liberty and Union, now and forever, one and inseparable"

J. Aloof New England president whose elitism made him unpopular in the era of popular democracy

K. Confusing four-way campaign that ended up in the House of Representatives

L. Corrupt New York customs collector whose thefts symbolized the abuses that came along with the spoils system

M. Frontier aristocrat, military folk hero, hickory-tough president

N. Jackson's "magician" secretary of state and his most effective cabinet member

O. Female target of vicious mudslinging campaign in election of 1828

E. Putting Things in Order

Put the following events in correct order by numbering them from 1 to 5.

____ An increasingly sectionalist South Carolinian resigns as Jackson's vice president after a cabinet crisis set off by social gossip.

____ A strange four-way election puts an icy New Englander in office amid charges of a "corrupt bargain."

____ A New England–backed high tariff raises howls of protest and talk of nullification in the South.

___ A slave rebellion in South Carolina raises southern fears of abolitionism and federal power.

___ Two eloquent senatorial orators debate sectionalism, nationalism, and the nature of the Constitution.

PART III: Applying What You Have Learned

1. What was the New Democracy, and why did it arise in the 1820s?
2. How did the election and administration of John Quincy Adams arouse Jacksonian wrath and provide fuel for the new antielitist forces in American politics?
3. How did Jackson and his "Revolution of 1828" represent the spirit of the New Democracy, and how did they apply it to the federal government?
4. Why did Calhoun and the South see the Tariff of 1828 as such an "abomination" and raise threats of nullification over it?
5. What were the benefits and liabilities of the Jacksonian New Democracy?

14

★★★★★★★★★

Jacksonian Democracy at Flood Tide,

1830–1840

PART I: Reviewing the Chapter

A. Checklist of Learning Objectives

After mastering this chapter, you should be able to

1. describe how Jackson thwarted the radical nullifiers in South Carolina, while making some political concessions to the South.
2. explain how and why Jackson attacked and destroyed the Bank of the United States and indicate the political and economic effects of his action.
3. analyze the political innovations of the 1830s, including national conventions, the birth of the Whig party, and the second two-party system.
4. describe the changes affecting Native American life, including Jackson's removal policies.
5. explain the settlement of Texas, the Texas revolution, and the admission of Texas as a U.S. state.
6. describe the economic and political woes of Jackson's successor, Van Buren.
7. describe how the Whigs effectively appropriated the popular campaign techniques of the New Democracy and used them to defeat the Democrats in 1840.

B. Glossary

To build your social science vocabulary, familiarize yourself with the following terms.

1. **impost** A tax, particularly a tariff or duty on imported goods. ". . . it did lower the imposts. . . ." (p. 182)
2. **appeasement** The policy of giving in to demands of a hostile or dangerous power in hopes of avoiding conflict. "Later generations . . . have condemned the 'appeasement' of South Carolina in 1833 as sheer folly." (p. 183)
3. **plutocratic** Concerning an extremely wealthy ruling class. "The Old Hero assailed the plutocratic and monopolistic bank as unconstitutional." (p. 184)

4. **prejudice** Unreasonable suspicion, bias, or hatred directed at members of a group. ". . . Jackson succeeded in mobilizing the prejudices of the West against the East." (p. 184)

5. **evangelical** Concerning religious belief, commonly Protestant, that emphasizes personal salvation, individual and voluntary religious commitment, and the authority of Scripture. "Moreover, the Anti-Masons attracted support from many evangelical Protestant groups. . . ." (p. 185)

6. **platform** A statement of the principles or positions of a political party. ". . . National Republicans added still another innovation when they adopted formal platforms. . . ." (p. 185)

7. **mandate** Something authoritatively commanded or required. "He was convinced that he now had a 'mandate' from the voters. . . ." (p. 185)

8. **trammels** Something that confines, restrains, or shackles. "Hardy Texan pioneers . . . resent[ed] the trammels imposed by a 'foreign' government." (p. 189)

9. **prolific** Producing abundant young. "Energetic and prolific, Texas-Americans numbered about thirty thousand by 1835." (p. 189)

10. **favorite sons** In American politics, presidential candidates who are nominated by their own state, primarily out of local loyalty, but who have little chance to win. "Their long-shot strategy was instead to run several prominent 'favorite sons,' who would . . . scatter the vote. . . ." (p. 191)

PART II: Checking Your Progress

A. True-False

Where the statement is true, mark **T**. Where it is false, mark **F**, and correct it in the space immediately below.

_____ 1. President Jackson used military force to end South Carolina's threat of nullification and secession.

_____ 2. All the other southern states strongly backed South Carolina's act of nullification against the federal government.

_____ 3. Jackson used his veto of the bill to recharter the Bank of the United States to mobilize the common people of the West against the financial elite of the East.

_____ 4. The Anti-Masonic third party of 1832 appealed strongly to American suspicion of secret societies and to anti-Jackson Protestant evangelicals.

_____ 5. Jackson finally destroyed the Bank of the United States by replacing it with an "independent treasury" staffed with his own political supporters.

_____ 6. President Jackson defied a Supreme Court ruling and ordered Native Americans from the Southeast removed to Oklahoma.

_____ 7. The Cherokee, Seminole, and Chief Black Hawk all accepted their removal across the Mississippi peacefully.

_____ 8. American settlers in Texas clashed with the Mexican government over issues of slavery, immigration, and legal rights.

_____ 9. Jackson refused to recognize Texas's independence but did support the entry of Texas into the Union.

____ 10. The Whig party eventually coalesced in the 1830s into a strong party with a generally nationalistic outlook.

____ 11. President Van Buren reaped the economic benefits of Jackson's bitter battle to destroy the Bank of the United States.

____ 12. The fact of William Henry Harrison's poverty-stricken background formed the basis for the Whigs' appeal to the common voter in 1840.

____ 13. Van Buren lost the election of 1840 partly because voters connected him with the hard times caused by the panic of 1837.

____ 14. In general, the Democratic party stood for social harmony and an active government, while the Whigs emphasized individual liberty and the dangers of a privileged elite.

____ 15. The two-party system placed a premium on political compromise within each party and thus tended to reduce the ideological conflict between the parties.

B. Multiple Choice

Select the best answer and put the proper letter in the space provided.

____ 1. The nullification crisis in South Carolina ended when

    a. Andrew Jackson used military force to crush the nullifiers.
    b. Henry Clay pushed through a compromise tariff that enabled South Carolina to save face.
    c. Jackson was forced to back down and accept the basic principle of nullification.
    d. South Carolina Unionists seized power within the state and repealed the nullification ordinance.

____ 2. Jackson's veto of the bank recharter bill represented

    a. a bold assertion of presidential power on behalf of western farmers and other debtors.
    b. an attempt to assure bankers and creditors that the federal government had their interests at heart.
    c. a concession to Henry Clay and his National Republican followers.
    d. a gain for sound banking and a financially stable currency system.

____ 3. Among the new political developments that appeared in the election of 1832 were

    a. political parties and direct popular voting for president.
    b. newspaper endorsements and public financing of presidential campaigns.
    c. nomination by congressional caucus and voting by the Electoral College.
    d. third-party campaigning, national conventions, and party platforms.

____ 4. Jackson's Specie Circular declared that

    a. all federal deposits had to be removed from the Bank of the United States.
    b. the Treasury would distribute surplus federal funds to the states.
    c. all public lands would have to be purchased with "hard" or metallic money.
    d. all paper currency had to be backed with gold or silver.

5. The end result of Jackson's policies toward Native Americans was

    a. the flourishing of the southeastern tribes on their ancestral lands.

    b. a united Indian military confederacy led by Chief Tecumseh and his brother.

    c. the forcible removal of most of the southeastern Indians to Oklahoma.

    d. the assimilation of most Native Americans into the white population.

6. A particular source of friction between the government of Mexico and the immigrant settlers in Texas was

    a. the price of land.

    b. the settlers' importation of slaves.

    c. the treatment of women.

    d. the issue of settler voting rights.

7. In the aftermath of the successful Texas Revolution,

    a. Texas petitioned to join the United States but was refused admission.

    b. Texas immediately joined the United States as a slave state.

    c. Mexico and the United States agreed to a joint protectorate over Texas.

    d. Britain threatened the United States with war over Texas.

8. The Panic of 1837 and subsequent depression were caused by

    a. the stock-market collapse and a sharp decline in grain prices.

    b. a lack of new investment in industry and technology.

    c. the threat of war with Mexico over Texas.

    d. overspeculation and Jackson's financial policies.

9. Prominent leaders of the Whig party included

    a. Martin Van Buren and John C. Calhoun.

    b. Henry Clay and Daniel Webster.

    c. Andrew Jackson and William Henry Harrison.

    d. Stephen Austin and Henry Clay.

10. In general, the Whig party tended to favor

    a. individual liberty and states' rights.

    b. the protection of slavery and southern interests.

    c. a strong federal role in economic and moral issues.

    d. the interests of the working people and farmers against the interests of the upper classes.

C. Identification

Supply the correct identification for each numbered description.

1. State where a radical convention nullified the "Tariff of Abominations" and nearly provoked Jackson to military action

2. Compromise protection law, sponsored by Henry Clay, that helped defuse the nullification crisis

_____ 3. Legislation called the "Bloody Bill" by radical nullifiers that authorized the president to use the army and navy to collect tariffs

_____ 4. The "moneyed monster" that Clay tried to preserve and that Jackson killed with his veto in 1832

_____ 5. Ritualistic secret societies that became the target of a momentarily powerful third party in 1832

_____ 6. Religious believers, originally attracted to the Anti-Masonic party and then to the Whigs, who sought to use political power for moral and religious reform

_____ 7. State financial institutions where Jackson deposited federal funds after removing them from the Bank of the United States

_____ 8. Jackson's Treasury Department decree that required all public lands to be purchased with "hard" money (coins)

_____ 9. Cherokee leader who devised an alphabet for his people

_____ 10. The sorrowful path along which thousands of southeastern Indians were moved to Oklahoma

_____ 11. Florida tribe that refused to accept peaceful removal and waged a bitter war against the American army from 1835 to 1837

_____ 12. The nation from which Texas won its independence in 1836

_____ 13. Anti-Jackson political party that generally stood for national community and an activist government

_____ 14. System of keeping government funds in separate vaults, established by Van Buren's "Divorce Bill" in 1840

_____ 15. Popular symbols of the somewhat bogus but effective campaign the Whigs used to elect "poor boy" William Henry Harrison in 1840

D. Matching People, Places, and Events

Match the person, place, or event in the left column with the proper description in the right column by inserting the correct letter on the blank line.

____ 1. John C. Calhoun

____ 2. Henry Clay

A. Southeastern Indian tribe whose rights were upheld by the Supreme Court but who were nevertheless forcibly removed to Oklahoma

B. Political party that generally stressed individual liberty, the rights of the common people, and hostility to privilege

___ 3. Nicholas Biddle	C. Seminole leader whose warriors killed 1,500 American soldiers in years of guerrilla warfare
___ 4. Cherokees	D. Former Tennessee governor whose victory at San Jacinto in 1836 won Texas its independence
___ 5. Black Hawk	E. Mexican general and dictator whose large army failed to defeat the Texans
___ 6. Osceola	F. Former vice president, leader of South Carolina nullifiers, bitterly hated by Andrew Jackson
___ 7. Stephen Austin	G. Political party that favored a more activist government, high tariffs, internal improvements, and moral reforms
___ 8. Sam Houston	H. Original leader of American settlers in Texas who obtained a huge land grant from the Mexican government
___ 9. Alamo and Goliad	I. Sites of the greatest Mexican victories during the war for Texan independence
___ 10. Santa Anna	J. "Old Tippecanoe," who was portrayed by Whig propagandists as a hard-drinking common man of the frontier
___ 11. Martin Van Buren	K. Jackson's rival for the presidency in 1832, who failed to save the Bank of the United States
___ 12. Panic of 1837	L. The "wizard of Albany," whose economically troubled presidency was served in the shadow of Jackson
___ 13. William Henry Harrison	M. Talented but high-handed bank president who fought a bitter and losing battle with the president of the United States
___ 14. Whigs	N. Illinois-Wisconsin-area Indian chief whose warriors were defeated by regular and militia soldiers in 1832
___ 15. Democrats	O. Severe economic crisis that caused low prices, factory closings, and unemployment

E. Putting Things in Order

Put the following events in correct order by numbering them from 1 to 5.

___ A southern state declares a federal tariff law invalid but finally submits to federal pressure.

___ A financial collapse causes a prolonged economic crisis and widespread suffering.

___ The federal government establishes a system of separate vaults to hold treasury deposits.

___ President Jackson and Senator Clay lock horns in a bitter battle over rechartering a national bank.

___ U.S. settlers in a Latin American country stage a successful rebellion to win their independence.

PART III: Applying What You Have Learned

1. How did President Jackson use his power and strong public support to overcome both the South Carolina nullifiers and the Bank of the United States?
2. What were the economic issues in the Bank War, and how did they contribute to the panic of 1837?
3. How did attitudes of both "assimilation" and "removal" affect Native American life in the 1820s and 1830s?
4. How did American settlers in Mexico create an independent Texas, and why did Jackson refuse to incorporate Texas into the United States?
5. Was Andrew Jackson a good president who brought popular democracy and Western directness to the presidency, or a manipulator of public opinion who undermined the public virtues that the founding fathers believed essential to free government?

15
★★★★★★★★

Forging the National Economy,

1790–1860

PART I: Reviewing the Chapter

A. Checklist of Learning Objectives

After mastering this chapter, you should be able to

1. describe the American migration westward and life on the frontier.
2. describe the effects of population growth and immigration on American society, including anti-immigrant nativism.
3. describe the early development of the factory system and Eli Whitney's system of interchangeable parts.
4. indicate the nature of early industrial labor and explain its effects on workers.
5. describe the effects of an increasingly specialized market economy on American society, especially its impact on women workers and the family.
6. describe the impact of new technology and transportation systems on American business and agriculture, particularly in expanding the market economy and creating a sectional division of labor.
7. describe the sequence of major transportation systems that developed from 1790 to 1860 and indicate their economic consequences.

B. Glossary

To build your social science vocabulary, familiarize yourself with the following terms.

1. **nativist** One who advocates favoring native-born citizens over aliens or immigrants. "The invasion of this so-called immigrant rabble . . . inflamed the hates of American 'nativists.'" (p. 203)
2. **factory** An establishment for the manufacturing of goods, including buildings and substantial machinery. "The factory system gradually spread from England—'the world's workshop'—to other lands." (p. 205)
3. **trademark** A distinguishing symbol or word used by a manufacturer on its goods, usually registered by law to protect against imitators. ". . . unscrupulous Yankee manufacturers . . . stamped their own products with faked English trademarks." (p. 205)
4. **liability** Legal responsibility for loss or damage. "The principle of limited liability aided the concentration of capital. . . ." (p. 208)

5. **incorporation** The formation of individuals into a legally organized group. ". . . businesspeople could create corporations. . . ." (p. 208)

6. **labor union** An organization of workers—usually wage-earning workers—to promote the interests and welfare of its members, often by collective bargaining with employers. "They were forbidden by law to form labor unions. . . ." (p. 208)

7. **strike** An organized work stoppage by employees in order to obtain better wages, working conditions, and so on. "Not surprisingly, only twenty-four recorded strikes occurred before 1835." (p. 208)

8. **capitalist** An individual or group who uses private property to produce for profit in an open market. "It made ambitious capitalists out of humble plowmen. . . ." (p. 211)

9. **turnpike** A toll road. "The highly successful Lancaster turnpike returned dividends. . . ." (p. 211)

10. **productivity** In economics, the relative capacity to produce goods and services, measured in terms of the number of workers and machines needed to create goods in a certain length of time. "The principle of division of labor, which spelled productivity and profits. . . ." (p. 213)

PART II: Checking Your Progress

A. True-False

Where the statement is true, mark **T.** Where it is false, mark **F,** and correct it in the space immediately below.

____ 1. American frontier life was often grim and plagued by poverty and illness.

____ 2. The influx of Irish immigrants contributed to America's tolerance of ethnic and religious pluralism.

____ 3. Most early American manufacturing was concentrated in the South.

____ 4. The principle of "general incorporation" permitted individual businesspeople to apply for limited-liability corporate charters from the state legislature.

____ 5. The early Industrial Revolution greatly benefited workers by opening up well-paying factory jobs.

____ 6. Early labor unions made very slow progress, partly because the strike weapon was illegal and ineffective.

____ 7. The steel plow and mechanical reaper helped turn American farmers from subsistence farming to commercial, market-oriented agriculture.

____ 8. By 1840, most women who entered the work force were married.

____ 9. The Erie Canal's great economic effect was to create strong east-west commercial and industrial links between the Northeast and the West (Midwest).

____ 10. The railroad gained immediate acceptance as a more efficient and flexible alternative to water-bound transportation.

____ 11. The South generally provided raw materials to the Northeast in exchange for manufactured goods, transportation, and commercial services.

___ 12. Economic and social changes affecting women contributed to a sharp decline in the birthrate and the average size of the American family.

___ 13. The new developments in manufacturing and transportation decreased the gap between rich and poor in America.

___ 14. American industrial cities were the sites of a slow but steady rise in wage rates for most workers.

___ 15. By the time of the Civil War, over half of the American economy was significantly dependent on foreign trade with Europe.

B. Multiple Choice

Select the best answer and put the proper letter in the space provided.

___ 1. Two major sources of European immigration to America in the 1840s and 1850s were

    a. France and Italy.
    b. Germany and France.
    c. Germany and Ireland.
    d. Ireland and Norway.

___ 2. One consequence of the influx of new immigrants was

    a. a decline in the birthrate of native-born Americans.
    b. an upsurge of anti-Catholicism.
    c. a virtual end to westward migration.
    d. a national decline in wage rates.

___ 3. Admiration for the wild beauty of the American West contributed especially to

    a. more positive attitudes toward the Indians.
    b. the belief that the West should not be economically developed.
    c. the movement to preserve wildlife and nature, including the national parks.
    d. the development of federal environmental legislation.

___ 4. The first industry to be shaped by the new factory system of manufacturing was

    a. textiles.
    b. the telegraph.
    c. agriculture.
    d. iron making.

___ 5. Wages for most American workers rose in the early nineteenth century, but the most exploited workers were

    a. immigrants and westerners.
    b. textile and transportation workers.
    c. single men and women.
    d. women and children.

_____ 6. A major change affecting the American family in the early nineteenth century was

    a. the rise of an organized feminist movement.
    b. the movement of most women into the work force.
    c. increased conflict between parents and children over moral questions.
    d. a decline in the average number of children per household.

_____ 7. The first major improvements in the American transportation system were

    a. canals and railroads.
    b. railroads and clipper ships.
    c. steamboats and highways.
    d. keelboats and Conestoga wagons.

_____ 8. The new regional "division of labor" created by improved transportation meant that

    a. the South specialized in cotton, the West in grain and livestock, and the East in manufacturing.
    b. the South specialized in manufacturing, the West in transportation, and the East in grain and livestock.
    c. the South specialized in cotton, the West in manufacturing, and the East in finance.
    d. the South specialized in grain and livestock, the West in cotton, and the East in transportation.

_____ 9. One effect of industrialization was

    a. an increasing economic equality among all citizens.
    b. a strengthening of the family as an economic unit.
    c. an increasingly stable labor force.
    d. a rise in the gap between rich and poor.

_____ 10. A new technological development that linked America more closely to Europe was

    a. the McCormick reaper.
    b. the transatlantic cable.
    c. the telephone.
    d. the railroad.

C. Identification

Supply the correct identification for each numbered description.

_____ 1. Nation whose potato famine of the 1840s led to a great migration of its people to America

_____ 2. Term applied by historians to the heedless destruction of wildlife like the beaver, buffalo, and sea otter

_____ 3. Liberal German refugees who fled failed democratic revolutions and came to America

_____ 4. Americans who protested and sometimes rioted against Roman Catholic immigrants

_____ 5. The transformation of manufacturing, involving steam power and factory production, that began in Britain about 1750

_____ 6. Whitney's invention that enhanced cotton production and gave new life to black slavery

_____ 7. Principle that permitted individual investors to risk no more capital in a business venture than their own share of a corporation's stock

_____ 8. Morse's invention that provided instant communication across distance

_____ 9. Common source of early factory labor, often underpaid, whipped, and brutally beaten

_____ 10. Working people's organizations, often considered illegal under early American law

_____ 11. McCormick's invention that vastly increased the productivity of the American grain farmer

_____ 12. The only major highway constructed by the federal government before the Civil War

_____ 13. Fulton's invention that made river transportation a two-way affair

_____ 14. "Clinton's Big Ditch" that transformed transportation and economic life from New York City across the Great Lakes to Chicago

_____ 15. Beautiful but short-lived American ships, replaced by less elegant but more reliable British "tramp steamers"

D. Matching People, Places, and Events

Match the person, place, or event in the left column with the proper description in the right column by inserting the correct letter on the blank line.

____ 1. Samuel Slater

____ 2. Eli Whitney

____ 3. Elias Howe

____ 4. Samuel F. B. Morse

____ 5. Know-Nothings

____ 6. George Caitlin

____ 7. Cyrus McCormick

A. Inventor of the mechanical reaper that transformed grain growing into a business
B. New York governor who built the enormously successful Erie Canal
C. Inventor of a machine that revolutionized the ready-made clothing industry
D. Agitators against immigrants and Roman Catholics
E. Wealthy New York manufacturer who laid the first transatlantic cable in 1858
F. Immigrant mechanic who started American industrialization by setting up his cotton-spinning factory in 1791
G. Painter turned inventor who developed the first reliable system for instant communication across distance
H. Developer of a "folly" that made rivers two-way streams of transportation

_____ 8. Robert Fulton

_____ 9. Cyrus Field

_____ 10. Lancaster Turnpike

_____ 11. DeWitt Clinton

I. First successful toll road, built across Pennsylvania

J. Yankee mechanical genius who revolutionized cotton production and created the system of interchangeable parts

K. Notable American painter and student of Native American life who advocated national parks

E. Putting Things in Order

Put the following events in correct order by numbering them from 1 to 5.

_____ First telegraph message—"What hath God wrought?"—is sent from Baltimore to Washington.

_____ Industrial revolution begins in Britain.

_____ Telegraph lines are stretched across Atlantic Ocean and North American continent.

_____ Major water transportation route connects New York City to Lake Erie and points west.

_____ Invention of cotton gin and system of interchangeable parts revolutionizes southern agriculture and northern industry.

PART III: Applying What You Have Learned

1. How did the migration westward affect U.S. society? What was its effect on the western environment?
2. What were the effects of the new factory and corporate systems of production on early industrial workers, and how did they respond to these conditions?
3. How did the series of new transportation systems create a commercially linked national economy and a specialized sectional division of labor?
4. What was the impact of the new economic developments on the distribution of wealth between owners and workers and between sections?
5. In what ways did the changes in the economy affect the condition and status of women in American society?

16

★★★★★★★★★

The Ferment of Reform and Culture,

1790–1860

PART I: Reviewing the Chapter

A. Checklist of Learning Objectives

After mastering this chapter, you should be able to

1. describe the changes in American religion and their effects on culture and social reform.
2. describe the major changes that occurred in American education.
3. describe the cause of the most important American reform movements of the period.
4. explain the origins of American feminism and describe its various manifestations.
5. describe the utopian and communitarian experiments of the period.
6. point out the early American achievements in the arts and sciences.
7. understand the American literary flowering of the early nineteenth century, especially in relation to transcendentalism and other ideas of the time.

B. Glossary

To build your social science vocabulary, familiarize yourself with the following terms.

1. **polygamy** The practice or condition of having two or more spouses at one time. "Accusations of polygamy likewise arose and increased in intensity. . . ." (p. 220)
2. **theocracy** Literally, rule by God; the term is often applied to a state where religious leaders exercise direct or indirect political authority. ". . . the community became a prosperous frontier theocracy and a cooperative commonwealth." (p. 220)
3. **zealot** One who is carried away by a cause to an extreme or excessive degree. "But less patient zealots came to believe that temptation should be removed by legislation." (p. 224)
4. **communistic** Referring to the theory or practice in which the means of production are owned by the community as a whole. "Various reformers . . . set up more than forty communities of a . . . communistic . . . nature." (p. 226)

5. **communitarian** Referring to the belief in or practice of the superiority of community life or values over individual life, but not necessarily the common ownership of material goods. "Various reformers . . . set up more than forty communities of a . . . 'communitarian' nature." (p. 226)

6. **free love** The principle or practice of sexual relations unrestricted by law, marriage, or religious constraints. "It practiced free love ('complex marriage'). . . ." (p. 226)

7. **eugenic** Concerning the improvement of the human species through selective breeding or genetic control. "It practiced . . . the eugenic selection of parents to produce superior offspring." (p. 226)

8. **monogamy** The belief in or practice of marrying only one spouse at a time. "In 1879–1880 the group embraced monogamy and abandoned communism." (p. 226)

9. **classical** Concerning the culture of ancient Greece and Rome, or any artistic or cultural values presumed to be based on those enduring ancient principles. "He brought a classical design to his Virginia hilltop home, Monticello. . . ." (p. 226)

10. **mystical** The belief in the direct personal apprehension of God or divine mystery, without reliance on reason or public religious tradition. "These mystical doctrines of transcendentalism defied precise definition. . . ." (p. 228)

11. **nonconformist** One who refuses to follow established or conventional ideas or habits. "Henry David Thoreau . . . was . . . a poet, a mystic, a transcendentalist, and a nonconformist." (p. 228)

12. **providential** Under the care or direction of God or other benevolent natural or supernatural forces. ". . . he lived among cannibals, from whom he providentially escaped uneaten." (p. 230)

PART II: Checking Your Progress

A. True-False

Where the statement is true, mark **T.** Where it is false, mark **F**, and correct it in the space immediately below.

____ 1. The Second Great Awakening largely reversed the trends toward religious indifference and rationalism of the late eighteenth century.

____ 2. The religious revivals of the Second Great Awakening tended to break down regional, denominational, and social-class divisions in favor of a common Christianity.

____ 3. The Mormon church migrated to Utah to escape persecution and to establish its tightly organized cooperative social order without interference.

____ 4. The common public schools aimed at the goal, however imperfectly realized, of educating all citizens for participation in democracy, without regard to wealth.

____ 5. Women quickly achieved equality with men in higher education before the Civil War.

____ 6. Many early American reformers were middle-class idealists inspired by evangelical religion who often failed to take account of the new forces of industrialization.

____ 7. The temperance movement first attempted to prohibit all liquor by law but then turned to an emphasis on individual pledges of moderate consumption.

____ 8. The more radical early American feminists attacked the dominant nineteenth-century doctrine that a woman's place was in the home.

____ 9. Most early American utopian experiments involved attempts to create a perfect society based on brotherly love and communal ownership of property.

____ 10. Early American science was stronger in biology, botany, and geology than it was in basic theoretical science or medicine.

____ 11. The first American national literature by Washington Irving and James Fenimore Cooper came in the aftermath of the American Revolution.

____ 12. Although it rejected the general American emphasis on materialism and practical concerns, transcendentalism strongly reflected American individualism, love of liberty, and hostility to formal institutions or authority.

____ 13. Ralph Waldo Emerson taught the doctrines of simple living and nonviolence, while his friend Henry David Thoreau emphasized self-improvement and the development of American scholarship.

____ 14. Walt Whitman's *Leaves of Grass* revealed his love of democracy, the frontier, and the common people.

____ 15. Most early American imaginative writers and historians came from the Midwest and the South.

B. Multiple Choice

Select the best answer and put the proper letter in the space provided.

____ 1. The tendency toward rationalism and indifference in religion was reversed about 1800 by

    a. the rise of Deism and Unitarianism.
    b. the rise of new groups like the Mormons and Christian Scientists.
    c. the revivalist movement called the Second Great Awakening.
    d. the influx of religiously conservative immigrants.

____ 2. Two denominations that especially gained adherents among the common people of the West and South were

    a. Episcopalians and Unitarians.
    b. Congregationalists and Mormons.
    c. Transcendentalists and Adventists.
    d. Methodists and Baptists.

____ 3. The major promoter of an effective tax-supported system of public education for all American children was

    a. Joseph Smith.
    b. Horace Mann.
    c. Noah Webster.
    d. Susan B. Anthony.

____ 4. Reformer Dorothea Dix worked for the cause of
   a. women's rights.
   b. peace.
   c. better treatment of the mentally ill.
   d. temperance.

____ 5. One cause of women's subordination in nineteenth-century America was
   a. the sharp division of labor that kept women at home and men working outside the home.
   b. women's primary concern for causes other than women's rights.
   c. the higher ratio of females to males in many communities.
   d. the prohibition against women's participation in religious activities.

____ 6. The Seneca Falls Convention launched the modern women's rights movement, especially with its call for
   a. equal pay for equal work.
   b. an equal rights amendment to the Constitution.
   c. women's voting rights.
   d. access to public education for women.

____ 7. Many of the American utopian experiments of the early nineteenth century focused on
   a. communal economics and alternative sexual arrangements.
   b. temperance and diet reforms.
   c. advanced scientific and technological systems.
   d. free-enterprise economics and trade.

____ 8. One area of American science that made very little progress before the Civil War was
   a. oceanography.
   b. medicine.
   c. geology.
   d. biology and botany.

____ 9. The "Knickerbocker" group of American writers included
   a. Henry David Thoreau, Thomas Jefferson, and Susan B. Anthony.
   b. George Bancroft, Ralph Waldo Emerson, and Herman Melville.
   c. Washington Irving, James Fenimore Cooper, and William Cullen Bryant.
   d. Walt Whitman, Henry Wadsworth Longfellow, and Edgar Allan Poe.

____ 10. The "transcendentalist" writers such as Emerson and Thoreau stressed the ideas of
   a. inner truth and individual self-reliance.
   b. political community and economic progress.
   c. personal guilt and fear of death.
   d. love of chivalry and return to the medieval past.

C. Identification

Supply the correct identification for each numbered description.

_____ 1. Liberal religious belief, held by many of the founding fathers, that stressed rationalism and moral behavior rather than Christian revelation

_____ 2. Religious revival that began on the frontier and swept eastward, stirring an evangelical spirit in many areas of American life

_____ 3. The *two* religious denominations that benefited most from the evangelical revivals of the early nineteenth century

_____ 4. Religious group founded by Joseph Smith that eventually established a cooperative commonwealth in Utah

_____ 5. Memorable 1848 meeting in New York where women made an appeal based on the Declaration of Independence

_____ 6. Commune established in Indiana by Scottish industrialist Robert Owen

_____ 7. Intellectual commune in Massachusetts based on "plain living and high thinking"

_____ 8. Jefferson's stately home in Virginia, which became a model of American classical architecture

_____ 9. New York literary movement that drew on both local and national themes

_____ 10. Philosophical and literary movement, centered in New England, that greatly influenced many American writers of the early nineteenth century

_____ 11. The doctrine, promoted by American writer Henry David Thoreau in an essay of the same name, that later influenced Mohandas Gandhi

_____ 12. Walt Whitman's initially shocking collection of emotional poems

_____ 13. Nathaniel Hawthorne's disturbing New England masterpiece about adultery and guilt in the old Puritan era

_____ 14. The great but commercially unsuccessful novel about Captain Ahab's obsessive pursuit of a white whale

_____ 15. The title bestowed on George Bancroft for his multivolume history of the United States

D. Matching People, Places, and Events

Match the person, place, or event in the left column with the proper description in the right column by inserting the correct letter on the blank line.

___ 1. Dorothea Dix

___ 2. Brigham Young

___ 3. Elizabeth Cady Stanton

___ 4. Lucretia Mott

___ 5. Elizabeth Blackwell

___ 6. Charles G. Finney

___ 7. Robert Owen

___ 8. Oneida colony

___ 9. Shakers

___ 10. Washington Irving

___ 11. James Fenimore Cooper

___ 12. Ralph Waldo Emerson

___ 13. Walt Whitman

___ 14. Edgar Allan Poe

___ 15. Herman Melville

A. Radical New York commune that practiced "complex marriage" and eugenic birth control

B. Bold, unconventional poet who celebrated American democracy

C. The "Mormon Moses," who led persecuted Latter-Day Saints to their promised land in Utah

D. Influential evangelical revivalist of the Second Great Awakening

E. New York writer whose romantic sea tales were more popular than his dark literary masterpiece

F. Long-lived early American religious sect that attracted thousands of members to its celibate communities

G. Idealistic Scottish industrialist whose attempt at communal utopia failed

H. Second-rate poet and philosopher, but first-rate promoter of transcendentalist ideas and American culture and scholarship

I. Eccentric southern-born genius whose tales of mystery, suffering, and the supernatural departed from general American literary trends

J. Quietly determined reformer who substantially improved conditions for the mentally ill

K. First female graduate of an American medical school

L. Leading feminist who wrote the "Declaration of Sentiments" in 1848 and pushed for women's suffrage

M. First American to win international literary fame with his tales of old Dutch New York

N. Path-breaking American novelist who contrasted the natural person of the forest with the values of modern civilization

O. Quaker women's rights advocate who also strongly supported abolition of slavery

E. Putting Things in Order

Put the following events in correct order by numbering them from 1 to 5.

___ A leading New England transcendentalist appeals to American writers and thinkers to turn away from Europe and develop their own literature and culture.

___ A determined reformer appeals to a New England legislature to end the cruel treatment of the insane.

___ A gathering of female reformers in New York declares that the ideas of the Declaration of Independence apply to *both* sexes.

_____ Great evangelical religious revival begins in western camp meetings.

_____ A visionary New Yorker creates a controversial new religion.

PART III: Applying What You Have Learned

1. What major changes in American religion occurred in the early nineteenth century, and how did they affect American culture and reform?
2. What changes affected American education in the early nineteenth century? Include both elementary and higher education in your answer.
3. How did the first American feminists propose altering the condition of women, and what success did they have?
4. What were the major features of the American literary flowering of the early nineteenth century?
5. It is often said that Americans are a practical and materialistic people. Yet many of the reform and cultural movements of the early 1800s were highly idealistic and even utopian. How do you explain this seeming contradiction?

17

★★★★★★★★★

The South and the Slavery Controversy,

1793–1860

PART I: Reviewing the Chapter

A. Checklist of Learning Objectives

After mastering this chapter, you should be able to

1. point out the economic strengths and weaknesses of the cotton kingdom.
2. describe the southern planter aristocracy and explain its strengths and weaknesses.
3. describe the nonslaveholding white majority of the South and explain its relations with both the planter elite and the black slaves.
4. describe the nature of African-American life, both free and slave, before the Civil War.
5. describe the effects of the "peculiar institution" of slavery on both blacks and whites.
6. explain the rise of abolitionism and the reactions to it in both the North and the South.

B. Glossary

To build your social science vocabulary, familiarize yourself with the following terms.

1. **oligarchy** Rule by a small elite. ". . . the South was not in some respects so much a democracy as an oligarchy." (p. 237)
2. **commission** Fee paid to an agent in a transaction, usually as a percentage of the sale. "They were pained by the heavy outward flow of commissions. . . ." (p. 238)
3. **racism** Belief in the superiority of one race over another or behavior reflecting such a belief. "Thus did the logic of economics join with the illogic of racism in buttressing the slave system." (p. 240)
4. **overseer** Someone who governs or directs the work of another. ". . . under the watchful eyes and ready whip-hand of a white overseer or black 'driver.'" (p. 241)
5. **sabotage** Intentional destruction or damage of goods, machines, or productive processes. "They sometimes sabotaged expensive equipment. . . ." (p. 243)
6. **incendiary** A person who willfully stirs up riot or rebellion. "The nullification crisis . . . conjuring up nightmares of black incendiaries and abolitionist devils." (p. 244)

PART II: Checking Your Progress

A. True-False

Where the statement is true, mark **T.** Where it is false, mark **F,** and correct it in the space immediately below.

____ 1. After about 1800, the prosperity of both North and South became heavily dependent on growing, manufacturing, and exporting cotton.

____ 2. The southern planter aristocracy was strongly attracted to medieval cultural ideals.

____ 3. The growing of cotton on large plantations was economically efficient and agriculturally sound.

____ 4. Most southern slaveowners owned ten or more slaves.

____ 5. In 1860, three-fourths of all white southerners owned no slaves at all.

____ 6. Poor whites supported slavery because it made them feel racially superior and because they hoped someday to be able to buy slaves.

____ 7. The one group of southern whites who opposed slavery consisted of those who lived in mountain areas far from plantations and from blacks.

____ 8. Free blacks enjoyed considerable status and wealth in both the North and the South before the Civil War.

____ 9. Slaveowners generally treated their black slaves as a valuable economic investment.

____ 10. Slavery almost completely destroyed the black family.

____ 11. American slaves used many methods of resistance to demonstrate their hatred of slavery and their yearning for freedom.

____ 12. Abolitionists like William Lloyd Garrison quickly attained great popularity in the North.

____ 13. Black abolitionists like Frederick Douglass favored antislavery political parties while white abolitionists like Garrison opposed all political action.

____ 14. After about 1830, the South no longer tolerated even moderate pro-abolitionist discussion.

____ 15. Southern whites increasingly argued that their slaves were happier and better off than northern wage earners.

B. Multiple Choice

Select the best answer and put the proper letter in the space provided.

____ 1. The primary market for southern cotton production was

    a. the North.
    b. France.
    c. Latin America.
    d. Britain.

____ 2. The South's cotton economy contributed to

    a. increasing immigration of laborers from Europe.
    b. a dependence on the North for trade and manufacturing.
    c. a stable system of credit and finance.
    d. a relatively equal distribution of property and wealth.

____ 3. Most southern slaveowners held

    a. over a hundred slaves.
    b. over fifty slaves.
    c. fewer than ten slaves.
    d. only one slave.

____ 4. Even if they owned no slaves, most poorer southern whites supported the slave system because

    a. they were bribed by the planter class.
    b. they enjoyed the economic benefits of slavery.
    c. they felt racially superior to blacks and hoped to be able to buy slaves.
    d. they disliked the northern abolitionists.

____ 5. Most slaveowners treated their slaves as

    a. objects to be beaten and brutalized as often as possible.
    b. economically profitable investments.
    c. democratic equals.
    d. sources of technological innovation.

____ 6. The African-American family under slavery was

    a. generally stable and supportive of its members.
    b. almost nonexistent.
    c. largely female-dominated.
    d. seldom able to raise children to adulthood.

7. Most of the early abolitionists were motivated by

    a. a desire to see an independent black republic in America.
    b. anger at the negative economic consequences of slavery.
    c. religious feeling against the "sin" of slavery.
    d. a philosophical commitment to racial integration.

8. The most prominent black abolitionist leader was

    a. Theodore Dwight Weld.
    b. David Walker.
    c. William Lloyd Garrison.
    d. Frederick Douglass.

9. After about 1830, most southerners came to look on slavery as

    a. a curse on their region.
    b. a necessary evil.
    c. a positive good.
    d. a threat to their social ideals.

10. By the 1850s, most northerners could be described as

    a. opposed to slavery but also hostile to immediate abolitionists.
    b. fervently in favor of immediate abolition.
    c. sympathetic to white southern arguments in defense of slavery.
    d. inclined to let the slaveholding South break apart the Union.

C. Identification

Supply the correct identification for each numbered description.

1. Term for the South that emphasized its economic dependence on a single staple product

2. Prosouthern New England textile owners who were economically tied to the southern "lords of the lash"

3. Derogatory term for the most economically deprived southern whites; also called "crackers" or "clay eaters"

4. The poor, vulnerable group that was the object of prejudice in the North and despised as a "third race" in the South

5. Theodore Dwight Weld's powerful antislavery work

6. The area of the South where most slaves were held, stretching from South Carolina across to Louisiana

7. Organization founded in 1817 to send blacks back to Africa

_____   8. The group of students, led by Theodore Dwight Weld, who were expelled from their seminary for their abolitionist activity

_____   9. William Lloyd Garrison's fervent abolitionist newspaper that preached an immediate end to slavery

_____   10. Garrisonian abolitionist organization that included the eloquent Wendell Phillips among its leaders

_____   11. Strict rule passed by prosouthern Congressmen in 1836 to prohibit all discussion of slavery in the House of Representatives

_____   12. Northern antislavery people, like Abraham Lincoln, who rejected radical abolitionism but sought to prohibit the expansion of slavery in the western territories

D. Matching People, Places, and Events

Match the person, place, or event in the left column with the proper description in the right column by inserting the correct letter on the blank line.

___ 1. Lyman Beecher

___ 2. Harriet Beecher Stowe

___ 3. Nat Turner

___ 4. Liberia

___ 5. Theodore Dwight Weld

___ 6. Denmark Vesey

___ 7. Lane Theological Seminary

___ 8. William Lloyd Garrison

___ 9. David Walker

___ 10. Sojourner Truth

___ 11. Martin Delany

___ 12. Frederick Douglass

___ 13. Virginia

A. Free black who organized a slave rebellion in Charleston in 1822

B. Visionary black preacher whose bloody slave rebellion in 1831 tightened the reins of slavery in the South

C. Midwestern institution whose president expelled eighteen students for organizing a debate on slavery

D. New York free black woman who fought for emancipation and women's rights

E. Leading radical abolitionist who burned the Constitution as "a covenant with death and an agreement with hell"

F. Author of an abolitionist novel that portrayed the separation of slave families by auction

G. Site of Nat Turner's slave rebellion and the last major southern debate over slavery and emancipation, 1831–1832

H. President of Lane Theological Seminary, father of Harriet Beecher Stowe

I. Black abolitionist who visited West Africa in 1859 to examine sites where African-Americans might relocate

J. Former president who fought for the right to discuss slavery in Congress

K. Illinois editor whose death at the hands of a mob made him an abolitionist martyr

L. West African republic founded in 1822 by freed blacks from the United States

M. Escaped slave and great black abolitionist who fought to end slavery through political action

____ 14. John Quincy Adams   **N.** Black abolitionist writer who called for a bloody end to slavery in an appeal of 1829

____ 15. Elijah Lovejoy   **O.** Leader of the "Lane Rebels" who wrote the powerful antislavery work *American Slavery As It Is*

E. Putting Things in Order

Put the following events in correct order by numbering them from 1 to 5.

____ The last slaves to be legally imported from Africa enter the United States.

____ A radical abolitionist editor is murdered, and so becomes a martyr to the antislavery cause.

____ A radical abolitionist newspaper and a slave rebellion spread fear through the South.

____ A new invention increases the efficiency of cotton production, laying the basis for the vast cotton kingdom.

____ A group of seminary students expelled for their abolitionist views spread the antislavery gospel far and wide.

PART III: Applying What You Have Learned

1. Describe the complex structure of southern society. What role did plantation owners, small slaveholders, independent white farmers, poor whites, free blacks, and black slaves each have in the southern social order?
2. Why did most nonslaveholding southern whites support a slave system that harmed them economically?
3. How did slavery affect the lives of African-Americans in both the South and the North?
4. Discuss the following proposition: Abolitionism had a more significant impact on the South than on the North.
5. In what ways did slavery make the South a fundamentally different kind of society from the North?

18
★★★★★★★★★

Manifest Destiny and Its Legacy,

1841–1848

PART I: Reviewing the Chapter

A. Checklist of Learning Objectives

After mastering this chapter, you should be able to

1. explain the spirit of "Manifest Destiny" that inspired American expansionism in the 1840s.
2. indicate how American anti-British feeling led to various conflicts over debts, Maine, Canadian rebellion, Texas, and Oregon.
3. explain why the movement to annex Texas gained new momentum and why the issue aroused such controversy.
4. indicate how the issues of Oregon and Texas became central in the election of 1844 and why Polk's victory was seen as a mandate for "Manifest Destiny."
5. describe how the issues of California and the Texas boundary created conflict and war with Mexico.
6. describe how the American victory in the Mexican War led to the large territorial acquisition of the whole Southwest.
7. explain the consequences of the Mexican War, especially its effect on the slavery question.

B. Glossary

To build your social science vocabulary, familiarize yourself with the following terms.

1. **protectorate** The relation of a strong nation to a weak one under its control and protection. ". . . Texas was driven to open negotiations . . . in the hope of securing the defensive shield of a protectorate." (p. 251)
2. **colossus** Anything of extraordinary size and power. "Such a republic would check the southward surge of the American colossus. . . ." (p. 251)
3. **resolution** In government, a formal statement of policy or judgment by a legislature, but requiring no statute. ". . . annexation by a joint resolution." (p. 252)
4. **intrigue** A plot or scheme formed by secret, underhanded means. ". . . the Lone Star Republic had become a danger spot, inviting foreign intrigue that menaced the American people." (p. 252)
5. **barter** To exchange goods or services without money. "Spain . . . bartered away . . . claims to the United States. . . ." (p. 252)

PART II: Checking Your Progress

A. True-False

Where the statement is true, mark **T**. Where it is false, mark **F**, and correct it in the space immediately below.

____ 1. The new president John Tyler carried on the strong Whig policies of leaders like Clay and Webster.

____ 2. By the 1840s, America and Britain had reconciled and become allies in international affairs.

____ 3. The "Aroostook War" over the Maine boundary was settled by territorial compromise in the Webster-Ashburton Treaty.

____ 4. A primary motive driving Americans to annex Texas was fear that the Lone Star Republic would become an ally or protectorate of Britain.

____ 5. Texas was annexed to the United States by a simple majority resolution of both houses of Congress.

____ 6. In the dispute with Britain over Oregon, the United States repeatedly demanded control of the whole territory as far north as "fifty-four forty."

____ 7. In the election of 1844, Clay lost to Polk partly because he tried to straddle the Texas annexation issue and thus lost antislavery support.

____ 8. Polk's victory in 1844 was interpreted by the Democrats as a mandate for Manifest Destiny.

____ 9. The Polk administration was frustrated by its inability to purchase California from Mexico.

____ 10. The immediate cause of the Mexican War was an attempt by Mexico to reconquer Texas.

____ 11. Polk's primary goal in the Mexican War was to take California.

____ 12. The overwhelming American military victory over Mexico led some Americans to call for the United States to take over all of Mexico.

____ 13. The Treaty of Guadalupe Hidalgo gave the United States only small territorial gains.

____ 14. The Mexican War began an era of continuing bad feeling between the United States and Latin America.

____ 15. The Wilmot Proviso prohibiting slavery in territory acquired from Mexico helped shove the slavery issue out of sight.

B. Multiple Choice

Select the best answer and put the proper letter in the space provided.

____ 1. The conflict between President Tyler and Whig leaders like Henry Clay took place over issues of

    a. slavery and expansion.
    b. banking and tariff policy.
    c. foreign policy.
    d. agriculture and transportation policy.

____ 2. One major source of tension between Britain and the United States in the 1840s was

    a. American involvement in Mexican affairs.
    b. British refusal to support American abolitionists.
    c. a conflict over the Maine boundary with Canada.
    d. American intervention in the British West Indies.

____ 3. Texas was finally admitted to the Union in 1844 as a result of

    a. the Mexican War.
    b. the Texans' willingness to abandon slavery.
    c. President Tyler's interpretation of the election of 1844 as a "mandate" to acquire Texas.
    d. a compromise agreement with Britain.

____ 4. "Manifest Destiny" represented the widespread American belief that

    a. Americans were destined to uphold democracy and freedom.
    b. there was bound to be a civil war over slavery in the future.
    c. new western territory could be acquired only by war.
    d. God had destined the United States to expand across the whole North American continent.

____ 5. Henry Clay lost the election of 1844 to James Polk because

    a. his attempt to "straddle" the Texas issue lost him votes to the antislavery Liberty party in New York.
    b. his strong stand for expansion in Texas and Oregon raised fears of war with Britain.
    c. he supported lower tariffs and an independent treasury system.
    d. he lacked experience in presidential politics.

____ 6. The result of the British-American conflict over Oregon in 1844–1846 was

    a. American success in winning the goal of a boundary at "fifty-four forty."
    b. an agreement to continue the joint occupation of Oregon for twenty years more.
    c. a compromise agreement on a border at the forty-ninth parallel.
    d. an outbreak of war between the two nations.

7. The immediate cause of the Mexican War was

a. American refusal to pay Mexican claims for damages to its citizens.
b. Mexican refusal to sell California and a dispute over the Texas boundary.
c. Mexican support for the antislavery movement in Texas.
d. American determination to establish democracy in northern Mexico.

8. The main American military campaign that finally captured Mexico City was commanded by

a. General Stephen W. Kearny.
b. Captain John C. Frémont.
c. General Zachary Taylor.
d. General Winfield Scott.

9. The Treaty of Guadalupe Hidalgo ending the Mexican War provided for

a. a return to the status quo that had existed before the war.
b. the American acquisition of all of Mexico.
c. American acquisition of nearly half of Mexico and payment of several million dollars in compensation.
d. a small territorial adjustment in the southern boundary of Texas.

10. The most ominous domestic consequence of the Mexican War was

a. the decline of the Democratic party.
b. a sharp revival of the issue of slavery.
c. a large influx of Hispanic immigrants into the southern United States.
d. a significant increase in taxes to pay the costs of the war.

C. Identification

Supply the correct identification for each numbered description.

_____ 1. Popular nickname for Whig president who died after only four weeks in office

_____ 2. State where the "Aroostook War" was fought over a disputed boundary with Canada

_____ 3. Nation that strongly backed independence for Texas, hoping to turn it into an economic asset and antislavery bastion

_____ 4. Antislavery Whigs who opposed both the Texas annexation and the Mexican War on moral grounds

_____ 5. Act of both houses of Congress by which Texas was annexed

_____ 6. Northern boundary of Oregon, advocated by Democratic party and others as the desired line of American expansion

_____ 7. Two-thousand-mile-long path along which thousands of Americans journeyed to the Willamette Valley in the 1840s

_____ 8. The widespread American belief that God had ordained the United States to occupy all the territory of continental North America

_____ 9. Small antislavery party that took enough votes from Henry Clay to cost him the election of 1844

_____ 10. Final compromise line that settled the Oregon boundary dispute in 1846

_____ 11. Rich Mexican province that Polk tried to buy and Mexico refused to sell

_____ 12. River that Mexico claimed as the Texas-Mexico boundary, crossed by Taylor's troops in 1846

_____ 13. Resolutions offered by Congressman Abraham Lincoln demanding to know the precise location where Mexicans had allegedly shed American blood on "American" soil

_____ 14. Treaty ending Mexican War and granting vast territories to the United States

_____ 15. Controversial congressional amendment stipulating that slavery should be forbidden in all territory acquired from Mexico

D. Matching People, Places, and Events

Match the person, place, or event in the left column with the proper description in the right column by inserting the correct letter on the blank line.

____ 1. John Tyler

____ 2. Henry Clay

____ 3. Aroostook War

____ 4. Daniel Webster

____ 5. Texas

____ 6. Oregon

____ 7. James K. Polk

____ 8. Election of 1844

____ 9. Abraham Lincoln

____ 10. Rio Grande

A. Congressional author of the "spot resolutions" criticizing the Mexican War

B. "Old Fuss and Feathers," whose conquest of Mexico City brought U.S. victory in the Mexican War

C. Leader of Senate Whigs and unsuccessful presidential candidate against Polk in 1844

D. Long-winded American diplomat who negotiated the Treaty of Guadalupe Hidalgo

E. Whig leader and secretary of state who negotiated an end to Maine boundary dispute in 1842

F. Claimed by United States as southern boundary of Texas

G. Won by the party stressing expansionism and lost by the party divided over slavery and Texas

H. Clash between Canadians and Americans over disputed timber country

I. Mexican military leader who failed to stop humiliating American invasion of his country

J. Independent nation that was the object of British, Mexican, and French scheming in the early 1840s

____	11. Zachary Taylor	**K.** American military hero who invaded northern Mexico from Texas in 1846–1847
____	12. Winfield Scott	**L.** Congressional author of resolution forbidding slavery in territory acquired from Mexico
____	13. Santa Anna	**M.** Dark-horse presidential winner of 1844 who effectively carried out ambitious expansionist plans
____	14. Nicholas Trist	**N.** Northwestern territory in dispute between Britain and United States, subject of "Manifest Destiny" rhetoric in 1844
____	15. David Wilmot	**O.** Leader who was elected on the Whig ticket in 1840 but spent most of his presidency in bitter feuds with his fellow Whigs

E. Putting Things in Order

Put the following events in correct order by numbering them from 1 to 5.

____   United States ends a long courtship by incorporating an independent republic that had once been part of Mexico.

____   The first American president to die in office is succeeded by his controversial vice president.

____   A treaty adding vast territory to the United States is hastily pushed through the Senate.

____   American and Mexican troops clash in disputed border territory, leading to a controversial declaration of war.

____   An ambitious "dark horse" wins an election against an opponent trapped by the Texas annexation issue.

PART III: Applying What You Have Learned

1. What led to the rise of the spirit of "Manifest Destiny" in the 1840s, and how did that spirit show itself in the American expansionism of the decade?
2. Why were the issues of Texas annexation and the Texas boundary so central to the politics of the 1840s? Why were the debates about the Oregon territory not nearly so volatile?
3. Why did the crucial election of 1844 come to be fought over expansionism, and how did Polk exercise his "mandate" for expansion in his attempt to obtain California?
4. What were the short- and long-term causes and consequences of the Mexican War? Could the war have been avoided?
5. How did the "Manifest Destiny" of the 1840s—particularly the expansion into Texas and Mexico—intensify the sectional conflict over slavery?

19
★★★★★★★★

Renewing the Sectional Struggle,

1848–1854

PART I: Reviewing the Chapter

A. Checklist of Learning Objectives

After mastering this chapter, you should be able to

1. explain how the issue of slavery in the territories acquired from Mexico disrupted American politics from 1848 to 1850.
2. point out the major terms of the Compromise of 1850 and indicate how this agreement attempted to deal with the issue of slavery.
3. indicate how the Whig party disintegrated and disappeared because of its divisions over slavery.
4. describe how the Pierce administration engaged in various prosouthern overseas and expansionist ventures.
5. describe Douglas's Kansas-Nebraska Act and explain why it stirred the sectional controversy to new heights.

B. Glossary

To build your social science vocabulary, familiarize yourself with the following terms.

1. **self-determination** In politics, the right of a people to assert its own national identity or form of government without outside influence. "The public liked it because it accorded with the democratic tradition of self-determination." (p. 263)
2. **sanctuary** A place of refuge or protection, where people are safe from punishment by the law. ". . . scores of . . . runaway slaves . . . were spirited . . . to the free-soil sanctuary of Canada." (p. 264)
3. **fugitive** A person who flees from danger or prosecution. ". . . southerners were demanding a new and more stringent fugitive-slave law." (p. 264)
4. **isthmian** Concerning a narrow strip of land connecting two larger bodies of land. ". . . neither America nor Britain would secure exclusive control over any future isthmian waterway." (p. 269)
5. **filibustering** Referring to adventurers who conduct a private war against a foreign country. "During 1850–1851 two 'filibustering' expeditions . . . descended upon Cuba." (p. 269)
6. **cloak-and-dagger** Concerning the activities of spies or undercover agents, especially involving elaborate deceptions. "An incredible cloak-and-dagger episode followed." (p. 269)

7. **leak** To accidentally or deliberately disclose information supposed to be kept secret. "The secret Ostend Manifesto quickly leaked out." (p. 269)

8. **booster** One who promotes a person or enterprise, especially in a highly enthusiastic way. "An ardent booster for the West, he longed to . . . stretch a line of settlements across the continent." (p. 271)

9. **truce** A temporary suspension of warfare by agreement of the hostile parties. "This bold step Douglas was prepared to take, even at the risk of shattering the uneasy truce patched up by the Great Compromise of 1850." (p. 271)

PART II: Checking Your Progress

A. True-False

Where the statement is true, mark **T.** Where it is false, mark **F,** and correct it in the space immediately below.

____ 1. Democratic politicians and others attempted to avoid the issue of slavery in the territories by saying it should be left to "popular sovereignty."

____ 2. The Free Soil party's primary goal was to obtain homesteads for western farmers.

____ 3. California was admitted to the Union as a slave state immediately after the Mexican War.

____ 4. Southerners demanded a more effective fugitive-slave law to stop the Underground Railroad from running escaped slaves to Canada.

____ 5. In the Senate debate of 1850, the primary spokesman for sectional compromise was Senator John C. Calhoun.

____ 6. In the key provisions of the Compromise of 1850, New Mexico and Utah were admitted as slave states, while California was left open to popular sovereignty.

____ 7. The provision of the Compromise of 1850 that aroused the fiercest northern opposition was the Fugitive Slave Law.

____ 8. The political winner in the Compromise of 1850 was the South.

____ 9. The Whig party disappeared because its northern and southern wings were too deeply split over the Fugitive Slave Law and other sectional issues.

____ 10. The Pierce administration's expansionist efforts in Central America, Cuba, and the Gadsden Purchase were basically designed to serve southern proslavery interests.

____ 11. The Gadsden Purchase resulted in a general national agreement to build the transcontinental railroad along the southern route.

____ 12. Douglas's Kansas-Nebraska Act was intended to organize western territories so that a transcontinental railroad could be built along a northern route.

____ 13. Both southerners and northerners alike refused to accept Douglas's plan to repeal the Missouri Compromise.

____ 14. The Kansas-Nebraska Act wrecked the Compromise of 1850 and created deep divisions within the Democratic party.

____ 15. The Republican party was initially organized as a northern protest against Douglas's Kansas-Nebraska Act.

B. Multiple Choice

Select the best answer and put the proper letter in the space provided.

____ 1. "Popular sovereignty" was the idea that

   a. the government of the United States should be elected by the people.
   b. western settlers should be able to organize their own territorial governments.
   c. the people of a territory should determine for themselves whether or not to permit slavery.
   d. people in the territories acquired from Mexico should decide whether they would accept U.S. rule.

____ 2. In the election of 1848, the response of the Whig and Democratic parties to the rising controversy over slavery was

   a. a strong proslavery stance by the Democrats and a strong antislavery stance by the Whigs.
   b. to join together in opposing the antislavery Free Soil party.
   c. to attempt to ignore the issue.
   d. to grant permission for each candidate to take his own stand on the issue.

____ 3. The admission of California to the Union was controversial because

   a. its entry as a free state would destroy the balance between slave and free states in the U.S. Senate.
   b. of the threat that Mexico would try to reconquer California.
   c. proslavery and antislavery settlers had formed competing territorial governments.
   d. of the very large and unruly population drawn into the state by the discovery of gold.

____ 4. The existence of the Underground Railroad added to southern demands for

   a. the admission of new slave states to the Union.
   b. the death penalty for abolitionists.
   c. a stricter federal Fugitive Slave Law.
   d. the enslavement of all blacks North and South.

____ 5. Among the notable advocates of compromise in the controversy over slavery in 1850 were

   a. William Seward and Abraham Lincoln.
   b. Henry Clay and Daniel Webster.
   c. John C. Calhoun and Zachary Taylor.
   d. Stephen Douglas and Harriet Tubman.

6. Under the terms of the Compromise of 1850,

   a. California was admitted to the Union as a free state, and slavery in the Utah and New Mexico territories would be left to popular sovereignty.
   b. California was admitted as a free state, and Utah and New Mexico as slave states.
   c. California was admitted as a free state and slavery was permitted in the District of Columbia.
   d. New Mexico and Texas were admitted as slave states and Utah and California as free states.

7. One of the primary effects of the Fugitive Slave Law passed as part of the Compromise of 1850 was

   a. a virtual end to slave escapes and the Underground Railroad.
   b. popular northern support for the capture of runaway slaves.
   c. a sharp rise in northern antislavery feeling.
   d. an increase in violent slave rebellions.

8. The conflict over slavery after the election of 1852 led shortly to

   a. the death of the Whig party.
   b. the death of the Democratic party.
   c. the death of the Republican party.
   d. the rise of the Free Soil party.

9. Southerners seeking to expand the territory of slavery were especially interested in acquiring

   a. Canada and Alaska.
   b. Venezuela and Colombia.
   c. Nicaragua and Cuba.
   d. Hawaii and Japan.

10. Douglas's Kansas-Nebraska Act stirred anger in the North especially because

   a. it aimed to build a transcontinental railroad.
   b. it might make Douglas a large personal profit.
   c. it repealed the Missouri Compromise.
   d. it would bring Kansas into the Union as a slave state.

C. Identification

Supply the correct identification for each numbered description.

_____ 1. Hotheaded southern agitators who pushed southern interests and favored secession from the Union

_____ 2. The doctrine that the issue of slavery should be decided by the residents of a territory themselves, not by the federal government

_____ 3. The boundary line between slave and free states in the East; originally the southern border of Pennsylvania

_____ 4. The informal network that conducted runaway slaves from the South to Canada

_____ 5. Senator William Seward's doctrine that slavery should be excluded from the territories because it was contrary to God's moral law, which he considered above the Constitution

_____ 6. The provision of the Compromise of 1850 that comforted southern slave-catchers and angered northern abolitionists

_____ 7. Third-party entry in the election of 1848 that advocated prohibiting slavery in the territories

_____ 8. An agreement between North and South that temporarily dampened the slavery controversy and led to a short-lived "Era of Good Feelings"

_____ 9. Political party that fell apart and disappeared after losing the election of 1852

_____ 10. Central American nation where proslavery American expansionists seized power in 1856

_____ 11. A top-secret dispatch, drawn up by American diplomats in Europe, that called for seizing Cuba from Spain

_____ 12. Southwestern territory acquired by the Pierce administration to facilitate a southern transcontinental railroad

_____ 13. The sectional agreement of 1820, repealed by the Kansas-Nebraska Act

_____ 14. The political party that was deeply divided by Douglas's Kansas-Nebraska Act

_____ 15. A new political party organized as a protest against the Kansas-Nebraska Act

D. Matching People, Places, and Events

Match the person, place, or event in the left column with the proper description in the right column by inserting the correct letter on the blank line.

___ 1. William Walker

___ 2. Zachary Taylor

___ 3. California

___ 4. District of Columbia

___ 5. Harriet Tubman

___ 6. Daniel Webster

A. American naval commander who opened Japan to the West in 1854

B. Brazen American adventurer who invaded Nicaragua and made himself its president

C. Weak Democratic president whose prosouthern cabinet pushed aggressive expansionist schemes

D. Famous "conductor" on the Underground Railroad who rescued more than three hundred slaves from bondage

E. Illinois politician who helped smooth over sectional conflict in 1850 but then reignited it in 1854

F. Central American nation sought by proslavery expansionists in the 1850s

_____ 7. William Seward

_____ 8. Utah and New Mexico

_____ 9. Franklin Pierce

_____ 10. Winfield Scott

_____ 11. Nicaragua

_____ 12. Matthew Perry

_____ 13. Cuba

_____ 14. Kansas and Nebraska

_____ 15. Stephen A. Douglas

G. Military hero of the Mexican War who became the Whigs' last presidential candidate in 1852

H. Whig president who nearly wrecked the Compromise of 1850 before he died in office

I. Rich Spanish island colony coveted by American proslavery expansionists in the 1850s

J. Federal territory where the slave trade was ended by the Compromise of 1850

K. Areas organized as territories under Douglas's controversial law of 1854 leaving their decision on slavery up to popular sovereignty

L. New York senator who argued that the expansion of slavery was forbidden by a "higher law"

M. Areas organized as territories under the Compromise of 1850, leaving their decision on slavery up to popular sovereignty

N. Massachusetts senator whose support for the Compromise of 1850 earned him the hatred of abolitionists

O. Area acquired from Mexico in 1848 and admitted as a free state in 1850 without ever having been a territory

E. Putting Things in Order

Put the following events in correct order by numbering them from 1 to 5.

_____ A series of delicate agreements between the North and South temporarily smooths over the slavery conflict.

_____ A Mexican War hero is elected president, as the issue of how to deal with slavery in the territory acquired from Mexico arouses national controversy.

_____ A spectacular growth of settlement in the Far West creates demand for admission of a new free state and agitates the slavery controversy.

_____ Stephen Douglas's scheme to build a transcontinental railroad leads to repeal of the Missouri Compromise, which reopens the slavery controversy and spurs the formation of a new party.

_____ The Pierce administration acquires a small Mexican territory to encourage a southern route for the transcontinental railroad.

PART III: Applying What You Have Learned

1. Why did the results of the Mexican War cause a crisis over slavery?
2. How did the Compromise of 1850 attempt to deal with the most difficult issues concerning slavery? What were the actual effects of the compromise?
3. Why were proslavery southerners so eager to push for further expansion in Nicaragua, Cuba, and elsewhere in the 1850s?
4. What were the causes and consequences of the Kansas-Nebraska Act?
5. What was the primary factor that undermined the Compromise of 1850?

20
★★★★★★★★★

Drifting Toward Disunion,

1854–1861

PART I: Reviewing the Chapter

A. Checklist of Learning Objectives

After mastering this chapter, you should be able to
1. relate the sequence of major crises that led from the Kansas-Nebraska Act to secession.
2. explain how and why "Bleeding Kansas" became a dress rehearsal for the Civil War.
3. trace the growing power of the Republican party in the 1850s and the increasing divisions and helplessness of the Democrats.
4. explain how the Dred Scott decision and Brown's Harpers Ferry raid deepened sectional antagonism.
5. trace the rise of Lincoln as the leading exponent of the Republican doctrine of no expansion of slavery.
6. analyze the complex election of 1860 in relation to the sectional crisis.
7. describe the movement toward secession, the formation of the Confederacy, and the failure of the last compromise effort.

B. Glossary

To build your social science vocabulary, familiarize yourself with the following terms.
1. **puppet government** A government set up and controlled by outside forces. ". . . set up their own puppet government at Shawnee Mission." (p. 277)
2. **bandwagon** In politics, a movement or candidacy that gains rapid momentum because of people's desire to join a successful cause. "After mounting the Republican bandwagon, he emerged as one of the foremost politicians. . . ." (p. 280)
3. **arsenal** A military installation where weapons are stored. "He seized the federal arsenal at scenic Harpers Ferry. . . ." (p. 281)
4. **fire-eaters** In nineteenth-century politics, radical southerners who favored immediate secession from the Union. ". . . but southern 'fire-eaters' regarded him as a traitor." (p. 282)
5. **vassalage** The service and homage given by a feudal subordinate to an overlord. ". . . secession [w]as a golden opportunity to cast aside their generations of 'vassalage' to the North." (p. 285)

PART II: Checking Your Progress

A. True-False

Where the statement is true, mark **T.** Where it is false, mark **F,** and correct it in the space immediately below.

___ 1. *Uncle Tom's Cabin* effectively stirred the northern and European public against the evils of slavery.

___ 2. Prosouthern Kansas pioneers brought a large number of slaves with them in order to guarantee that Kansas would become a slave state.

___ 3. The violence in Kansas was provoked by both radical abolitionists and militant proslavery forces.

___ 4. By opposing the proslavery Lecompton Constitution, Senator Stephen Douglas was able to unite the Democratic party.

___ 5. Both South Carolina and Massachusetts defiantly reelected the principal figures in the Brooks-Sumner beating incident.

___ 6. Although Republican John Frémont lost to Democrat James Buchanan, the election of 1856 demonstrated the growing power of the Republican party.

___ 7. The Dred Scott decision upheld the doctrine of popular sovereignty—the right of the people of a territory to determine whether or not to permit slavery.

___ 8. Republicans considered the Supreme Court's Dred Scott decision invalid and vowed to defy it.

___ 9. In the Lincoln-Douglas debates, Lincoln forced Douglas to abandon his support for popular sovereignty.

___ 10. John Brown's raid at Harpers Ferry failed to set off a slave uprising.

___ 11. Northern Democrats walked out of the Democratic party in 1860 when southerners nominated Stephen A. Douglas for president.

___ 12. The election of 1860 was really two campaigns, Lincoln versus Douglas in the North, and Bell versus Breckenridge in the South.

___ 13. Lincoln won a solid majority of the popular vote but only a minority in the Electoral College.

___ 14. Seven states seceded and formed the Confederate States of America during the "lame duck" period between Lincoln's election and his inauguration.

___ 15. Lincoln made a strong effort to get the South to accept the Crittenden compromise.

B. Multiple Choice

Select the best answer and put the proper letter in the space provided.

____   1. Harriet Beecher Stowe's *Uncle Tom's Cabin*

      a.. greatly strengthened northern antislavery feeling.
      b. portrayed nonslaveholding whites as the primary victims of slavery.
      c. increased the desire for sectional compromise on the issue of slavery.
      d. was based on Stowe's long personal experience with slavery in the Deep South.

____   2. The conflict over slavery in Kansas

      a. was caused by the growing number of slaves being brought into the territory.
      b. was one of the goals Douglas had sought in the Kansas-Nebraska Act.
      c. was temporarily resolved by the Compromise of 1850.
      d. was greatly escalated by abolitionist-funded antislavery settlers and proslavery "border ruffians" from Missouri.

____   3. As presented to Congress, the Lecompton Constitution provided for

      a. the admission of Kansas as a free state.
      b. a statewide referendum on slavery to be held after Kansas's admission to the Union.
      c. a prohibition against either New England's or Missouri's involvement in Kansas politics.
      d. the admission of Kansas as a slave state.

____   4. The election of 1856 was most noteworthy for

      a. the Democrats' surprising win of the White House.
      b. the support demonstrated for immigrants and Catholics by all the parties.
      c. the dramatic rise of the Republican party.
      d. the absence of the slavery issue from the campaign.

____   5. In the *Dred Scott* case, the Supreme Court

      a. avoided controversy by ruling that the slave Dred Scott had no right to sue in federal court.
      b. ruled that the Kansas-Nebraska Act was unconstitutional.
      c. ruled that Congress could not prohibit slavery in the territories because slaves were private property.
      d. ruled that slaves could sue in federal court only if their masters permitted them to do so.

____   6. The panic of 1857 encouraged the South to believe that

      a. its economy was fundamentally stronger than that of the North.
      b. it ought to take new steps to develop its own banking and manufacturing institutions.
      c. it would be wise to support the Homestead Act.
      d. its economic future was closely tied to that of the North.

7. A key issue between Lincoln and Douglas in their debates was

    a. whether secession from the Union was legal.
    b. whether the people of a territory could prohibit slavery in light of the Dred Scott decision.
    c. whether Illinois should continue to prohibit slavery.
    d. whether Kansas should be admitted to the Union as a slave or a free state.

8. The South was particularly enraged by the John Brown affair because

    a. so many slaves had joined the insurrection.
    b. they believed Brown's violent abolitionist sentiments were shared by the whole North.
    c. Brown had expressed his contempt for the southern way of life.
    d. Brown escaped punishment by pleading insanity.

9. Lincoln won the presidency

    a. with an electoral majority derived only from the North.
    b. with a majority of both the electoral and the popular vote.
    c. primarily because of the divisions in the Democratic party.
    d. with an electoral majority evenly derived from all sections of the nation.

10. Lincoln rejected the proposed Crittenden compromise because

    a. it did not deal with the issue of the future of slavery.
    b. it permitted the further extension of slavery south of the line of 36°30′.
    c. it represented a further extension of Douglas's popular sovereignty idea.
    d. the Supreme Court would probably have ruled it unconstitutional.

C. Identification

Supply the correct identification for each numbered description.

1. Antislavery novel that altered the course of American politics

2. A book by a southern writer that said slavery oppressed poor whites

3. Rifles paid for by New England abolitionists and brought to Kansas by antislavery pioneers

4. Term that described the prairie territory where a small-scale civil war erupted in 1856

5. Tricky document designed to bring Kansas into the Union as a slave state, but blocked by Stephen Douglas

6. Anti-immigrant and anti-Catholic party headed by former President Fillmore that competed in the election of 1856

7. Controversial Supreme Court ruling that blacks had no rights and that Congress could not prohibit slavery in the territories

_____ 8. Sharp economic decline that increased northern demands for a high tariff and convinced southerners that the North was economically vulnerable

_____ 9. Thoughtful political discussions during an Illinois Senate campaign that focused on the issues concerning slavery

_____ 10. Middle-of-the-road party of elderly politicians that sought compromise in 1860 but carried only three border states

_____ 11. First state to secede from the Union, in December 1860

_____ 12. A new "nation" that proclaimed its independence in Montgomery, Alabama, in 1861

_____ 13. Last-ditch compromise proposal to save the Union by providing guarantees for slavery in the territories

_____ 14. Four-way race for the presidency that resulted in the election of a sectional minority president

_____ 15. Period between Lincoln's election and his inauguration, during which the ineffectual President Buchanan remained in office.

D. Matching People, Places, and Events

Match the person, place, or event in the left column with the proper description in the right column by inserting the correct letter on the blank line.

____ 1. Harriet Beecher Stowe

____ 2. Hinton R. Helper

____ 3. New England Emigrant Aid Company

____ 4. John Brown

____ 5. James Buchanan

____ 6. Charles Sumner

____ 7. Preston Brooks

____ 8. John C. Frémont

____ 9. Dred Scott

A. Southern congressman whose bloody attack on a northern senator fueled sectional hatred

B. Leading northern Democrat whose presidential hopes fell victim to the conflict over slavery

C. Black slave whose unsuccessful attempt to win his freedom deepened the sectional controversy

D. Former United States senator who became the president of a "new nation" in 1861

E. "The little woman who wrote the book that made this great war" (the Civil War)

F. Fanatical and bloody-minded abolitionist admired in the North and hated in the South

G. Southern-born author of a book attacking slavery's effects on poor whites

H. Scene of militant abolitionist John Brown's massacre of proslavery men in 1856

I. Site where seven seceding states united to declare their independence from the United States

____ 10. Harpers Ferry

____ 11. Stephen A. Douglas

____ 12. Osawatomie Creek, Kansas

____ 13. John C. Breckenridge

____ 14. Montgomery, Alabama

____ 15. Jefferson Davis

J. Romantic western hero and first Republican candidate for president

K. Abolitionist senator whose verbal attack on the South provoked a physical assault that severely injured him

L. Site of a federal arsenal where a militant abolitionist attempted to start a slave rebellion in 1859

M. Buchanan's vice president, nominated for president in 1860 by breakaway southern Democrats

N. Weak Democratic president whose manipulation by proslavery forces divided his own party

O. Abolitionist group that sent settlers and weapons to oppose slavery in Kansas

E. Putting Things in Order

Put the following events in correct order by numbering them from 1 to 6.

____   A black slave's attempt to win freedom produces a controversial Supreme Court decision.

____   A newly organized territory becomes a bloody battleground between proslavery and antislavery forces.

____   The hanging of a fanatically violent abolitionist makes him a martyr in the North and a hated symbol in the South.

____   The minority sectional victory of a "black Republican" in a presidential election provokes southern secession.

____   The fictional tale of a black slave's vicious treatment by the cruel Simon Legree touches millions of northern hearts and creates stronger opposition to slavery.

____   A group of states calling itself a new southern nation declares its independence and chooses its first president.

PART III: Applying What You Have Learned

1. How did each of the crisis events of the 1850s help lead toward the Civil War?
2. What role did violence in Kansas and at Harpers Ferry play in increasing the sectional conflict?
3. How did the political developments of the period work to fragment the Democratic party and benefit the Republicans?
4. Why did the seven southern states secede from the Union after Lincoln's election, even though Lincoln promised he would not interfere with slavery where it existed?
5. In 1820 and 1850 severe conflict between North and South was resolved by compromise. Why was no compromise workable in 1860? (Consider the Crittenden compromise as one specific attempt that failed.)

21

★★★★★★★★

Girding for War: The North and the South,

1861–1865

Part I: Reviewing the Chapter

A. Checklist of Learning Objectives

After mastering this chapter, you should be able to

1. explain how the firing on Fort Sumter and Lincoln's call for troops galvanized both sides for war.
2. describe the crucial early struggle for the border states.
3. indicate the strengths and weaknesses of both sides as they went to war.
4. describe the diplomatic struggle for the sympathies of the European powers.
5. describe the politics of the war in both North and South.
6. describe how the war affected society in both North and South, including the role of women.

B. Glossary

To build your social science vocabulary, familiarize yourself with the following terms.

1. **balance of power** The distribution of political or military strength among several nations so that no one of them becomes too strong or dangerous. "They could gleefully transplant to America their hoary concept of the balance of power." (p. 289)
2. **martial law** The imposition of military rule above or in place of civil authority during times of war and emergency. "In Maryland he declared martial law where needed. . . ." (p. 290)
3. **ultimatum** A final proposal, as by one nation to another, that if rejected, will likely lead to war. "The London Foreign Office prepared an ultimatum. . . ." (p. 293)
4. **loopholed** Characterized by small exceptions or conditions that enable escape from the general rule or principle. "These vessels were not warships within the meaning of the loopholed British law. . . ." (p. 293)
5. **squadron** A special unit of warships assigned to a particular naval task. ". . . they probably would have sunk the blockading squadrons. . . ." (p. 294)

6. **envoy** An official government representative to a foreign nation. "But America's envoy . . . took a hard line. . . ." (p. 294)
7. **quota** The proportion or share of a larger number of things that a smaller group is assigned to contribute. ". . . each state [was] assigned a quota based on population." (p. 295)
8. **greenback** United States paper money, especially that printed before the establishment of the Federal Reserve System. "Greenbacks thus fluctuated with the fortunes of Union arms. . . ." (p. 296)

PART II: Checking Your Progress

A. True-False

Where the statement is true, mark **T.** Where it is false, mark **F,** and correct it in the space immediately below.

____ 1. Lincoln successfully prevented any more states from seceding after his inauguration.

____ 2. In order to appease the border states, Lincoln first insisted that the North was fighting only to preserve the Union and not to abolish slavery.

____ 4. The South's advantage in the Civil War was that it only had to stalemate the war on its own territory, while the North had to fight a war of conquest against a hostile population.

____ 4. The North generally had superior military leadership, while the South struggled to find successful commanders for its armies.

____ 5. In the long run, northern economic and human-resources advantages effectively wore down southern resistance.

____ 6. The northern sea blockade helped to strangle the southern economy.

____ 7. Although officially neutral, Britain sometimes engaged in acts that aided the South.

____ 8. Northern pressure forced the British to stop the *Alabama* from raiding Union shipping.

____ 9. The U.S. minister C. F. Adams threatened war with Britain over the "Laird ram" affair.

____ 10. Once the Civil War was over, the threat of U.S. intervention forced Napoleon III to withdraw his support of Maximilian in Mexico.

____ 11. The Civil War draft reflected the North's commitment to fighting a war based on fair and equal treatment of all citizens, rich and poor.

____ 12. The North effectively financed its Civil War effort through an income tax, higher tariffs, and the sale of federal government bonds.

____ 13. The South in effect used severe inflation as a means of financing its war effort.

____ 14. The suppliers of goods to the Union armies were noted for their efficiency and integrity.

___ 15. One consequence of the Civil War was the development of nursing as a respected profession for women.

B. Multiple Choice

Select the best answer and put the proper letter in the space provided.

___ 1. The firing on Fort Sumter had the effect of

a. pushing Missouri, Kentucky, and Maryland to join South Carolina in seceding from the Union.
b. causing Lincoln to declare a war to free the slaves.
c. strengthening many northerners' view that the South should be allowed to secede.
d. strengthening northern support for a war to put down southern "rebellion."

___ 2. Among the states that joined the Confederacy only after Lincoln's call for troops were

a. Florida, Louisiana, and Texas.
b. Virginia, Arkansas, and Tennessee.
c. Missouri, Maryland, and Delaware.
d. South Carolina, North Carolina, and Mississippi.

___ 3. Lincoln at first declared that the war was being fought

a. only to save the Union and not to free the slaves.
b. in order to end slavery only in the border states.
c. only in order to restore the Missouri Compromise.
d. only to punish South Carolina for firing on Fort Sumter.

___ 4. Among the potential advantages held by the Confederacy at the beginning of the Civil War was

a. a stronger and more balanced economy than the North's.
b. a stronger navy than the North's.
c. better trained officers and soldiers than the North's.
d. a larger reserve of manpower than the North's.

___ 5. Among the potential advantages held by the Union at the beginning of the Civil War was

a. better preparation of its ordinary soldiers for military life.
b. a continuing influx of immigrant manpower from Europe.
c. more highly educated and experienced generals.
d. the ability to fight a primarily defensive war.

___ 6. Europe's response to the Civil War was

a. almost unanimous support for the North.
b. support for the South among the upper classes and for the North among the working classes.
c. almost unanimous support for the South.
d. support for the South among the working classes and for the North among the upper classes.

7. The South's weapon of "King Cotton" failed to draw Britain into the war on the side of the Confederacy because

 a. the British switched to producing other fabrics like wool and nylon.
 b. the British were able to grow sufficient cotton themselves.
 c. the British found sufficient cotton from previous stockpiles and new sources in Egypt and India.
 d. the threat of war with France distracted British attention.

8. The success of the Confederate raider *Alabama* highlighted the issue of

 a. northern inferiority on the high seas.
 b. Britain's prosouthern policy allowing Confederate ships to be built in its naval yards.
 c. the British navy's ability to break the Union blockade of southern ports.
 d. the superiority of Confederate ironclad ships over the Union's wooden vessels.

9. One political problem that severely crippled Confederate President Jefferson Davis was

 a. that he could not logically justify suppressing states' rights within the Confederacy.
 b. a portion of the South did not believe in defending slavery.
 c. he had no sympathizers in Europe.
 d. Lincoln's appeal for a slave rebellion forced Davis to keep troops away from the front.

10. The Civil War agency that became a primary instrument for women's organizational activity was

 a. the Treasury Department.
 b. the U.S. Sanitary Commission.
 c. the American Nursing Association.
 d. the Women's Army Corps (WAC).

C. Identification

Supply the correct identification for each numbered description.

1. Five crucial states where secession failed but slavery still survived

2. The effective northern naval effort to strangle the South's economy and dethrone "King Cotton"

3. A ship from which two Confederate diplomats were removed, creating a major crisis between London and Washington

4. Vessel built in Britain that wreaked havoc on northern shipping until it was finally sunk in 1864

5. Ironclad warships that were kept out of Confederate hands by Minister Adams's stem protests to the British government

6. Provision established by Congress in 1863, after volunteers ran out, that provoked violent protests in northern cities

_____ 7. Slippery northern men who collected fees for enlisting in the Union army and then deserted

_____ 8. Paper currency printed by the Union government

_____ 9. Financial system set up by the United States to sell government bonds and stabilize the currency

_____ 10. Scornful term for northern manufacturers who made quick fortunes out of selling inferior goods to the U.S. Army

D. Matching People, Places, and Events

Match the person, place, or event in the left column with the proper description in the right column by inserting the correct letter on the blank line.

___ 1. Napoleon III

___ 2. Charles Francis Adams

___ 3. Mexico

___ 4. Archduke Maximilian

___ 5. New York City

___ 6. Britain

___ 7. Abraham Lincoln

___ 8. Jefferson Davis

___ 9. Elizabeth Blackwell

___ 10. Clara Barton

A. American envoy whose shrewd diplomacy kept the United States and Britain from war

B. An Old World aristocrat, manipulated as a puppet in Mexico, who was shot when his puppet-master deserted him

C. A leader inexperienced in military affairs but a genius at inspiring and directing the Union cause

D. Leader whose rigid personality harmed his ability to direct the southern war effort

E. Nation whose upper classes hoped for a Confederate victory, while its working classes sympathized with the antislavery North

F. Slippery French dictator who ignored the Monroe Doctrine by intervening in Mexican politics

G. Nation where the French emperor installed a puppet government while America was preoccupied with the Civil War

H. Person who helped transform nursing into a respected profession during the Civil War

I. Scene of the largest northern antidraft riot in 1863

J. First woman physician, organizer of the United States Sanitary Commission

E. Putting Things in Order

Put the following events in correct order by numbering them from 1 to 5.

___ Enactment of military draft causes major riot in New York City.

___ Napoleon III's puppet emperor is removed from power in Mexico under threat of American intervention.

_____ The firing on Fort Sumter unifies the North and leads to Lincoln's call for troops.

_____ The *Alabama* escapes from a British port and begins wreaking havoc on northern shipping.

_____ Charles Francis Adams's successful diplomacy prevents the Confederacy from obtaining two Laird ram warships.

PART III: Applying What You Have Learned

1. How did the Civil War change from a limited war to preserve the Union into a "total war" to abolish slavery?
2. How did careful Union diplomacy end British flirtations with the Confederacy?
3. How did the North and the South each handle their economic and manpower needs?
4. In what ways did the Civil War affect both North and South similarly, and in what ways were its social and economic effects very different for the two sides?
5. Given the balance of forces at the beginning, how might the South have won the Civil War? Why did the Confederacy lose the war?

22

★★★★★★★★

The Furnace of Civil War,

1861–1865

Part I: Reviewing the Chapter

A. Checklist of Learning Objectives

After mastering this chapter, you should be able to

1. describe the failure of the North to gain its expected early victory in 1861.
2. explain the significance of Antietam and the northern turn to a "total war" against slavery.
3. describe the role that African-Americans played during the war.
4. describe the military significance of the battles of Gettysburg in the East and Vicksburg in the West.
5. describe the political struggle between Lincoln's Union party and the antiwar Copperheads.
6. describe the consequences of the Civil War.

B. Glossary

To build your social science vocabulary, familiarize yourself with the following terms.

1. **mediation** The attempt to resolve a dispute through the intervention or counsel of a third party. "The British and French governments were on the verge of diplomatic mediation. . . ." (p. 302)
2. **proclamation** An official announcement or publicly declared order. "Thus, the Emancipation Proclamation was stronger on proclamation than emancipation." (p. 303)
3. **flank** The side of an army, where it is vulnerable to attack. "Lee . . . sent Stonewall Jackson to attack the Union flank." (p. 305)
4. **court martial** A military court, or a trial held in such a court under military law. "Resigning from the army to avoid a court martial for drunkenness, he failed at various business ventures. . . ." (p. 305)
5. **garrison** A military fortress, or the troops stationed at such a fortress, usually designed for defense or occupation of a territory. "Vicksburg at length surrendered . . . , with the garrison reduced to eating mules and rats." (p. 306)
6. **morale** The condition of courage, confidence, and willingness to endure hardship. "His major purposes were . . . to weaken the morale of the men at the front by waging war on their homes." (p. 307)
7. **pillaging** Plundering, looting, destroying property by violence. ". . . the army . . . engaged in an orgy of pillaging." (p. 307)

8. **running mate** In politics, the candidate for the lesser of two offices when they are decided together—for example, the U.S. vice presidency. "Lincoln's running mate was ex-tailor Andrew Johnson." (p. 309)

PART II: Checking Your Progress

A. True-False

Where the statement is true, mark **T.** Where it is false, mark **F,** and correct it in the space immediately below.

_____ 1. The First Battle of Bull Run proved to be the turning point of the Civil War.

_____ 2. The Emancipation Proclamation was more important for its political effects on the North and Europe than because it actually freed large numbers of slaves.

_____ 3. The Union's greatest military breakthroughs came on the eastern front in Virginia and Maryland.

_____ 4. The Battle of Antietam was a turning point of the war because it forestalled British and French recognition of the Confederacy.

_____ 5. Lincoln's decision to fight a war against slavery strengthened his popularity in the North.

_____ 6. The use of black soldiers in the Union Army proved militarily ineffective.

_____ 7. Lee's invasion of Pennsylvania in 1863 was intended to encourage the northern peace movement and promote foreign intervention.

_____ 8. The northern victories at Vicksburg and Gettysburg spelled doom for the Confederacy.

_____ 9. In the final year of the conflict, Grant and Sherman waged a "total war" that was immensely destructive of southern lives and property.

_____ 10. The northern Democrats were deeply divided between "War Democrats" who backed the war and "Copperheads" who favored peace negotiations with the South.

_____ 11. The formation of the "Union party" in 1864 was a political device by Lincoln to gain the support of prowar Democrats.

_____ 12. Lincoln was opposed by some members of his own party throughout the Civil War.

_____ 13. The South hoped that the victory of a "Peace Democrat" in the northern election of 1864 would enable it to achieve its political goals without a military victory.

_____ 14. Although they cheered it at the time, most southerners later came to see Lincoln's assassination as a tragedy for them.

_____ 15. The Civil War failed to settle the central issues of slavery, states' rights, and secession that caused the war.

B. Multiple Choice

Select the best answer and put the proper letter in the space provided.

____ 1. One effect of the early Battle of Bull Run was

    a. to convince the North that victory would be relatively simple.
    b. to increase the South's already dangerous overconfidence.
    c. to demonstrate the superiority of southern volunteer soldiers over northern draftees.
    d. to cause a wave of new southern enlistments in the army.

____ 2. After the unsuccessful Peninsula Campaign, Lincoln and the Union turned to

    a. a new strategy based on "total war" against the Confederacy.
    b. a new strategy based on cavalry raids and guerrilla warfare.
    c. a pattern of defensive warfare designed to protect Washington, D.C.
    d. a reliance on the navy rather than the army to win the war.

____ 3. Antietam was probably the crucial battle of the Civil War because

    a. it ended any possibility of Confederate invasion of the North.
    b. it destroyed Lee's army in the East.
    c. it fundamentally undermined Confederate morale.
    d. it prevented British and French recognition of the Confederacy.

____ 4. Officially, the Emancipation Proclamation freed only

    a. slaves who had fled their masters and joined the Union Army.
    b. slaves in those Confederate states still in rebellion.
    c. slaves in the border states and areas under Union Army control.
    d. slaves in Washington, D.C.

____ 5. The thousands of black soldiers in the Union Army

    a. added a powerful new weapon to the antislavery dimension of the Union cause.
    b. were prevented from participating in combat.
    c. seldom fought effectively in battle.
    d. saw action in the very first days of the war.

____ 6. Lee's goal in invading the North in the summer of 1863 was

    a. to capture the major northern cities of Philadelphia and New York.
    b. to deflect attention from "Stonewall" Jackson's movements against Washington.
    c. to strengthen the northern peace movement and encourage foreign intervention in the war.
    d. to cut off northern supply lines and damage the Union's economic foundations.

___ 7. Grant's capture of Vicksburg was especially important because

    a. it quelled northern peace agitation and cut off Confederate trade along the Mississippi.
    b. it ended the threat of a Confederate invasion of southern Illinois and Indiana.
    c. it blocked possible French military support of the Confederacy from Mexico.
    d. it destroyed southern naval power.

___ 8. The "Copperheads" were

    a. northern Democrats who opposed the Union war effort.
    b. Republicans who opposed the Lincoln administration.
    c. Democrats who backed Lincoln and the war effort.
    d. radical Republicans who advocated a war to destroy slavery and punish the South.

___ 9. Andrew Johnson, Lincoln's running mate in 1864, was

    a. a Copperhead.
    b. a War Democrat.
    c. a conservative Republican.
    d. a radical Republican.

___ 10. Lincoln's election victory in 1864 was sealed by Union military successes at

    a. Gettysburg, Antietam, and Vicksburg.
    b. The Wilderness, Lookout Mountain, and Appomattox.
    c. Bull Run, the Peninsula, and Fredericksburg.
    d. Mobile, Atlanta, and the Shenandoah Valley.

C. Identification

Supply the correct identification for each numbered description.

_____ 1. First major battle of the Civil War, in which untrained northern troops and civilian picnickers were put to flight

_____ 2. McClellan's disastrously unsuccessful attempt to capture Richmond quickly along an invasion route between the York and James rivers

_____ 3. Battle that was probably the most decisive of the war because it forestalled European intervention and led to the Emancipation Proclamation

_____ 4. Document that did not touch slavery within the Union but "freed" the slaves in the rebellious Confederate states

_____ 5. General U. S. Grant's nickname, taken from his military demand to the enemy at Fort Donelson and elsewhere

_____ 6. Crucial Confederate fortress on the Mississippi whose fall to Grant in 1863 cut the South in two

_____ 7. Pennsylvania battle that ended Lee's last hopes of achieving victory through an invasion of the North

_____ 8. Mississippi site where black soldiers were massacred after their surrender

_____ 9. Northerners who openly obstructed the war effort and favored the South

_____ 10. Northern Democrats who supported Lincoln and the war effort

_____ 11. Georgia city captured and burned by Sherman just before the election of 1864

_____ 12. The 1864 political coalition of Republicans and War Democrats that backed Lincoln's reelection

_____ 13. Washington site where Lincoln was assassinated by Booth on April 14, 1865

_____ 14. Virginia site where Lee surrendered to Grant in April 1865

_____ 15. Romantic name given to the southern fight for independence

D. Matching People, Places, and Events

Match the person, place, or event in the left column with the proper description in the right column by inserting the correct letter on the blank line.

___ 1. Bull Run

___ 2. George McClellan

___ 3. Robert E. Lee

___ 4. Antietam

___ 5. "Stonewall" Jackson

___ 6. George Pickett

___ 7. Ulysses S. Grant

___ 8. Gettysburg

___ 9. Vicksburg

___ 10. William T. Sherman

___ 11. Clement Vallandigham

A. Daring southern commander killed at the Battle of Chancellorsville

B. Southern officer whose failed charge at Gettysburg marked "the high water mark of the Confederacy"

C. Ruthless northern general who waged a march through Georgia

D. Fortress whose capture split the Confederacy in two

E. Site where Lee's last major invasion of the North was turned back

F. Gentlemanly top commander of the Confederate army

G. Site of Grant's bloody attacks on Confederates near Richmond in 1864

H. Crucial battle in Maryland that staved off European recognition of the Confederacy

I. Lincoln's secretary of the treasury who hungered for the presidency in 1864

J. Fanatical actor whose act of violence harmed the South

K. Union commander who first made his mark with victories in the West

L. Pro-Union War Democrat from the South who ran as Lincoln's "Union party" vice-presidential candidate in 1864

M. Copperhead, convicted of treason, who ran for governor of Ohio while exiled in Canada

____ 12. Salmon P. Chase

____ 13. The Wilderness

____ 14. Andrew Johnson

____ 15. John Wilkes Booth

N. Former Union general who repudiated his party's Copperhead platform and polled 45 percent of the popular vote in the 1864 election

O. Site of Union defeat in very early battle of the war

E. Putting Things in Order

Put the following events in correct order by numbering them from 1 to 5.

____ Within one week, two decisive battles in Mississippi and Pennsylvania almost ensure the Confederacy's eventual defeat.

____ Defeat in a battle near Washington, D.C., ends Union military complacency.

____ A militarily indecisive battle in Maryland enables Lincoln to declare that the Civil War has become a
war on slavery.

____ The Civil War ends with the defeated army being granted generous terms of surrender.

____ In both Georgia and Virginia, determined northern generals wage bloody and destructive "total war"
against a weakened but still-resisting South.

PART III: Applying What You Have Learned

1. How did the military stalemate of 1861–1862 affect both sides in the Civil War?
2. What were the primary military strategies of each side, and how did each side attempt to carry them out?
3. What role did the "politics of slavery" play during the Civil War? How did the Emancipation Proclamation
   and the use of black soldiers affect the "meaning" of the war for both northerners and southerners?
4. The battles of Antietam, Gettysburg, and Atlanta are all regarded as crucial to the northern victory in the
   Civil War. Explain the military *and* political significance of each battle.
5. What were the significance and meaning of the Civil War? For the North? For the South? For blacks? For
   later generations of Americans?

23

★★★★★★★★★

The Ordeal of Reconstruction,

1865–1877

PART I: Reviewing the Chapter

A. Checklist of Learning Objectives

After mastering this chapter, you should be able to

1. define the major problems facing the South and the nation after the Civil War.
2. describe the condition of the newly freed slaves and indicate what efforts were made to assist them.
3. analyze the differences between the presidential and congressional approaches to Reconstruction.
4. explain how the blunders of President Johnson and the white South opened the door to more radical congressional Reconstruction policies.
5. describe the actual effects of congressional Reconstruction in the South.
6. indicate why the Republican attempt to empower southern blacks failed.
7. explain why the radical Republicans impeached Johnson.
8. explain why Reconstruction failed and why it left such a bitter legacy for the future.

B. Glossary

To build your social science vocabulary, familiarize yourself with the following terms.

1. **ringleader** A person who leads others, especially in unlawful acts or opposition to authority. "What should be done with the captured Confederate ringleaders . . . ?" (p. 315)
2. **civil disabilities** Legally imposed restrictions of a person's civil rights or liberties. "But Congress removed their remaining civil disabilities thirty years later. . . ." (p. 316)
3. **pocket veto** Term for the provision of the Constitution (Article I, Section 7) whereby a president can kill a law passed by Congress by failing to sign it at the end of a session. "Republicans were outraged when Lincoln "pocket-vetoed" this bill. . . ." (p. 319)
4. **lease** To enter into a contract by which one party gives another use of land, buildings, or other property for a fixed time and fee. ". . . some [codes] even barred [blacks] from renting or leasing land." (p. 319)
5. **sharecrop** An agricultural system in which a tenant receives land, tools, and seed on credit and pledges in return to give a share of the crop to the creditor. ". . . slipped into virtual peonage as sharecropper farmers. . . ." (p. 319)

6. **peonage** A system in which debtors are held in servitude and forced to labor for their creditors. "... slipped into virtual peonage...." (p. 319)

7. **scalawag** A white southerner who supported Republican Reconstruction after the Civil War. "... fell under the control of white 'scalawags.'..." (p. 323)

8. **carpetbagger** A northern politician who came south to exploit the unsettled conditions after the Civil War; hence, any politician who relocates for political advantage. "... 'carpetbaggers' [were] northerners...." (p. 323)

9. **felony** A major crime for which severe penalties are exacted under the law. "The crimes of the Reconstruction governments were no more outrageous than the scams and felonies being perpetrated in the North at the same time...." (p. 323)

10. **terror** Violence used in order to create intense fear and thus achieve political or other objectives. "Such terror tactics proved partially effective." (p. 324)

PART II: Checking Your Progress

A. True-False

Where the statement is true, mark **T.** Where it is false, mark **F,** and correct it in the space immediately below.

_____ 1. Southern agriculture was severely crippled by the Civil War.

_____ 2. Military defeat in the Civil War brought white southerners to accept the reality of northern political domination.

_____ 3. The primary social institution for newly freed slaves was the black church.

_____ 4. The greatest success of the Freedmen's Bureau came in providing "forty acres and a mule" to the former slaves.

_____ 5. Lincoln's "10 percent" Reconstruction plan was designed to return the southern states to the Union with few restrictions.

_____ 6. The disagreement between the president and Congress over Reconstruction arose only after Johnson succeeded Lincoln as president.

_____ 7. Radical Republicans expected that President Johnson would support their effort to severely punish the southern planter elite.

_____ 8. The enactment of the Black Codes in the South strengthened those who supported a moderate approach to Reconstruction.

_____ 9. Congressional Republicans demanded that the southern states ratify the Fourteenth Amendment in order to be readmitted to the Union.

_____ 10. Radical Republicans succeeded in their goal of redistributing land to the former slaves.

_____ 11. During Reconstruction, blacks controlled all the southern state legislatures except one.

___ 12. The passage of the Fourteenth and Fifteenth Amendments created conflicts between advocates of black rights and the women's suffrage movement.

___ 13. The Ku Klux Klan failed in its goal of intimidating blacks and preventing them from voting.

___ 14. Johnson's impeachment was essentially an act of political vindictiveness by radical Republicans.

___ 15. Reconstruction was more successful in healing the racial division between black and white than in healing the sectional division between North and South.

B. Multiple Choice

Select the best answer and put the proper letter in the space provided.

___ 1. After emancipation, many blacks traveled in order to

  a. return to Africa or the West Indies.
  b. seek a better life in northern cities.
  c. find lost family members or seek new economic opportunities.
  d. track down and punish cruel overseers.

___ 2. The Freedmen's Bureau was originally established to provide

  a. land and supplies for black farmers.
  b. labor registration.
  c. food, clothes, and education for emancipated slaves.
  d. political training in citizenship for black voters.

___ 3. Lincoln's original plan for Reconstruction in 1863 had provided that a state could be reintegrated into the Union when

  a. it withdrew its soldiers from the Confederate Army.
  b. 10 percent of its voters took an oath of allegiance to the Union and pledged to abide by emancipation.
  c. it formally adopted a plan guaranteeing black political and economic rights.
  d. it ratified the Fourteenth and Fifteenth Amendments to the Constitution.

___ 4. The Black Codes passed by many of the southern state governments in 1865

  a. provided for economic assistance to get former slaves started as sharecroppers.
  b. recognized slavery's end but legalized many other oppressive restrictions against blacks.
  c. permitted blacks to vote if they met certain educational or economic standards.
  d. gave blacks personal liberty but restricted political and economic rights.

___ 5. The congressional elections of 1866 resulted in

  a. a victory for Johnson and his prosouthern Reconstruction plan.
  b. a political stalemate between the Republicans in Congress and Johnson.
  c. a decisive defeat for Johnson and a veto-proof Republican Congress.
  d. a gain for northern Democrats and their moderate plan for Reconstruction.

6. In contrast to radical Republicans, moderate Republicans generally

    a. favored states' rights and opposed direct federal involvement in individuals' lives.
    b. favored the use of federal power to alter the southern economic system.
    c. favored emancipation but opposed the Fourteenth Amendment.
    d. favored returning the southern states to the Union without significant Reconstruction.

7. The "radical" Reconstruction regimes in the southern states

    a. took away white southerners' civil rights and voting rights.
    b. consisted almost entirely of blacks.
    c. were made up of white northerners, white southerners, and blacks.
    d. eliminated the public education systems in most southern states.

8. The Reconstruction effort to empower blacks politically

    a. created a stable base of black officeholders in the southern states through the early twentieth century.
    b. was undermined by the Ku Klux Klan and other efforts to destroy black rights.
    c. turned most blacks into supporters of the Democratic party.
    d. was strongly backed by most white northerners.

9. The radical Republican attempt to force Andrew Johnson out of the presidency resulted in

    a. Johnson's acceptance of the radicals' Reconstruction plan.
    b. a failure to remove Johnson by a margin of only one vote.
    c. Johnson's impeachment conviction on the charge of violating the Tenure of Office Act.
    d. Johnson's resignation and the appointment of Edwin Stanton as president.

10. The public eventually accepted Seward's unpopular purchase of Alaska partly because

    a. extensive oil deposits were discovered in the territory.
    b. it was considered strategically vital to American defense.
    c. the public shared Seward's enthusiasm for northward expansion.
    d. Russia had been the only great power friendly to the Union during the Civil War.

C. Identification

Supply the correct identification for each numbered description.

    1. Common term for the blacks newly liberated from slavery

    2. Federal agency that greatly assisted blacks educationally but failed in other aid efforts

    3. Lincoln's 1863 program for a rapid Reconstruction of the South

    4. A congressional bill of 1864, pocket-vetoed by Lincoln, that required 50 percent of southern voters to take an oath of allegiance before readmission to the Union

_____ 5. The constitutional amendment freeing all slaves

_____ 6. The harsh southern state laws of 1865 that limited black rights and imposed restrictions to ensure a stable black labor supply

_____ 7. The constitutional amendment granting civil rights to freed slaves and barring former Confederates from office

_____ 8. Republican Reconstructionists who opposed radical plans for drastic economic transformation of the South

_____ 9. Republican Reconstructionists who favored keeping the South out of the federal government until a complete social and economic revolution was accomplished in the region

_____ 10. The congressional committee, led by radical Thaddeus Stevens, that directed the program of military Reconstruction

_____ 11. Supreme Court ruling that military tribunals could not try civilians when the civil courts were open

_____ 12. Derogatory term for white southerners who cooperated with the Republican Reconstruction governments

_____ 13. Northerners who came to the South during Reconstruction and sometimes took part in Republican state governments

_____ 14. Organization that became the primary vehicle for black political and militia activity during Reconstruction

_____ 15. "Seward's Folly," acquired in 1867 from Russia

D. Matching People, Places, and Events

Match the person, place, or event in the left column with the proper description in the right column by inserting the correct letter on the blank line.

____ 1. Jefferson Davis

____ 2. Oliver O. Howard

____ 3. Andrew Johnson

____ 4. Abraham Lincoln

____ 5. Civil Rights Bill of 1866

A. A constitutionally questionable law whose violation by President Johnson formed the official basis for his impeachment

B. The first congressional attempt to guarantee black rights in the South, passed over Johnson's veto

C. Leader, born in poverty, who became the champion of the white South against radical Reconstruction

D. Secretary of state who arranged an unpopular but valuable land deal in 1867

E. Laws designed to stamp out Ku Klux Klan terrorism in the South

___ 6. Charles Sumner

___ 7. Thaddeus Stevens

___ 8. Military Reconstruction
       Act of 1867

___ 9. Hiram Revels

___ 10. Ku Klux Klan

___ 11. Force Acts of 1870 and
       1871

___ 12. Tenure of Office Act

___ 13. Johnson impeachment
       trial

___ 14. Benjamin Wade

___ 15. William Seward

F. Black senator from Mississippi, elected during Reconstruction
G. Secret organization that intimidated blacks and worked to restore white supremacy
H. Top rebel leader, imprisoned for two years after the Civil War, whose U.S. citizenship was posthumously restored
I. Congressional law that imposed military rule on the South and demanded harsh conditions for readmission of the seceded states
J. The leader of Senate radical Republicans during Reconstruction
K. Problack general who led an agency that tried to assist the freedmen
L. Effort led by radicals that fell only one vote short of removing their archenemy from office
M. Author of the moderate "10 percent" Reconstruction plan that ran into congressional opposition
N. The president pro tempore of the Senate who expected to become president of the United States after Johnson's impeachment conviction
O. The leader of radical Republicans in the House of Representatives

E. Putting Things in Order

Put the following events in correct order by numbering them from 1 to 5.

___ The Constitution is amended to guarantee former slaves the right to vote.

___ Lincoln announces a plan to rapidly restore southern states to the Union.

___ Northern troops are finally withdrawn from the South, and southern state governments are reconstituted without federal restraint.

___ An unpopular antiradical president escapes conviction and removal from office by one vote.

___ Johnson's attempt to restore the South to the Union is overturned because of congressional hostility to ex-Confederates and southern passage of the Black Codes.

PART III: Applying What You Have Learned

1. What were the major problems facing the South and the nation after the Civil War? How did Reconstruction address them, or fail to do so?
2. What were the most important social, economic, and political activities and organizations by which newly freed slaves attempted to assert their freedom and improve their condition?
3. What were the political differences among President Johnson, moderate Republicans, and radical Republicans regarding Reconstruction policy?

4. What were the actual effects of Reconstruction on the South?

5. Was Reconstruction a total failure or a partial success? Explain your answer. Include a discussion of both short- and long-term successes and failures.

24
★★★★★★★★★

Politics in the Gilded Age,

1869–1896

PART I: Reviewing the Chapter

A. Checklist of Learning Objectives

After mastering this chapter, you should be able to

1. describe the political corruptions of the Grant administration and the various efforts to clean up politics in the Gilded Age.
2. describe the economic slump of the 1870s and the growing conflict between "hard-money" and "soft-money" advocates.
3. indicate the reasons for the intense political involvements of the age, despite the agreement of the two parties on most issues.
4. explain the causes and results of the Compromise of 1877.
5. explain the importance of the spoils system in Gilded Age politics and how the Garfield assassination led to the beginnings of the civil service.
6. describe the economic and political effects of the Panic of 1893.
7. explain why the level of politics in the Gilded Age was generally so low.

B. Glossary

To build your social science vocabulary, familiarize yourself with the following terms.

1. **coalition** A temporary alliance of political factions or parties for some specific purpose. "The Republicans, now freed from the Union party coalition of war days, enthusiastically nominated Grant. . . ." (p. 333)
2. **corner** To gain exclusive control of a commodity in order to fix its price. "This crafty pair concocted a plot in 1869 to corner the gold market." (p. 333)
3. **eccentric** Deviating from the norm; peculiar, unconventional. ". . . the eccentric editor had long blasted them as traitors. . . . " (p. 334)
4. **amnesty** A general pardon for offenses or crimes against a government. "The Republican Congress in 1872 passed a general amnesty act. . . ." (p. 335)
5. **hard money** Scarce money with high purchase value. ". . . 'hard-money' people everywhere looked forward to [the] complete disappearance [of greenbacks]." (p. 335)

6. **kickback** The return of a portion of the money received in a sale or contract, often secretly or illegally, in exchange for favors. "The lifeblood of both parties was patronage—disbursing jobs by the bucketful in return for votes, kickbacks, and party service." (p. 336)

7. **consensus** Common or unanimous opinion. "How can this apparent paradox of political consensus and partisan fervor be explained?" (p. 336)

8. **pull** Political influence or special advantage. "It established a merit system of making appointments to office on the basis of aptitude rather than 'pull.'" (p. 341)

9. **laissez-faire** The doctrine of noninterference by the government in matters of economics or business. "[The new president was] a staunch apostle of the hands-off creed of *laissez-faire*. . . ." (p. 343)

10. **quorum** In parliamentary procedure, the minimum number of a body's membership who must be present for it legally to conduct business. "He ignored Democratic speakers who demanded quorum counts. . . ." (pp. 343–344)

PART II: Checking Your Progress

A. True-False

Where the statement is true, mark **T.** Where it is false, mark **F,** and correct it in the space immediately below.

____ 1. Ulysses Grant's status as a military hero enabled him to function successfully as a president above partisan politics.

____ 2. The scandals of the Grant administration included bribes and corrupt dealings reaching to the cabinet and the vice president of the United States.

____ 3. The political skill of the Liberal Republican movement enabled it to clean up corruption in the Grant administration.

____ 4. The severe economic downturn of the 1870s caused business failures, labor conflict, and battles over currency.

____ 5. The fiercely contested elections of the Gilded Age reflected the deep ideological divisions between Republicans and Democrats over national issues.

____ 6. The battles between the "Stalwart" and "Half-Breed" Republican factions were mainly over who would get patronage and spoils.

____ 7. The disputed Hayes-Tilden election was settled by a political deal in which Democrats got the presidency and Republicans got to appoint the Supreme Court.

____ 8. The Compromise of 1877 purchased political peace by sacrificing southern blacks, who lost their protection when federal troops were withdrawn from the South.

____ 9. White workers' hostility to Chinese immigrants eventually led Congress to ban all Chinese immigration to the United States.

___ 10. The president who took over after Garfield's assassination, Chester Arthur, had always been a strong supporter of civil-service reform.

___ 11. By reducing the use of patronage, the new civil-service system inadvertently made U.S. politicians more dependent on big-business campaign contributors.

___ 12. The Cleveland-Blaine campaign of 1884 was conducted primarily as a debate about the issues of taxes and the tariff.

___ 13. The Populist party attempted to get industrial workers to join forces with discontented farmers.

___ 14. Southern white conservatives effectively stopped the Populist effort to form an alliance of poor whites and blacks.

___ 15. The depression of the 1890s was partly alleviated by federal aid to farmers and unemployed workers.

B. Multiple Choice

Select the best answer and put the proper letter in the space provided.

___ 1. Financiers Jim Fisk and Jay Gould tried to involve the Grant administration in a corrupt scheme to

a. skim funds from the Bureau of Indian Affairs.
b. sell "watered" railroad stock at high prices.
c. corner the gold market.
d. bribe congressmen in exchange for federal land grants.

___ 2. Grant's greatest failing in the scandals that plagued his administration was

a. his refusal to turn over evidence to congressional investigators.
b. his toleration of corruption and his loyalty to crooked friends.
c. his acceptance of bribes in the White House.
d. his use of large amounts of "dirty" money in his political campaigns.

___ 3. Besides the Democrats, the third party that backed Horace Greeley against Grant in the election of 1872 was

a. the Union party.
b. the Greenback party.
c. the Liberal Republican party.
d. the Copperhead party.

___ 4. The depression of the 1870s led to increasing demands for

a. inflation of the currency by issuing more paper currency and silver money.
b. federal programs to create jobs for the unemployed.
c. restoration of sound money by backing all paper currency with gold.
d. the creation of a federal banking system.

5. The political system of the "Gilded Age" was generally characterized by

    a. "split-ticket" voting, low voter turnout, and single-issue special-interest groups.

    b. strong party loyalties, low voter turnout, and deep ideological differences.

    c. "third-party" movements, high voter turnout, and strong disagreement on foreign-policy issues.

    d. strong party loyalties, high voter turnout, and few disagreements on national issues.

6. The primary goal for which all factions in both political parties contended was

    a. racial justice.

    b. a sound financial and banking system.

    c. patronage.

    d. a more assertive American foreign policy.

7. In the key tradeoff featured in the Compromise of 1877,

    a. Republicans got the presidency in exchange for the final removal of federal troops from the South.

    b. Democrats got the presidency in exchange for federal guarantees of black civil rights.

    c. Republicans got the presidency in exchange for Democratic control of the cabinet.

    d. Democrats got the presidency in exchange for increased immigration quotas from Ireland.

8. For African-Americans, the final result of the Compromise of 1877 was

    a. a turn from the Republican to the Democratic party.

    b. a new movement to demand equal education and civil rights.

    c. a large-scale movement from the rural South to northern cities.

    d. increased poverty and loss of civil and political rights.

9. President James Garfield was assassinated by

    a. a fanatically anti-Republican Confederate veteran.

    b. a mentally unstable disappointed office seeker.

    c. an anticapitalist immigrant anarchist.

    d. a corrupt gangster under federal criminal indictment.

10. The Cleveland-Blaine campaign of 1884 was notable for

    a. its sharp division between conservative defenders of the gold standard and "soft money" silver advocates.

    b. the infusion of large amounts of corporate money into politics.

    c. the nasty mudslinging between the two sides.

    d. the intrusion of the "Chinese issue" into American politics.

11. The principal issue for which Congressman William McKinley first became widely known was

    a. civil service reform.

    b. the high tariff.

    c. support for Civil War veterans.

    d. free and unlimited coinage of silver.

___ 12. Among the radical policies advocated by the Populist party in the 1892 campaign was

    a. free homesteads for settlers in the West.
    b. an end to American overseas expansion.
    c. the cancellation of all farm debts.
    d. government ownership of the telephone, telegraph, and railroads.

___ 13. The primary reason that the Populists were ultimately unable to make substantial political gains in the South was

    a. the Midwestern Populists were too identified with the cause of northern (Union) veterans.
    b. they were unable to overcome the racial divisions among southern poor whites and blacks.
    c. the economics of cotton farming were very different from that of corn or wheat growing.
    d. southern Populists would not accept the idea of a larger federal government role in the economy.

___ 14. The deepest consequence of the Populist crusade in the South proved to be

    a. complete disenfranchisement and segregation for blacks.
    b. the growth of the Republican party in the South.
    c. an improvement in the status of poor whites.
    d. the end of northern Reconstruction efforts.

___ 15. The deep depression of the 1890s finally forced President Grover Cleveland to

    a. offer federal assistance to suffering workers and farmers.
    b. support a higher tariff to aid business recovery.
    c. seek a $65 million gold loan from J. P. Morgan to stop the loss of gold from the federal treasury.
    d. abandon the gold standard for U.S. currency.

C. Identification

Supply the correct identification for each numbered description.

_____ 1. The symbol of the Republican political tactic of attacking Democrats with reminders of the Civil War

_____ 2. Corrupt construction company whose bribes and payoffs to congressmen and others created a major Grant administration scandal

_____ 3. Short-lived third party of 1872 that attempted to curb Grant administration corruption

_____ 4. Precious metal that "soft-money" advocates demanded be coined again, after the "Crime of '73"

_____ 5. "Soft-money" third party that polled over a million votes and elected fourteen congressmen in 1878 by advocating inflation

_____ 6. Mark Twain's sarcastic name for the post–Civil War era, which emphasized its atmosphere of greed and corruption

_____ 7. Civil War veterans' organization that became a potent political bulwark of the Republican party in the late nineteenth century

_____ 8. Republican party faction, led by Senator Roscoe Conkling, that opposed all attempts at civil-service reform

_____ 9. Republican party faction, led by James G. Blaine, that gave lukewarm support to the civil-service idea while still battling for patronage and spoils

_____ 10. The complex political agreement between Republicans and Democrats that resolved the bitterly disputed election of 1876

_____ 11. Asian immigrant group that aroused discrimination on the West Coast

_____ 12. System of choosing federal employees on the basis of merit rather than patronage, introduced by the Pendleton Act of 1883

_____ 13. Term for laws that exempted from literacy tests anyone whose forebear had voted in 1860

_____ 14. Supreme Court decision that upheld segregation under the doctrine of "separate but equal"

_____ 15. Farmer-based political party that made dramatic gains in the early 1890s

D. Matching People, Places, and Events

Match the person, place, or event in the left column with the proper description in the right column by inserting the correct letter on the blank line.

____ 1. Ulysses S. Grant

____ 2. Jim Fisk

____ 4. Boss Tweed

____ 4. Horace Greeley

____ 5. Jay Cooke

____ 6. William McKinley

____ 7. Denis Kearney

____ 8. Roscoe Conkling

A. New York political boss whose widespread fraud landed him in jail in 1871

B. Unprincipled financier whose plot to comer the U.S. gold market nearly succeeded in 1869

C. The winner of a contested election in 1876 who presided over the end of Reconstruction

D. Great military leader whose presidency foundered in corruption and political ineptitude

E. Eloquent southern Populist who turned from interracial cooperation to vicious racism

F. Wealthy Wall Street banker to whom Cleveland turned for a controversial loan in 1895

G. President whose assassination after only a few months in office spurred the passage of a civil-service law

H. The "high priest of high protection" who successfully worked to raise protective tariffs

_____   9. James G. Blaine

_____   10. Rutherford B. Hayes

_____   11. James A. Garfield

_____   12. Tom Watson

_____   13. Grover Cleveland

_____   14. J. P. Morgan

_____   15. Benjamin Harrison

I. Irish-American agitator who opposed the Chinese in California

J. Wealthy New York financier whose bank collapsed in 1873, setting off an economic depression

K. Imperious New York senator and leader of the "Stalwart" faction of Republicans

L. First Democratic president since the Civil War

M. Presidential grandson of another president, who defeated Cleveland in the election of 1888

N. Colorful newspaper editor who carried the Liberal Republican and Democratic banners against Grant in 1872

O. Charming but corrupt "Half-Breed" Republican senator and presidential nominee in 1884

E. Putting Things in Order

Put the following events in correct order by numbering them from 1 to 5.

_____   A bitterly disputed presidential election is resolved by a complex political deal that ends Reconstruction in the South.

_____   Two unscrupulous financiers use corrupt means to manipulate New York gold markets and the U.S. Treasury.

_____   The assassination of a president by a disappointed office seeker creates political pressure for a civil-service law.

_____   Grant administration scandals split the Republican party, but Grant overcomes the inept opposition to win reelection.

_____   A radical Farmers' party makes a successful debut into national politics.

PART III: Applying What You Have Learned

1. What made politics in the Gilded Age extremely popular—with over 80 percent voter participation—yet so often corrupt and unconcerned with issues?
2. What were the causes and effects of the political scandals of the Grant administration?
3. What did Republicans and Democrats each gain from the Compromise of 1877, and why were southern blacks the real losers in the deal?
4. What were the causes and results of the Panic of 1893? Who gained politically from the depression, and who lost?
5. How and why were the issues of race effectively shoved aside during the Gilded Age? Could the Populists' attempt at an interracial alliance of farmers and workers have succeeded? Why or why not?

25
★★★★★★★★

Industry Comes of Age,

1865–1900

PART I: Reviewing the Chapter

A. Checklist of Learning Objectives

After mastering this chapter, you should be able to

1. explain how the transcontinental railroad network provided the basis for the great post–Civil War industrial transformation.
2. describe how the economy came to be dominated by giant "trusts," such as those headed by Carnegie and Rockefeller, in the steel and oil industries.
3. discuss the growing class conflict caused by industrial growth and combination, and the early efforts to alleviate it.
4. explain why the South was generally excluded from industrial development and fell into a "third world" economic dependency.
5. analyze the social changes brought by industrialization, particularly the altered position of working men and women.
6. describe the early efforts of labor to organize and counterbalance corporate power and why they generally failed.

B. Glossary

To build your social science vocabulary, familiarize yourself with the following terms.

1. **pool** In business, an agreement to divide a given market in order to avoid competition. "The earliest form of combination was the 'pool.'. . ." (p. 353)
2. **rebate** A return of a portion of the amount paid for goods or services. "Other rail barons granted secret rebates. . . . " (p. 353)
3. **free enterprise** An economic system that permits unrestricted entrepreneurial business activity; capitalism. "Dedicated to free enterprise. . . ." (p. 353)
4. **trust** A combination of corporations, usually in the same industry, in which stockholders trade their stock to a central board in exchange for trust certificates. "He perfected a device for controlling bothersome rivals—the 'trust.'" (p. 355)

5. **syndicate** An association of financiers organized to carry out projects requiring very large amounts of capital. "His prescribed remedy was to . . . ensure future harmony by placing officers of his own banking syndicate on their various boards of directors." (p. 355)

6. **patrician** Characterized by noble or high social standing. "An arrogant class of 'new rich' was now elbowing aside the patrician families. . . ." (p. 357)

7. **monopolistic** Concerning the control of an entire industry by a single corporation. "But the iron grip of monopolistic corporations was being threatened." (p. 358)

8. **Third World** The noncommunist and non-Western nations of the world, most of them formerly under colonial rule and still economically poor and dependent. "The net effect was to keep the South in a kind of 'Third World' servitude to the Northeast. . . ." (p. 358)

9. **lockout** The refusal by an employer to allow employees to work unless they agree to his or her terms. "Employers could lock the doors of a plant (the 'lockout'). . . ." (p. 360)

10. **yellow dog contract** A labor contract in which an employee must agree not to join a union as a condition of holding the job. "[Employers] could require them to sign 'yellow dog contracts.' . . ." (p. 360)

11. **cooperative** An organization for producing, marketing, or consuming goods in which the members share the benefits. ". . . they campaigned for . . . producers' cooperatives. . . ." (p. 361)

12. **anarchist** One who believes that formal, coercive government is wrong in principle. "Eight anarchists were rounded up. . . ." (p. 361)

13. **socialism** The ownership and control of the major means of production by the whole community rather than by individuals or corporations. "A bitter foe of socialism, he shunned politics for economic strategies and goals." (p. 362)

PART II: Checking Your Progress

A. True-False

Where the statement is true, mark **T**. Where it is false, mark **F**, and correct it in the space immediately below.

___ 1. Private railroad companies built the transcontinental rail lines without the assistance of the federal government.

___ 2. The expansion of the railroad industry was often accompanied by rapid mergers, bankruptcies, and reorganizations.

___ 3. The railroads contributed substantially to the growth of cities and to the surge of European immigration.

___ 4. Railroad owners were noted for the honesty of their dealings with shippers, the government, and the public.

___ 5. The weak early federal efforts at railroad regulation brought some order and stability to industrial competition.

___ 6. The Rockefeller oil company technique of "horizontal integration" involved combining all the phases of manufacturing, from the raw material to the customer, into a single organization.

___ 7. Rockefeller, Morgan, and others organized monopolistic trusts and "interlocking directorates" in order to eliminate cutthroat competition.

___ 8. Corporations effectively used the Fourteenth Amendment and sympathetic court rulings to prevent much effective government regulation of their activities.

___ 9. The proindustrial ideology of the "New South" enabled that region to make rapid economic gains by 1900.

___ 10. Two new inventions that brought large numbers of women into industry were the typewriter and the telephone.

___ 11. Industrialization generally gave the industrial wage earner greater status and control over his or her own life.

___ 12. In the late nineteenth century, the public generally sympathized with wage earners' attempts to organize unions in large industries.

___ 13. The Knights of Labor organized skilled and unskilled workers, blacks and whites, women and men.

___ 14. The Knights of Labor was severely damaged by the Haymarket Square episode, even though it had no connection with the bombing.

___ 15. The American Federation of Labor organized primarily skilled, white, male craft workers and ignored unskilled, female, and black workers.

B. Multiple Choice

Select the best answer and put the proper letter in the space provided.

___ 1. The federal government contributed to the building of the national rail network by

a. importing substantial numbers of Chinese immigrants to build the railroads.
b. providing free grants of federal land to the railroad companies.
c. building and operating the first transcontinental rail lines.
d. transporting the mail and other federal shipments over the rail lines.

___ 2. The most efficient and public-minded of the early railroad-building industrialists was

a. Collis P. Huntington.
b. Leland Stanford.
c. Cornelius Vanderbilt.
d. James J. Hill.

3. The railroad greatly stimulated American industrialization by

    a. opening up the West to settlement.
    b. creating a single national market for raw materials and consumer goods.
    c. eliminating the inefficient canal system.
    d. inspiring greater federal investment in technical research and development.

4. The railroad barons aroused considerable public opposition through such practices as

    a. forcing Indians off their traditional hunting grounds.
    b. refusing to pay their employees decent wages.
    c. refusing to build railroad lines in less settled areas.
    d. stock watering and bribery of public officials.

5. The first important federal effort at regulating industry was

    a. the Federal Communications Commission.
    b. the Pure Food and Drug Act.
    c. the Federal Commerce Commission.
    d. the Federal Trade Commission.

6. Financier J. P. Morgan attained much of his economic power by

    a. developing "horizontal integration" in the oil industry.
    b. lending money to the federal government.
    c. consolidating rival industries through "interlocking directorates."
    d. promoting American business in foreign countries.

7. The large trusts like Standard Oil and Swift and Armour felt their economic domination of industry was justifiable because

    a. government regulation guaranteed that they would serve the public interest.
    b. only large-scale methods of production and distribution could provide superior products at low prices.
    c. competition among many small firms violated the laws of economics.
    d. only large American industries could compete with British and German companies.

8. The attempt to create an industrialized "New South" in the late nineteenth century generally failed because

    a. the South was discriminated against and restricted to its role as supplier of raw materials to northern industry.
    b. southerners showed little interest in ending poverty and promoting economic development.
    c. continued political violence made the South an unattractive place for investment.
    d. there was little demand for southern products like cotton and sugar.

9. For American workers, industrialization generally led to

    a. a steady, long-term decline in wages and the standard of living.
    b. an opportunity to create small businesses that might eventually produce large profits.
    c. a long-term rise in the standard of living but a loss of independence and control of work.
    d. a stronger sense of identification with their jobs and employers.

___ 10. In contrast to the Knights of Labor, the American Federation of Labor advocated

  a. uniting both skilled and unskilled workers into a single large union.
  b. concentrating on improved wages and hours and avoiding general social reform.
  c. working for black and female labor interests as well as those of white men.
  d. using secrecy and violence against employers.

C. Identification

Supply the correct identification for each numbered description.

_____ 1. Federally owned acreage granted to the railroad companies in order to encourage the building of rail lines

_____ 2. The original transcontinental railroad, commissioned by Congress, which built its rail line west from Omaha

_____ 3. The California-based railroad company, headed by Leland Stanford, that employed Chinese laborers in building its lines across the mountains

_____ 4. The northernmost of the transcontinental railroad lines, organized by economically wise and public-spirited industrialist James J. Hill

_____ 5. Dishonest device by which railroad promoters artificially inflated the price of their stocks and bonds

_____ 6. Supreme Court case of 1886 that prevented states from regulating railroads or other forms of interstate commerce

_____ 7. Federal agency, originally intended to regulate railroads, that was often used by rail companies to stabilize the industry and prevent ruinous competition

_____ 8. Late-nineteenth-century invention that created a large new communication industry that relied heavily on female workers

_____ 9. First of the great industrial trusts, organized through a principle of "horizontal integration" that incorporated or destroyed competitors

_____ 10. The first billion-dollar American corporation, organized when J. P. Morgan bought out Andrew Carnegie

_____ 11. The idea, promoted by Henry Grady and other boosters, that the South should attempt to industrialize in order to compete economically with the North

_____ 12. The first major U.S. industrial labor organization, which collapsed during the depression of the 1870s

_____ 13. Secret, ritualistic labor organization that collapsed suddenly after the Haymarket Square bombing

_____ 14. Organizations of skilled laborers that were most successful in conducting strikes and raising wages

_____ 15. The conservative labor group that successfully organized a minority of American workers but left others out

D. Matching People, Places, and Events

Match the person, place, or event in the left column with the proper description in the right column by inserting the correct letter on the blank line.

___ 1. Leland Stanford

___ 2. Ogden, Utah

___ 3. James J. Hill

___ 4. Cornelius Vanderbilt

___ 5. Interstate Commerce Act

___ 6. Alexander Graham Bell

___ 7. Thomas Edison

___ 8. Andrew Carnegie

___ 9. John D. Rockefeller

___ 10. J. P. Morgan

___ 11. Henry Grady

___ 12. Terence V. Powderly

___ 13. Haymarket Square

___ 14. John P. Altgeld

___ 15. Samuel Gompers

A Inventive genius of industrialization who worked on devices such as the electric light, the phonograph, and the motion picture

B. The only businessperson in America wealthy enough to buy out Andrew Carnegie and organize the United States Steel Corporation

C. Illinois governor who pardoned the Haymarket anarchists

D. Southern newspaper editor who tirelessly promoted industrialization as the salvation of the economically backward South

E. Aggressive energy-industry monopolist who used tough means to build a trust based on "horizontal integration"

F. First federal effort to regulate railroads, used by the rail industry to its own advantage

G. Aggressive eastern railroad builder and consolidator who scorned the law as an obstacle to his enterprise

H. Site where the Union Pacific met the Central Pacific to unite the nation by rail

I. Scottish immigrant who organized a vast new industry on the principle of "vertical integration"

J. Former California governor and organizer of the Central Pacific Railroad

K. Organizer of a conservative craft-union group and advocate of "more" wages for skilled workers

L. Eloquent leader of a secretive labor organization that made substantial gains in the 1880s before it suddenly collapsed

M. Public-spirited railroad builder who assisted farmers in the region served by his rail lines

N. Site of a bombing, during a labor demonstration, that aroused public hysteria against strikes

O. Former teacher of the deaf whose invention created an entire new industry

E. Putting Things in Order

Put the following events in correct order by numbering them from 1 to 5.

____ J. P. Morgan buys out Andrew Carnegie to form the first billion-dollar U.S. corporation.

____ The first federal law regulating railroads is passed.

____ The killing of policemen during a labor demonstration results in the execution of radical anarchists and the decline of the Knights of Labor.

____ A teacher of the deaf invents a machine that greatly eases communication across distance.

____ A golden spike is driven, fulfilling the dream of linking the nation by rail.

PART III: Applying What You Have Learned

1. What was the impact of the transcontinental rail system on the American economy and society in the late nineteenth century?
2. How did the huge industrial trusts develop in industries such as steel and oil, and what was their effect on the economy?
3. How did the public react to the growth of the new industrial corporations, and to the abuses that frequently accompanied industrial expansion?
4. What was the effect of the new industrial revolution on American laborers, and how did various labor organizations attempt to respond to the new conditions?
5. How did the industrial transformation after the Civil War compare with the earlier phase of American economic development? (See Chapter 15.) Why were the economic developments of 1865–1900 often seen as a threat to American democracy, while those of 1815–1860 were not?

26

★★★★★★★★

America Moves to the City,

1865–1900

PART I: Reviewing the Chapter

A. Checklist of Learning Objectives

After mastering this chapter, you should be able to

1. describe the new industrial city and its impact on American society.
2. describe the New Immigration and explain why it aroused opposition from many native-born Americans.
3. discuss the efforts of social reformers and churches to aid the New Immigrants and alleviate urban problems.
4. analyze the changes in American religious life in the late nineteenth century.
5. explain the changes in American education from the elementary to the college level.
6. explain the growing national debates about morality in the late nineteenth century, particularly in relation to the changing roles of women and the family.
7. describe the literary, cultural, and recreational life of the period.

B. Glossary

To build your social science vocabulary, familiarize yourself with the following terms.

1. **megalopolis** An extensive, heavily populated area, containing several dense urban centers. "The . . . city gave way to the immense and impersonal megalopolis. . . ." (p. 366)
2. **tenement** A multidwelling building, often poor or overcrowded. ". . . the perfection in 1879 of the 'dumb-bell' tenement." (p. 366)
3. **affluence** An abundance of wealth. "These leafy 'bedroom communities' eventually ringed the brick-and-concrete cities with a greenbelt of affluence." (p. 367)
4. **sweatshop** A factory where employees are forced to work long hours under difficult conditions for meager wages. "The women of Hull House successfully lobbied in 1893 for an Illinois antisweatshop law that protected women workers. . . ." (p. 369)
5. **pauper** A poor person, often one who lives on tax-supported charity. "The first restrictive law . . . banged the gate in the faces of paupers. . . ." (p. 371)
6. **parochial** Concerning a parish or small district. ". . . brought vast new strength to the private Catholic parochial schools. . . ." (p. 372)

7. **Fundamentalist** A Protestant who rejects religious modernism and adheres to a literal interpretation of Christian doctrine and Scripture. "Conservative believers, or Fundamentalists, stood firmly on the Scripture. . . ." (p. 372)

8. **syndicated** In journalism, material that is sold by an organization for publication in several newspapers. "Bare-knuckle editorials were . . . being supplanted by feature articles and noncontroversial syndicated material." (p. 375)

9. **tycoon** A wealthy businessperson, especially one who openly displays power and position. "Two new journalistic tycoons emerged." (p. 376)

10. **taboo** A culturally prohibited object, practice, or verbal usage. "*A Modern Instance* dealt with the once-taboo subject of divorce." (p. 377)

PART II: Checking Your Progress

A. True-False

Where the statement is true, mark **T.** Where it is false, mark **F,** and correct it in the space immediately below.

_____ 1. Rapid and uncontrolled growth made late-nineteenth-century American cities both exciting and full of social problems.

_____ 2. After 1880, most immigrants to America came from northern and western Europe.

_____ 3. Most of the New Immigrants who arrived in America originally came from the slums of European cities.

_____ 4. Female social workers established settlement houses to aid the New Immigrants and promote social reform.

_____ 5. Many native-born Americans considered the New Immigrants a threat to American democracy and Anglo-Saxon purity.

_____ 6. Two religions that gained strength in the United States from the New Immigration were Roman Catholicism and Judaism.

_____ 7. The growth of Darwinian science contributed to the resurgence of religious belief in the late nineteenth century.

_____ 8. In the late nineteenth century, secondary (high school) education was increasingly carried on by private schools.

_____ 9. Booker T. Washington believed that blacks should try to achieve social equality with whites.

_____ 10. American higher education depended on both public "land-grant" funding and private donations for its financial support.

_____ 11. Urban newspapers often promoted "yellow journalism" that emphasized sensational events, scandals, and sexual affairs.

____ 12. Post–Civil War writers like Mark Twain and William Dean Howells turned from social realism toward romantic themes in their fiction.

____ 13. Late-nineteenth-century Americans generally agreed on matters of sexual morality and the social role of women.

____ 14. The new urban environment weakened the family but offered new opportunities for women to achieve social and economic independence.

____ 15. The late-nineteenth-century urban culture saw a movement from spectator sports and recreations to more active participation.

B. Multiple Choice

Select the best answer and put the proper letter in the space provided.

____ 1. Two technical developments of the late nineteenth century that contributed to the spectacular physical growth of American cities were

    a. the telegraph and the telephone.
    b. the compressor and the internal combustion engine.
    c. the electric trolley and the skyscraper.
    d. the oil furnace and the air conditioner.

____ 2. Countries from which many of the New Immigrants came included

    a. Sweden and Great Britain.
    b. Germany and Ireland.
    c. Poland and Italy.
    d. China and Japan.

____ 3. The primary factors that drove millions of European peasants from their homelands to America in the late nineteenth century were

    a. American food imports and religious persecution in their native lands.
    b. the Protestant Reformation and the rise of the papacy.
    c. the rise of Communist and Fascist regimes.
    d. major international and civil wars.

____ 4. Besides providing direct services to immigrants, the women of Hull House worked for other reforms like

    a. the secret ballot and direct election of senators.
    b. antisweatshop laws to protect woman and child laborers.
    c. social security and unemployment compensation.
    d. conservation and federal aid to farmers.

5. The one immigrant group that was totally banned from America after 1882 nativist restrictions was

   a. the Irish.
   b. the Greeks.
   c. the Africans.
   d. the Chinese.

6. Two religious groups that grew dramatically because of the New Immigration were

   a. Methodists and Baptists.
   b. Christian Scientists and the Salvation Army.
   c. Episcopalians and Unitarians.
   d. Jews and Roman Catholics.

7. Traditional American religion received a substantial blow from

   a. the psychological ideas of William James.
   b. the theological ideas of the Fundamentalists.
   c. the chemical theories of Charles Eliot.
   d. the biological ideas of Charles Darwin.

8. W. E. B. Du Bois advocated

   a. that blacks accept segregation in exchange for gaining the vote.
   b. complete integration and social equality for blacks.
   c. practical rather than theoretical education for blacks.
   d. that blacks remain in the South rather than move north.

9. Reformers like Henry George and Edward Bellamy were especially concerned with problems of

   a. poverty and economic injustice.
   b. immigration and race relations.
   c. agriculture and conservation.
   d. international relations and peace.

10. Authors like Mark Twain, Stephen Crane, and Jack London turned American literature toward a greater concern with

   a. close description and contemplation of nature.
   b. psychological investigations of the individual.
   c. fantasy and science fiction.
   d. social realism and contemporary problems.

C. Identification

Supply the correct identification for each numbered description.

_____ 1. High-rise urban buildings that provided barrackslike housing for urban slum dwellers

_____ 2. Term for the post-1880 newcomers who came to America primarily from southern and eastern Europe

_____ 3. Immigrants who came to America to earn money for a time and then returned to their native land

_____ 4. The religious doctrines preached by those who believed the churches should directly address economic and social problems

_____ 5. The settlement house in the Chicago slums that became a model for women's involvement in urban social reform

_____ 6. The profession established by Jane Addams and others that opened new opportunities for women in the modem city

_____ 7. Nativist organization that attacked New Immigrants and Roman Catholicism in the 1880s and 1890s

_____ 8. The church that became the largest American religious group, mainly as a result of the New Immigration

_____ 9. The new religious movement founded by Mary Baker Eddy in 1879

_____ 10. The organization founded by W. E. B. Du Bois and others to advance black social and economic equality

_____ 11. Henry George's best-selling book that advocated social reform through the imposition of a "single tax" on rising land values

_____ 12. A highly restrictive federal law that was used to prosecute moral and sexual dissidents

_____ 13. Charlotte Perkins Gilman's book urging women to enter the work force and advocating cooperative kitchens and child-care centers

_____ 14. Organization formed by Elizabeth Cady Stanton and others to promote the vote for women

_____ 15. Women's organization founded by reformer Frances Willard and others to oppose alcohol consumption

D. Matching People, Places, and Events

Match the person, place, or event in the left column with the proper description in the right column by inserting the correct letter on the blank line.

_____ 1. Louis Sullivan

_____ 2. Walter Rauschenbusch

A. Controversial author of *Progress and Poverty* who advocated solving problems of economic inequality by a tax on land

B. Midwestem-born writer and lecturer who created a new style of American literature based on social realism and humor

____ 3. Jane Addams

____ 4. Dwight L. Moody

____ 5. Mary Baker Eddy

____ 6. Booker T. Washington

____ 7. W. E. B. Du Bois

____ 8. William James

____ 9. Henry George

____ 10. Emily Dickinson

____ 11. Mark Twain

____ 12. Victoria Woodhull

____ 13. Anthony Comstock

____ 14. Charlotte Perkins Gilman

____ 15. Carrie Chapman Catt

C. Pragmatic women's suffrage leader who argued for the vote on the grounds of women's traditional duties rather than on the grounds of equality

D. Author and founder of a new religion based on principles of spiritual healing

E. Leading Protestant advocate of the "social gospel" who tried to make Christianity relevant to urban and industrial problems

F. Former slave who promoted industrial education but not social equality for blacks

G. Harvard scholar who made original contributions to modem psychology and philosophy

H. Radical feminist whose attacks on conventional morality shocked many Americans in the 1870s

I. Brilliant feminist writer who advocated cooperative cooking and child-care arrangements

J. Leading social reformer who pioneered new forms of activism for women

K. Crusader for sexual "purity" who used federal law to enforce his moral views

L. Harvard-educated advocate of full black social and economic equality through the leadership of a "talented tenth"

M. Chicago architect whose high-rise innovation allowed more people to crowd into limited urban space

N. Popular evangelical preacher who brought revivalism to the industrial city

O. Gifted New England poet, most of whose works were not published until after her death

E. Putting Things in Order

Put the following events in correct order by numbering them from 1 to 5.

____ Well-educated young midwesterner moves to the Chicago slums and creates a vital center of social reform and activism.

____ Introduction of a new form of high-rise slum housing drastically increases the overcrowding of the urban poor.

____ Nativist organization is formed to limit the New Immigration and attack Roman Catholicism.

____ The formation of a new national organization signals growing strength for the women's suffrage movement.

____ A western territory becomes the first American government to grant full voting rights to women.

PART III: Applying What You Have Learned

1. In what ways was the city a place of both opportunity and crisis in the late nineteenth century?
2. How did the New Immigration differ from the Old Immigration, and how did Americans respond to it?
3. How was American religion affected by the urban transformation, the New Immigration, and cultural and intellectual changes?
4. How and why did women assume a larger place in American society at this time? (Compare their status in this period with that of the pre-Civil War period described in Chapter 16.) How were changes in their condition related to changes in both the family and the larger social order?
5. How did the city alter American culture and recreational life? In what ways did the culture reflect urban problems, and in what ways did it try to escape them?

27
★★★★★★★★★

The Great West and the Agricultural Revolt,

1865–1900

PART I: Reviewing the Chapter

A. Checklist of Learning Objectives

After mastering this chapter, you should be able to

1. discuss the conquest of the Plains Indians, and what happened to the Indians after their military defeat.
2. describe the brief flowering and decline of the cattle and mining frontiers.
3. explain the impact of the closing of the frontier and the long-term significance of the frontier for American history.
4. describe the revolutionary changes in farming on the Great Plains.
5. explain why western farmers fell into economic bondage and describe their protest movement.
6. describe the issues in the key election of 1896, and explain why McKinley defeated Bryan.

B. Glossary

To build your social science vocabulary, familiarize yourself with the following terms.

1. **immunity** Freedom or exemption from some imposition. ". . . [the] militia massacred . . . 400 Indians who apparently thought they had been promised immunity." (p. 385)
2. **reservation** Public land designated for use by Native Americans. "The vanquished Native Americans were finally ghettoized in reservations. . . ." (p. 386)
3. **ward** Someone considered incompetent to manage his or her own affairs and therefore placed under the legal guardianship of another person or group. ". . . there [they had] to eke out an existence as wards of the government." (p. 386)
4. **probationary** Concerning a period of testing or trial, after which a decision is made based on performance. "The probationary period was later extended. . . ." (p. 389)
5. **folklore** The common traditions and stories of a people. "These bowlegged Knights of the Saddle . . . became an authentic part of American folklore." (p. 391)

6. **contiguous** Joined together by common borders. "Only Oklahoma, New Mexico, and Arizona remained to be formed into states from contiguous territory on the mainland of North America." (p. 392)

7. **safety valve** Anything, such as the American frontier, that allegedly serves as a necessary outlet for built-up pressure, energy, and so on. "But the safety-valve theory does have some validity." (p. 393)

8. **serfdom** The feudal condition of being permanently bound to land owned by someone else. ". . . a status suggesting Old World serfdom." (p. 395)

9. **prophet** A person believed to speak with divine power or special gifts. "Numerous . . . prophets sprang forward. . . ." (p. 396)

10. **injunction** A judicial order mandating or prohibiting a specific act, often but not necessarily in conjunction with litigation. ". . . who had defied a federal court injunction to cease striking. . . ." (p. 397)

PART II: Checking Your Progress

A. True-False

Where the statement is true, mark **T.** Where it is false, mark **F,** and correct it in the space immediately below.

___ 1. After the Civil War, the federal government attempted to concentrate all Native Americans in the Oklahoma Territory and the Dakota Territory.

___ 2. The Plains Indians were rather quickly and easily defeated by the U.S. Army.

___ 3. A crucial factor in defeating the Indians was the destruction of the buffalo.

___ 4. Humanitarian reformers respected the Native Americans' traditional culture and tried to preserve their tribal way of life.

___ 5. Individual gold and silver miners proved unable to compete with large mining corporations and trained engineers.

___ 6. Western cattlemen's prosperity depended on driving large beef herds great distances to railroad terminal points.

___ 7. More families acquired land under the Homestead Act than from the states and private owners.

___ 8. Much of the best land available under the Homestead Act was fraudulently obtained by speculators and unscrupulous corporations.

___ 9. One factor that made the West unique was the large role played by the federal government.

___ 10. Although very few city dwellers migrated west, the frontier "safety valve" did have some positive effects on eastern workers.

___ 11. The greatest problem facing the farmers was the rising cost of the machinery and supplies they had to buy.

___ 12. Republican leaders Mark Hanna and William McKinley believed that prosperity would "trickle down" to workers.

___ 13. Heavy contributions from silver-mining interests enabled Bryan to outspend McKinley in the election of 1896.

___ 14. McKinley's victory in 1896 marked the end of an era of Republican domination of American politics.

___ 15. The Republican victory in 1896 was a triumph for big business and urban middle-class values over farmers and agrarian values.

B. Multiple Choice

Select the best answer and put the proper letter in the space provided.

___ 1. Western Indians offered strong resistance to white expansion through their effective use of

    a. artillery and infantry tactics.
    b. techniques of siege warfare.
    c. nighttime and winter campaigning.
    d. repeating rifles and horses.

___ 2. Indian resistance was finally subdued because

    a. the Indians lost most of their effective leadership.
    b. the coming of the railroad led to the destruction of the buffalo and the Indians' way of life.
    c. most Indians lost the will to resist.
    d. the army developed effective techniques of guerrilla warfare.

___ 3. Both the mining and cattle frontiers saw

    a. an increase of ethnic and class conflict.
    b. sustained prosperity even during national depressions.
    c. a turn from large-scale investment to the individual entrepreneur.
    d. a movement from individual operations to large-scale corporate business.

___ 4. The growth of agriculture in the Great Plains and West was greatly aided by

    a. techniques of irrigation and "dry farming."
    b. the end of federal land grants to the railroads.
    c. the development of peaceable relations with the Native Americans.
    d. the use of tractors and combines.

___ 5. The "safety-valve" theory of the frontier is the idea that

    a. the most violent elements of the U.S. population migrated to the West.
    b. the conflict between farmers and ranchers was relieved by the Homestead Act.
    c. unemployed city dwellers moved west and thus relieved labor conflict in the East.
    d. political movements such as Populism provided release for the frustrations of western farmers.

6.By the 1880s, most western farmers faced hard times because

    a. there was no more free land available under the Homestead Act.
    b. they were unable to increase grain production to keep up with demand.
    c. they were being strangled by excessive federal regulation of agriculture.
    d. they were forced to sell their grain at low prices in a depressed world market.

____ 7. Farmers had great difficulty gaining relief from their grievances because

    a. they did not understand the real roots of their problems.
    b. they were too locked into support of the Republican party.
    c. they were highly individualistic and hard to organize.
    d. they were too small a minority of the population.

____ 8. The first organization to work on behalf of farmers was

    a. the Grange.
    b. the Populist party.
    c. the Greenback Labor party.
    d. the American Farm Bureau.

____ 9. One of the political goals of the Grangers was

    a. to gain control of the Republican party.
    b. to regulate railway rates and grain-storage fees through state laws.
    c. to develop federal loan programs for farmers.
    d. to push for deregulation and greater competition among the railroads.

____ 10. A leading Populist orator and organizer from Kansas was

    a. Ignatius Donnelly.
    b. James B. Weaver.
    c. Mary Elizabeth Lease.
    d. Oliver H. Kelley.

____ 11. Among the signs of deep unrest in the country in the 1890s were

    a. the Sherman Silver Purchase Act and the "billion-dollar Congress."
    b. Coxey's "Commonweal Army" and the Pullman strike.
    c. the Haymarket bombing and the rise of the American Federation of Labor.
    d. the campaign of 1892 and the passage of a federal income tax.

____ 12. The Pullman strike ended when

    a. the federal government sent troops to break the strike.
    b. the Illinois governor declared a state of martial law.
    c. railroad owners and workers agreed to a mediated settlement.
    d. the federal government assumed temporary ownership of the railroads.

___ 13. William Jennings Bryan gained the Democratic nomination of 1896 with his strong support of

    a. unlimited coinage of silver in order to inflate the currency.
    b. higher tariffs in order to protect the American farmer.
    c. government ownership of the railroads and the telegraph system.
    d. President Grover Cleveland's actions in the Pullman strike.

___ 14. McKinley defeated Bryan primarily because he was able to win the support of

    a. white southern farmers.
    b. eastern wage earners and city dwellers.
    c. urban and rural blacks.
    d. former Populists and Greenback Laborites.

___ 15. McKinley effectively carried out his campaign goals by enacting

    a. civil-service reform and controls on election spending.
    b. lower tariffs and a silver-backed dollar.
    c. higher tariffs and a gold-backed dollar.
    d. aid to labor and agricultural interests.

C. Identification

Supply the correct identification for each numbered description.

_____ 1. Major northern Plains tribe that fought and eventually lost a bitter war against the U.S. Army, 1876–1877

_____ 2. Southwestern tribe led by Geronimo that was finally conquered and forced to settle in Oklahoma

_____ 3. Generally poor areas where vanquished Native Americans were eventually confined under federal control

_____ 4. Indian protest movement, originating out of the sacred Ghost Dance, that the federal government attempted to stamp out in 1890

_____ 5. Federal law that attempted to dissolve tribal landholding and establish Native Americans as individual farmers

_____ 6. Federal law that offered generous land opportunities to poorer farmers

_____ 7. Former "Indian Territory" where "sooners" tried to get the jump on "boomers" in 1889

_____ 8. The theory that the availability of the frontier lessened social conflict in America by providing economic opportunities for eastern workers

_____ 9. Farmers' organization that began as a secret social group and expanded into politics

_____ 10. Short-lived profarmer third party that gained over a million votes and elected fourteen congressmen in 1878

_____ 11. A group of unemployed workers, led by an Ohio businessman, who marched on Washington during the depression of 1893

_____ 12. Bitter railway dispute of 1894 that ended when federal troops crushed the workers' protest

_____ 13. Tax set at a rate of 2 percent by the Wilson-Gorman Act of 1894 but overturned by the Supreme Court as unconstitutional

_____ 14. Popular Populist pamphlet of the 1890s that featured a brilliant prosilver advocate winning arguments against conservative bankers and economists

_____ 15. Bryan's eloquent prosilver speech to the 1896 Democratic convention that won him its nomination for president

D. Matching People, Places, and Events

Match the person, place, or event in the left column with the proper description in the right column by inserting the correct letter on the blank line.

___ 1. Sand Creek, Colorado

___ 2. Little Big Horn

___ 3. Sitting Bull

___ 4. Chief Joseph

___ 5. Geronimo

___ 6. Helen Hunt Jackson

___ 7. Battle of Wounded Knee

___ 8. James B. Weaver

___ 9. Mary E. Lease

___ 10. Ignatius Donnelly

___ 11. Jacob Coxey

___ 12. Eugene V. Debs

A. Leading Populist orator and congressman from Minnesota
B. Leader of the Nez Percé tribe who conducted a brilliant but unsuccessful military campaign in 1877
C. Populist author of a widely read pamphlet that denounced bankers and advocated free silver
D. Leader of the Pullman strike
E. Leader of the Sioux uprising, 1876–1877
F. Bloody affair that resulted when the federal government attempted to stamp out the Indians' sacred "Ghost Dance" in 1890
G. Leader of the Apaches of Arizona in their warfare with the whites
H. Site of Indian massacre by militia forces in 1864
I. Massachusetts writer whose books aroused white sympathy for the plight of the Native Americans
J. Site of serious but temporary U.S. Army defeat in the Sioux War of 1876–1877
K. Old Greenbacker who garnered a million votes as the Populist presidential candidate in 1892
L. Eloquent Kansas Populist who urged farmers to "raise less corn and more hell"
M. Ohio Republican businessman who engineered and lavishly funded McKinley's nomination and election in 1896
N. Ohio businessman who organized a march of unemployed workers on Washington during the depression of 1893

____ 13. William "Coin" Harvey **O.** Eloquent free-silver spokesman who waged a dramatic but unsuccessful campaign for the presidency

____ 14. Mark Hanna

____ 15. William Jennings Bryan

E. Putting Things in Order

Put the following events in correct order by numbering them from 1 to 7.

____ A federal law attempts to break tribal landholding patterns and make Native Americans live more like whites.

____ A federal law reverses the policy of the Dawes Act and permits Native Americans to retain their tribal organization and lands.

____ The violation of agreements with the Dakota Sioux leads to a major Indian war and a military disaster for the U.S. cavalry.

____ A federal law grants 160 acres of land to farmers at token prices, thus encouraging the rapid settlement of the Great West.

____ The U.S. Census Bureau declares that there is no longer a clear line of frontier settlement, ending a formative chapter of American history.

____ A Mark Hanna–run campaign based on the "full dinner pail" defeats the "Boy Orator of the Platte" and his cry of "free silver."

____ A deep depression sets off bitter labor strikes and prompts a march on Washington.

PART III: Applying What You Have Learned

1. How did whites finally overcome the resistance of the Plains Indians to western expansion? What were the consequences for both whites and Indians of these conflicts?
2. How did the successive phases of mining, cattle raising, and farming each contribute to the settlement of the Great West? In what way was the "farmers' frontier" different from other kinds of economic activity in the West?
3. What were the actual effects of the frontier on American society at different stages of its development? Is the Turner thesis of the frontier still helpful in understanding the historical evolution of American society?
4. Were the farmers and workers justified in their belief that the government was unfairly allied with big business against their interests? What evidence supports that view? Why, in 1896, did industrial workers vote for the probusiness McKinkey rather than Bryan?
5. Some historians have seen Bryan as the political heir of Jefferson and Jackson, and McKinley as the political descendant of Hamilton and the Whigs. Is this a valid comparison? Why or why not? (See Chapters 10, 12, and 13.)

28

★★★★★★★★★

The Path of Empire,

1890–1909

PART I: Reviewing the Chapter

A. Checklist of Learning Objectives

After mastering this chapter, you should be able to

1. explain why the United States suddenly abandoned its isolationism and turned outward at the end of the nineteenth century.
2. describe how America became involved with Cuba and explain why a reluctant President McKinley went to war with Spain.
3. explain McKinley's decision to keep the Philippines and the opposing arguments in the debate about imperialism.
4. analyze the long-term consequences of the Spanish-American War.
5. explain the growing U.S. involvement in Latin America and East Asia.
6. indicate the significance of the proimperialist Republican victory in 1900 and the rise of Theodore Roosevelt as a strong advocate of American power in international affairs.
7. describe the building of the Panama Canal and Roosevelt's "corollary" to the Monroe Doctrine.

B. Glossary

To build your social science vocabulary, familiarize yourself with the following terms.

1. **reconcentration** The policy of forcibly removing a population to confined areas in order to deny support to enemy forces. "He undertook to crush the rebellion by herding many civilians into barbed-wire reconcentration camps." (p. 408)
2. **atrocity** A specific act of extreme cruelty. "Where atrocity stories did not exist, they were invented." (p. 409)
3. **proviso** An article or clause in a statute, treaty, or contract establishing a particular stipulation or condition affecting the whole document. "This proviso proclaimed . . . that when America had overthrown Spanish misrule, she would give the Cubans their freedom. . . ." (p. 410)
4. **sphere of influence** The territory of weaker states where a powerful state exercises the dominant control. ". . . they began to tear away . . . economic spheres of influence from the Manchu government." (p. 416)

5. **blueblood** Person descended from nobility or aristocracy. "What manner of man was Theodore Roosevelt, the red-blooded blueblood?" (p. 419)
6. **bellicose** Disposed to fight or go to war. "Incurably boyish and bellicose, Roosevelt . . . [denounced] civilized softness. . . ." (p. 419)
7. **corollary** A secondary inference or deduction from a main proposition that is taken as established or proven. "He therefore devised a devious policy of 'preventive intervention,' better known as the Roosevelt corollary of the Monroe Doctrine." (p. 421)

PART II: Checking Your Progress

A. True-False

Where the statement is true, mark **T.** Where it is false, mark **F,** and correct it in the space immediately below.

____ 1. The once-isolationist United States became involved in a number of international disputes in the late 1880s and 1890s.

____ 2. Alfred T. Mahan argued in his book that the acquisition of colonies to provide raw materials and markets was the key to world history.

____ 3. President Cleveland refused to annex Hawaii because he believed that the white planters there had unjustly deposed Queen Liliuokalani.

____ 4. Americans strongly sympathized with the Cubans' revolt against imperialist Spain.

____ 5. The Hearst press worked to promote a peaceful, negotiated settlement involving Cuban self-government under Spanish rule.

____ 6. Admiral Dewey's squadron attacked Spanish forces in the Philippines because of secret orders given by Assistant Navy Secretary Theodore Roosevelt.

____ 7. American forces were aided in capturing Manila by native Filipinos who were rebelling against Spain.

____ 8. McKinley decided to keep the Philippines for religious, economic, and strategic reasons.

____ 9. The acquisition of the Philippines as a U.S. colony was almost unanimously approved by Americans.

____ 10. The Supreme Court decided in the insular cases that American constitutional law and rights applied fully in the U.S. colonial possessions of Puerto Rico and the Philippines.

____ 11. The Filipino insurrection against U.S. rule was larger and more costly in lives than the Spanish-American War.

____ 12. John Hay's Open Door notes called for an international force to suppress the Boxer Rebellion and guarantee stability in China.

___ 13. Roosevelt actively promoted the Panamanian revolution against Colombia in 1903.

___ 14. The Roosevelt corollary to the Monroe Doctrine stated that the United States alone had the right to intervene in Latin American nations' affairs.

___ 15. The San Francisco school crisis of 1906 eventually led to an agreement halting Japanese immigration to the United States.

B. Multiple Choice

Select the best answer and put the proper letter in the space provided.

___ 1. Alfred Thayer Mahan helped promote American interest in overseas expansion by

    a. developing a lurid "yellow press" that stimulated popular support for imperialism.
    b. arguing that sea power was the key to world domination.
    c. provoking naval incidents with Germany and Britain in the Pacific.
    d. arguing that the Monroe Doctrine implied American control of Latin America.

___ 2. The end result of the Venezuela-Guiana crisis with Britain was

    a. a series of battles between British and American naval forces.
    b. the intervention of the German kaiser in Latin America.
    c. American colonial control of Guiana.
    d. British retreat and growing American-British friendship.

___ 3. President Cleveland refused to annex Hawaii because

    a. white planters had illegally overthrown Queen Liliuokalani against the wishes of most native Hawaiians.
    b. there was no precedent for the United States to acquire territory except by purchase.
    c. the Germans and British threatened possible war.
    d. he knew the public disapproved and the Senate would not ratify a treaty of annexation.

___ 4. Americans first became concerned with the situation in Cuba because

    a. Spanish control of Cuba was a violation of the Monroe Doctrine.
    b. imperialists and business leaders were looking to acquire colonial territory for the United States.
    c. Americans sympathized with Cuban rebels in their fight for freedom from Spanish rule.
    d. the Battleship *Maine* exploded in Havana harbor.

___ 5. Even after the *Maine* exploded, the United States was slow to declare war on Cuba because

    a. the public was reluctant to get into a war.
    b. President McKinley was reluctant to get into a war.
    c. the Cubans were hostile to the idea of American intervention in their revolution.
    d. there was no clear evidence that the Spanish had really blown up the *Maine*.

___ 6. Emilio Aguinaldo was

    a. the leader of the Cuban insurgents against Spanish rule.
    b. the leader of the Filipino insurgents against Spanish rule.
    c. the commander of the Spanish navy in the Battle of Manila Bay.
    d. the publisher of a pro-Cuban newspaper in New York.

___ 7. The largest cause of American deaths in Cuba was

    a. the direct-charge tactics of Theodore Roosevelt's Rough Riders.
    b. the effective artillery bombardments of the Spanish navy.
    c. armed clashes with Cuban rebels and civilians.
    d. bad food, disease, and unsanitary conditions.

___ 8. Among prominent Americans who opposed annexation of the Philippines were

    a. Leonard Wood and Walter Reed.
    b. Theodore Roosevelt and Alfred Thayer Mahan.
    c. Mark Twain and William James.
    d. Mark Hanna and "Czar" Thomas Reed.

___ 9. Among the arguments used by the advocates of American imperialism in the Philippines were

    a. patriotism and economic opportunities.
    b. the Monroe Doctrine and national security.
    c. the Declaration of Independence and the wishes of the Philippine people.
    d. overpopulation and the need to acquire new land for American settlers.

___ 10. The Platt Amendment provided that

    a. the people of Puerto Rico would become citizens of the United States.
    b. the United States would eventually grant independence to the Philippines and Puerto Rico.
    c. no European power could establish new bases or colonies in the Pacific.
    d. the United States had the right to intervene in Cuba and maintain military bases there.

___ 11. The immediate consequence of American acquisition of the Philippines was

    a. the establishment of Manila as a crucial American defense post in East Asia.
    b. an agreement between Americans and Filipinos to move toward Philippine independence.
    c. a guerrilla war between the United States and Filipino rebels.
    d. an attempt by Japan to seize the Philippines from American control.

___ 12. In the Open Door notes, Secretary of State John Hay called on all the imperial powers to

    a. guarantee American control of the Philippines.
    b. reduce the arms race in China and the Pacific.
    c. respect Chinese rights and avoid the colonial division of China.
    d. grant the United States an equal share in the colonization of China.

___ 13. Roosevelt overcame the Colombian refusal to approve a canal treaty by

   a. increasing the amount of money the United States was willing to pay for a canal zone.
   b. encouraging Panamanian rebels to revolt and declare independence from Colombia.
   c. looking for another canal site elsewhere in Central America.
   d. seeking mediation of the dispute by other Latin American nations.

___ 14. The Roosevelt corollary to the Monroe Doctrine declared that

   a. no European powers could intervene in or colonize Latin America.
   b. the United States had a right to build, maintain, and defend the Panama Canal.
   c. the United States would take no more territory in Latin America except Puerto Rico.
   d. the United States had the right to intervene in Latin American countries to maintain financial and political order.

___ 15. The "Gentlemen's Agreement" between the United States and Japan provided that

   a. the Americans and Japanese would each guarantee the other's right in China.
   b. the San Francisco schools would be integrated and Japan would stop the flow of Japanese immigrants to America.
   c. Japan would recognize American control of the Philippines and the United States would accept Japan's control of Manchuria.
   d. Japanese would be able to work in the United States but not to stay permanently.

C. Identification

Supply the correct identification for each numbered description.

_____ 1. The principle of American foreign policy invoked by Secretary of State Olney to justify American intervention in the Venezuelan boundary dispute

_____ 2. Valuable naval base acquired by the United States from the Hawaiian government in 1887

_____ 3. Term for the sensationalistic and jingoistic journalism practiced by W. R. Hearst and Joseph Pulitzer

_____ 4. American battleship sent on a "friendly" visit to Cuba that ended in disaster and war

_____ 5. Amendment to the declaration of war with Spain that stated the United States would grant Cubans their freedom

_____ 6. Site of the dramatic American naval victory that led to the colonial acquisition of a group of rich Spanish-owned islands

_____ 7. Colorful volunteer regiment of the Spanish-American War led by a politically influential colonel

_____ 8. The important Caribbean island conquered from Spain in 1898 that became an American colony

_____ 9. Group that battled against American colonization of the Philippines

_____ 10. Supreme Court cases of 1901 that determined that the U.S. Constitution did not apply in all territories under the American flag

_____ 11. John Hay's clever diplomatic efforts to preserve Chinese territorial integrity and maintain American access to China

_____ 12. Antiforeign Chinese revolt of 1900 that brought military intervention by Western troops, including Americans

_____ 13. Proverbial symbol of Roosevelt's belief that presidents should engage in diplomacy but also maintain a strong military readiness to back up their policy

_____ 14. Agreement between the United States and the revolutionary government of Panama granting America the right to build a canal

_____ 15. Extension of the Monroe Doctrine that declared an American right to intervene in Latin American nations under certain circumstances

D. Matching People, Places, and Events

Match the person, place, or event in the left column with the proper description in the right column by inserting the correct letter on the blank line.

____ 1. Alfred Thayer Mahan

____ 2. Queen Liliuokalani

____ 3. Grover Cleveland

____ 4. "Butcher" Weyler

____ 5. William R. Hearst

____ 6. William McKinley

____ 7. George E. Dewey

____ 8. Leonard Wood

____ 9. William James

____ 10. Walter Reed

A. Assistant navy secretary, Rough Rider, presidential advocate of the "big stick"

B. Harvard philosopher and one of the leading anti-imperialists opposing U.S. acquisition of the Philippines

C. Spanish general whose brutal tactics against Cuban rebels outraged American public opinion

D. Native Hawaiian ruler overthrown in a revolution led by white planters and aided by U.S. troops

E. Commander in Spanish-American War, who later organized the efficient American military government of Cuba

F. American naval officer who wrote influential books emphasizing sea power and advocating a big navy

G. Naval commander whose spectacular May Day victory in 1898 opened the doors to U.S. imperialism in East Asia

H. Sensationalistic "yellow" journalist and active promoter of war with Spain

I. American doctor who led the medical effort to conquer yellow fever during the U.S. occupation of Cuba

J. Scheming French engineer who helped stage a revolution in Panama and then became the new country's "instant" foreign minister

____ 11. Emilio Aguinaldo

____ 12. John Hay

____ 13. William Jennings Bryan

____ 14. Theodore Roosevelt

____ 15. Philippe Bunau-Varilla

K. Secretary of state who promoted the Open Door policy with China

L. President who initially opposed war with Spain but eventually supported U.S. acquisition of the Philippines

M. Leading Democratic politician whose intervention narrowly tipped the Senate vote in favor of acquiring the Philippines in 1899

N. American president who refused to annex Hawaii on the grounds that the native ruler had been unjustly deposed

O. Leader of the Filipino insurgents who aided Americans in defeating Spain and taking Manila

E. Putting Things in Order

Put the following events in correct order by numbering them from 1 to 10.

____ American rebels in Hawaii seek annexation by the United States, but the American president turns them down.

____ A battleship explosion arouses fury in America and leads the nation into a "splendid little war" with Spain.

____ TR mediates a peace treaty between two combatants in the Far East.

____ A Chinese uprising against foreigners brings American troops to Beijing (Peking).

____ "That damn cowboy" becomes president of the United States after an assassination.

____ A school-spawned crisis leads to an end to Japanese immigration to America and a flurry of diplomacy to smooth relations between the United States and Japan.

____ Questionable actions by Roosevelt in Central America help create a new republic and pave the way for a U.S.-built canal.

____ A South American boundary dispute leads to an aggressive American assertion of the Monroe Doctrine against Britain.

____ Americans grant Cuba self-government but retain naval bases and the right to intervene.

____ The U.S. Senate narrowly approves a treaty giving the United States a major colony off the coast of Asia.

PART III: Applying What You Have Learned

1. What were the causes and signs of America's sudden turn toward international involvement at the end of the nineteenth century?

2. How did the United States get into the Spanish-American War over the initial objections of President McKinley?

3. What were the surprising results of the Spanish-American War, and how did various Americans react to them?
4. How did Theodore Roosevelt use both diplomacy and growing U.S. power to expand America's role in international affairs?
5. Was the burst of American overseas expansion and involvement from 1890 to 1909 a violation of America's basic democratic heritage, or a necessary step in the development of the United States as a great world power?

29

★★★★★★★★★

Progressivism and the Republican Roosevelt,

1901–1912

PART I: Reviewing the Chapter

A. Checklist of Learning Objectives

After mastering this chapter, you should be able to

1. discuss the origins and nature of the progressive movement.
2. describe how the early progressive movement developed its roots at the city and state level.
3. indicate how President Roosevelt began applying progressive principles to the national economy.
4. explain why Taft's policies offended progressives, including Roosevelt.
5. describe how Roosevelt led a progressive revolt against Taft that openly divided the Republican party.

B. Glossary

To build your social science vocabulary, familiarize yourself with the following terms.

1. **progressive** In politics, one who believes in continuing progress, improvement, or reform. "The new crusaders, who called themselves 'progressives,' waged war on many evils. . . . (p. 426)
2. **exposé** A disclosure or revelation considered embarrassing to those involved. ". . . Ida M. Tarbell . . . published a devastating but factual exposé of the Standard Oil Company." (p. 428)
3. **direct primary** In politics, the nomination of a party's candidates for office through a special election of that party's voters. ". . . ardent reformers pushed for direct primary elections. . . ." (p. 428)
4. **initiative** In politics, the procedure whereby voters can, through petition, present proposed legislation directly to the electorate. "They favored the 'initiative' so that voters could directly propose legislation. . . ." (p. 428)
5. **referendum** The submission of a law, proposed or already in effect, to a direct vote of the electorate. "Progressives also agitated for the 'referendum.' " (p. 428)
6. **recall** In politics, a procedure for removing an official from office through popular election or other means. "The recall would enable the voters to remove faithless elected officials. . . ." (p. 428)

7. **city manager** An administrator appointed by the city council or other elected body to manage affairs, supposedly in a nonpartisan or professional way. "Other communities adopted the city-manager system. . . ." (p. 429)

8. **slumlord** A landlord who owns and profits from slum properties, often by charging excessive rents or neglecting maintenance and repairs. "Urban reformers likewise attacked 'slumlords.' . . ." (p. 430)

9. **red-light district** A section of a city where prostitution is officially or unofficially tolerated. ". . . wide-open prostitution (vice-at-a-price) . . . flourished in red-light districts. . . ." (p. 430)

10. **franchise** In government or business, a special privilege or license granted to a company or group to perform a specific function. "Public-spirited city dwellers also moved to halt the corrupt sale of franchises for streetcars. . . ." (p. 430)

11. **reclamation** The process of bringing or restoring wasteland to productive use. "Settlers repaid the cost of reclamation. . . ." (p. 433)

12. **collectivism** A political or social system in which individuals are subordinated to mass organization and direction. "He strenuously sought the middle road between unbridled individualism and paternalistic collectivism." (p. 435)

PART II: Checking Your Progress

A. True-False

Where the statement is true, mark **T.** Where it is false, mark **F,** and correct it in the space immediately below.

____ 1. The progressive movement was basically hostile to federal government intervention in social and economic affairs.

____ 2. Muckraking journalists, social-gospel ministers, and women reformers all helped stir Americans' concern about economic and social problems.

____ 3. Progressive reformers gained their strongest support among immigrants and urban industrial workers.

____ 4. Progressivism first gained strength at the city and state levels before it became a national movement.

____ 5. President Theodore Roosevelt ended the anthracite coal strike by threatening to use federal troops to break the miners' union.

____ 6. Roosevelt promoted stronger federal legislation to regulate the railroads and other major industries.

____ 7. Roosevelt believed that all the monopolistic trusts should be broken up and competition restored.

____ 8. Upton Sinclair's *The Jungle* was originally intended to arouse consumers' concern about unsanitary practices in the meat industry.

____ 9. Roosevelt's conservation policies attempted to strike a balance between exploitation of natural resources and pure "preservation" of nature.

____ 10. Some of Roosevelt's greatest successes came in environmental and consumer protection.

____ 11. Roosevelt effectively used the power of the presidency to tame unrestricted capitalism while not really threatening basic business interests.

____ 12. Taft proved more successful than Roosevelt in maintaining Republican political unity.

____ 13. Progressives became angry with Taft because he did not follow Roosevelt's policy of "trust-busting."

____ 14. The Ballinger-Pinchot conservation controversy pushed Taft into alliance with the Republican "Old Guard" against the pro-Roosevelt progressives.

____ 15. President Taft used his control of the party machinery to deny Roosevelt the Republican nomination in 1912.

B. Multiple Choice

Select the best answer and put the proper letter in the space provided.

____ 1. The primary emphasis of the progressive movement was on

   a. freeing local governments from federal control.
   b. providing more freedom for individual farmers and businesspeople.
   c. strengthening government as an instrument of social improvement and reform.
   d. organizing industrial workers into a unified political party.

____ 2. Prominent among those who aroused the progressive movement by stirring the public's sense of social concern were

   a. socialists, social gospelers, women, and journalists.
   b. union leaders, politicians, immigrants, and nurses.
   c. bankers, college professors, engineers, and scientists.
   d. athletes, entertainers, filmmakers, and musicians.

____ 3. Most progressives were

   a. farmers.
   b. urban workers.
   c. urban middle-class people.
   d. businesspeople.

____ 4. Among political reforms sought by the progressives were

   a. political conventions, direct election of representatives to Congress, and an end to political parties.
   b. an Equal Rights Amendment, federal financing of elections, and restrictions on negative campaigning.
   c. civil-service reform, racial integration, and free silver.
   d. initiative and referendum, direct election of senators, and women's suffrage.

_____ 5. The states where progressivism first gained influence were

    a. Massachusetts, Maine, and New Hampshire.
    b. Wisconsin, Oregon, and California.
    c. Indiana, Texas, and Nevada.
    d. New York, Florida, and Louisiana.

_____ 6. Roosevelt ended the Pennsylvania coal strike by

    a. letting the strike take its course.
    b. passing federal legislation to legalize unions.
    c. forcing mediation by threatening to seize the coal mines and operate them with federal troops.
    d. declaring a national state of emergency and ordering the miners back to work.

_____ 7. Two areas where Roosevelt's progressivism made substantial headway were

    a. agricultural and mining legislation.
    b. stock-market and securities legislation.
    c. immigration and racial legislation.
    d. consumer and conservation legislation.

_____ 8. As president, William Howard Taft was expected to

    a. continue and extend Roosevelt's progressive policies.
    b. forge a coalition with William Jennings Bryan and the Democrats.
    c. swing the Republican party in a sharply radical direction.
    d. turn away from Roosevelt and toward the conservative wing of the Republican party.

_____ 9. Progressive Republicans grew disillusioned with Taft primarily over the issues of

    a. dollar diplomacy and military intervention in the Caribbean and Central America.
    b. labor union rights and women's concerns.
    c. trust-busting, tariffs, and conservation.
    d. regulation of the banking and railroad industries.

_____ 10. Roosevelt finally decided to break with the Republicans and form a third party because

    a. he had never really been committed to Republican principles.
    b. he could no longer stand to be in the same party with Taft.
    c. Taft used his control of the Republican convention to deny Roosevelt the nomination.
    d. Roosevelt believed that he would have a better chance of winning the presidency as a third-party candidate.

C. Identification

Supply the correct identification for each numbered description.

_____ 1. The largely middle-class movement that aimed to use the power of government to correct the economic and social problems of industrialism

_____ 2. Popular journalists who used publicity to expose corruption and attack abuses of power in business and government

_____   3. Progressive proposal to allow voters to bypass state legislatures and propose legislation themselves

_____   4. Progressive device that enabled voters to remove corrupt or ineffective officials from office

_____   5. Roosevelt's policy of having the federal government promote the public interest by dealing evenhandedly with both labor and business

_____   6. Effective railroad-regulation law of 1906 that greatly strengthened the Interstate Commerce Commission

_____   7. Powerful northwestern railroad monopoly broken up by Roosevelt's trust-busting

_____   8. Upton Sinclair's muckraking novel that inspired proconsumer federal laws regulating meat, food, and drugs

_____   9. Brief but sharp economic downturn of 1907, blamed by conservatives on the supposedly dangerous president

_____   10. Generally unsuccessful Taft foreign policy in which government attempted to encourage overseas business ventures

_____   11. Powerful corporation broken up by a Taft-initiated antitrust suit in 1911

_____   12. Roosevelt's doctrine that the national government should be strengthened in order to regulate business and correct economic and social abuses

D. Matching People, Places, and Events

Match the person, place, or event in the left column with the proper description in the right column by inserting the correct letter on the blank line.

____ 1. Jacob Riis

____ 2. Lincoln Steffens

____ 3. Ida Tarbell

____ 4. Seventeenth Amendment

____ 5. Robert La Follette

____ 6. Triangle Shirtwaist Company fire

A. Decent but politically inept Roosevelt successor who ended up as the ally of the reactionary Republican "Old Guard"

B. Leading advocate of "preservationist" approach to saving America's natural heritage

C. New York City disaster that underscored urban workers' need for government protection and regulation

D. The most influential of the state-level progressive governors and a presidential aspirant in 1912

E. Author of *How the Other Half Lives,* a shocking portrayal of the New York slums

F. Muckraker who attacked the Standard Oil Company's abuse of power

___ 7. Anthracite coal strike	**G.** Proconservation federal official whose dismissal by Taft angered Roosevelt progressives
___ 8. Meat Inspection Act of 1906	**H.** Dangerous labor conflict resolved by Rooseveltian negotiation and threats against businesspeople
___ 9. John Muir	**I.** Early muckraker who exposed the political corruption in American cities
___ 10. William Howard Taft	**J.** Progressive law aimed at curbing practices like those exposed in Upton Sinclair's *The Jungle*
___ 11. Payne-Aldrich Bill	**K.** Progressive measure that required U.S. senators to be elected directly by the people rather than by state legislatures
___ 12. Gifford Pinchot	**L.** High-tariff law of 1909 that revealed Taft's political ineptitude and outraged Republican progressives

E. Putting Things in Order

Put the following events in correct order by numbering them from 1 to 5.

___ A former president opposes his handpicked successor for the Republican presidential nomination.

___ Sensational journalistic accounts of corruption and abuse of power in politics and business spur the progressive movement.

___ A progressive forestry official feuds with Taft's secretary of the interior, deepening the division within the Republican party.

___ A novelistic account of Chicago's meat-packing industry sparks new federal laws to protect consumers.

___ A brief but sharp financial crisis leads to conservative criticism of Roosevelt's progressive policies.

PART III: Applying What You Have Learned

1. What caused the progressive movement, and how did it get under way?
2. What did the progressive movement accomplish at the local, state, and national levels?
3. How did Theodore Roosevelt effectively use the federal government as an instrument of moderate progressive reform?
4. How did the movements for environmental and consumer protection reflect the progressive outlook? What conflicting interests did they attempt to deal with?
5. Did progressivism actually improve the industrial, social, or political problems it identified? Or did it tend to focus on verbal or "moral" solutions that left the deeper conditions mostly unchanged?

30
★★★★★★★★

Wilsonian Progressivism
at Home and Abroad,

1912–1916

PART I: Reviewing the Chapter

A. Checklist of Learning Objectives

After mastering this chapter, you should be able to

1. discuss the important 1912 election and the basic principles of Wilsonian progressivism.
2. describe how Wilson successfully reformed the "triple wall of privilege."
3. state the basic features of Wilson's foreign policy and explain why he intervened in Latin America.
4. describe America's response to World War I and indicate the difficulties of remaining neutral.
5. explain how German submarine warfare threatened to draw America into war.
6. analyze Wilson's narrow electoral victory in 1916 in the context of domestic progressivism and World War I.

B. Glossary

To build your social science vocabulary, familiarize yourself with the following terms.

1. **entrepreneurship** The process whereby an individual initiates a business at some risk in order to expand it and thereby earn a profit. "Wilson's New Freedom . . . favored small enterprise [and] entrepreneurship. . . ." (p. 442)
2. **piety** Devotion to religious duty and practices. ". . . Wilson was reared in an atmosphere of fervent piety." (p. 443)
3. **graduated income tax** A tax on income in which the taxation rates are progressively higher for those with higher income. "Congress enacted a graduated income tax. . . ." (p. 443)
4. **levy** A forcible tax or other imposition. ". . . [the] income tax [began] with a modest levy on incomes over $3,000. . . ." (p. 443)
5. **inelasticity** The inability to expand or contract rapidly. "[The] most serious shortcoming [of the country's financial structure] was the inelasticity of the currency." (p. 443)

6. **commercial paper** Any business document having monetary or exchangeable value. "The . . . paper money [was] backed by commercial paper. . . ." (p. 444)

7. **promissory note** A written pledge to pay a certain person a specified sum of money at a certain time. "The . . . paper money [was] backed by commercial paper, such as the promissory notes of businesspeople." (p. 444)

8. **adulteration** Debasing a product or substance by substituting poorer quality components or ingredients. ". . . unfair trade practices . . . include[d] . . . mislabeling, adulteration, and bribery." (p. 444)

9. **gringo** Contemptuous Latin American term for North Americans. "Villa punished the 'gringos' by killing sixteen young American mining engineers." (p. 446)

10. **censor** An official who examines publications, mail, literature, and so forth in order to remove or prohibit the distribution of material deemed dangerous or offensive. "Their censors sheared away war stories harmful to the Allies. . . ." (p. 447)

11. **torpedo** To launch from a submarine or airplane a self-propelled underwater explosive designed to detonate on impact. ". . . the British passenger liner *Lusitania* was torpedoed and sank. . . ." (p. 447)

12. **draft** In politics, to choose an individual to run for office without that person's prior solicitation of the nomination. "Instead, they drafted Supreme Court Justice Charles Evans Hughes. . . ." (p. 448)

PART II: Checking Your Progress

A. True-False

Where the statement is true, mark **T.** Where it is false, mark **F,** and correct it in the space immediately below.

____ 1. Wilson won the election of 1912 largely because of the division within the Republican party.

____ 2. In the 1912 campaign, Wilson's New Freedom favored preserving large regulated trusts, while Roosevelt's New Nationalism favored breaking up big business by antitrust action.

____ 3. Wilson believed that the president should provide national leadership by appealing directly to the people over the heads of Congress.

____ 4. Wilson successfully used his popular appeal to push through progressive reforms of the tariff, monetary system, and trusts.

____ 5. Wilson's progressive outlook included taking small steps on behalf of civil rights for blacks.

____ 6. Wilson attempted to reverse the big-stick and dollar-diplomacy foreign policies of Roosevelt and Taft, especially in Latin America.

____ 7. Wilson consistently refused to intervene militarily in the Caribbean.

____ 8. In his policy toward the revolutionary Mexican government of Huerta, Wilson attempted to walk a middle line between recognition and intervention.

____ 9. The mediation of other Latin American nations saved Wilson from a full-scale war with Mexico.

____ 10. General Pershing's expedition was sent into Mexico to support the pro-American faction there.

___   11. In the early days of World War I, more Americans sympathized with Germany than with Britain.

___   12. The American economy benefited greatly from supplying goods to the Allies.

___   13. After the *Lusitania*'s sinking, the Midwest and West favored war with Germany, while the East generally favored attempts at negotiation.

___   14. After the sinking of the *Sussex*, Wilson successfully pressured Germany into refraining from submarine attacks against neutral shipping.

___   15. In the 1916 campaign, Wilson emphasized his peacemaking efforts, while his opponent Hughes tried to straddle the war issue.

B. Multiple Choice

Select the best answer and put the proper letter in the space provided.

___   1. The basic contrast between the two progressive candidates, Roosevelt and Wilson, was that

   a. Roosevelt wanted major political and social reforms, while Wilson wanted only to end obvious corruption.
   b. Roosevelt wanted to promote free enterprise and competition, while Wilson wanted the federal government to regulate the economy and promote social welfare.
   c. Roosevelt wanted the federal government to regulate the economy and promote social welfare, while Wilson wanted to restore free enterprise and competition.
   d. Roosevelt wanted to focus on issues of jobs and economic growth, while Wilson wanted more social legislation affecting women, children, and city dwellers.

___   2. Wilson won the election of 1912 primarily because

   a. his policies were more popular with the public.
   b. Taft and Roosevelt split the former Republican vote.
   c. the Socialists took too many votes from Roosevelt.
   d. Roosevelt was able to carry only the solid South.

___   3. Wilson's primary weakness as a politician was

   a. his lack of skill in public speaking.
   b. his inability to grasp the complexity of governmental issues.
   c. his tendency to be inflexible and refuse to compromise.
   d. his lack of overarching political ideals.

___   4. Wilson effectively reformed the banking and financial system by

   a. establishing a new Bank of the United States to issue and regulate the currency.
   b. taking the United States off the gold standard.
   c. establishing a publicly controlled Federal Reserve Board with regional banks under banker control.
   d. deregulating federal government control of money.

___ 5. Wilson's progressive measures substantially aided all of the following groups *except*

    a. workers.
    b. blacks.
    c. farmers.
    d. women and children.

___ 6. Wilson's initial policy toward the Mexican revolutionary government was

    a. refusal to recognize the legitimacy of General Huerta's regime.
    b. willingness to intervene with troops on behalf of threatened American business interests.
    c. strong support and economic assistance to the Huerta regime.
    d. to mobilize other Latin American governments to help oust Huerta.

___ 7. General Pershing's expedition into Mexico came as a particular response to

    a. the refusal of Huerta to abandon power.
    b. the threat of German intervention in Mexico.
    c. the arrest of American sailors in the Mexican port of Tampico.
    d. the killing of American citizens in New Mexico by "Pancho" Villa.

___ 8. Most Americans' sympathy for the Allies and hostility to Germany was strengthened by

    a. the unwillingness of the Germans to trade with neutral America.
    b. the Germans' involvement in overseas imperialism.
    c. the German invasion of neutral Belgium.
    d. the German threat to seize American economic interests in Europe.

___ 9. After the *Lusitania, Arabic,* and *Sussex* sinkings, Wilson successfully pressured the German government to

    a. end the use of the submarine against British warships.
    b. end its attempt to blockade the British Isles.
    c. publish warnings to all Americans considering traveling on unarmed ships.
    d. cease from sinking merchant and passenger ships without warning.

___ 10. One of Wilson's effective slogans in the campaign of 1916 was

    a. "The full dinner pail."
    b. "Free and unlimited coinage of silver in the ratio of sixteen to one."
    c. "A war to make the world safe for democracy."
    d. "He kept us out of war."

C. Identification

Supply the correct identification for each numbered description.

_____ 1. Four-footed symbol of Roosevelt's Progressive third party in 1912

_____ 2. Wilson's political philosophy of restoring democracy through trust-busting and economic competition

_____ 3. The low-tariff measure enacted after Wilson aroused favorable public opinion

_____ 4. A twelve-member agency appointed by the president to oversee the banking system under a new federal law of 1913

_____ 5. New federal regulatory commission designed to prevent monopoly and guard against unethical trade practices

_____ 6. Wilsonian law that tried to curb business monopoly while encouraging labor and agricultural organization

_____ 7. Wilsonian reform law that implemented the old Populist idea of government-backed low-interest loans to farmers

_____ 8. Two troubled Caribbean island nations where Wilson sent in American marines to take control in 1914–1916

_____ 9. Tenn for the three Latin American nations whose mediation may have prevented war between the United States and Mexico in 1914

_____ 10. World War I alliance headed by Germany and Austria-Hungary

_____ 11. The coalition of powers—led by Britain, France, and Russia—that opposed Germany and its allies in World War I

_____ 12. New underwater weapon that threatened neutral shipping and apparently violated traditional norms of international law

_____ 13. Large British passenger liner whose sinking in 1915 prompted some Americans to call for war against Germany

_____ 14. Germany's qualified agreement in 1916 not to sink passenger and merchant vessels without warning

_____ 15. Key electoral state whose tiny majority for Wilson tipped the balance against Hughes in 1916

D. Matching People, Places, and Events

Match the person, place, or event in the left column with the proper description in the right column by inserting the correct letter on the blank line.

____ 1. Thomas Woodrow Wilson

____ 2. Theodore Roosevelt

A. Small European nation attacked by Austria-Hungary, leading to the outbreak of World War I

B. Mexican revolutionary whose assaults on American citizens and territory provoked a U.S. expedition into Mexico

___ 3. Samuel Gompers	C. Port cities where clashes between Mexicans and American military forces nearly led to war in 1914
___ 4. Louis D. Brandeis	D. Caribbean islands purchased by the United States from Denmark in 1917
___ 5. Virgin Islands	E. Narrowly unsuccessful presidential candidate whose campaign was plagued by confusion on the issue of American policy toward Germany
___ 6. General Huerta	
___ 7. Venustiano Carranza	F. Small European nation whose neutrality was violated by Germany in the early days of World War I
___ 8. Tampico and Vera Cruz	G. Commander of the American military expedition into Mexico in 1916–1917
___ 9. "Pancho" Villa	H. Southern-born intellectual who pursued strong moral goals in politics and the presidency
___ 10. John J. Pershing	I. Leading progressive reformer and the first Jew named to the U.S. Supreme Court
___ 11. Belgium	J. Wilson's secretary of state, who resigned rather than risk war over the *Lusitania* affair
___ 12. Serbia	K. Energetic progressive and vigorous nationalist who waged a third-party campaign in 1912 but refused to do so again in 1916
___ 13. Kaiser Wilhelm II	L. Labor leader who hailed the Clayton Anti-Trust Act as the "Magna Carta of labor"
___ 14. William Jennings Bryan	M. Huerta's successor as Mexican president who strongly resisted American military intervention in Mexico
___ 15. Charles Evans Hughes	N. Autocratic German ruler who symbolized ruthlessness and arrogance to many pro-Allied Americans
	O. Mexican revolutionary whose bloody regime Wilson refused to recognize

E. Putting Things in Order

Put the following events in correct order by numbering them from 1 to 5.

___ Wilson extracts a German agreement to halt submarine warfare.

___ Wilson pushes major reforms of the tariff and monetary system through Congress.

___ The Progressive bull moose and the Republican elephant are both electorally defeated by a Democratic donkey bearing the banner "New Freedom."

___ The heavy loss of American lives to German submarines nearly leads the United States into war with Germany.

___ Wilson's occupation of a Mexican port raises the threat of war.

PART III: Applying What You Have Learned

1. What were the essential qualities of Wilson's presidential leadership, and how did he display them in 1913–1914?
2. What were the results of Wilson's great reform assault on the "triple wall of privilege"—the tariff, the banks, and the trusts?
3. Why did Wilson's attempts to promote a new foreign policy fail to prevent further American interventions in Latin America?
4. Was Wilson's policy toward the warring European powers really "neutral" in the period 1914–1917? What Wilsonian actions demonstrated a genuine desire to stay out of war? Why did they ultimately fail?
5. In what ways was Wilson's foreign policy an extension of the idealistic progressivism he pursued in domestic policy? How significantly did Wilson's foreign policy differ from that of the other great progressive president, Theodore Roosevelt? (See Chapter 28.)

31
★★★★★★★★

The War to End War,

1917–1918

PART I: Reviewing the Chapter

A. Checklist of Learning Objectives

After mastering this chapter, you should be able to

1. explain the American entry into World War I.
2. describe how Wilsonian idealism turned the war into an ideological crusade.
3. discuss the mobilization of America for war.
4. describe America's role in the war and relations with its Allies.
5. analyze Wilson's attempt to forge a peace based on his Fourteen Points and explain why developments at home and abroad forced him to compromise.
6. discuss the opposition of Lodge and others to Wilson's League and indicate how Wilson's refusal to compromise doomed the Treaty of Versailles.

B. Glossary

To build your social science vocabulary, familiarize yourself with the following terms.

1. **maelstrom** A violently turbulent and dangerous state of affairs. "... America could [not] pursue the profits of neutral trade without being sucked into the ghastly maelstrom." (p. 454)
2. **depredation** A destructive assault or plundering. "President Wilson had drawn a clear ... line against the depredations of the submarine." (p. 454)
3. **mobilization** The organization of a nation and its armed forces for war. "Creel typified American war mobilization. ..." (p. 456)
4. **pardon** The official release of a person from punishment for a crime. "... presidential pardons were rather freely granted. ..." (p. 457)
5. **Bolshevik** The radical majority faction of the Russian Socialist party that seized power in the October 1917 revolution; it later took the name *Communist.* "As the communistic Bolsheviks removed their beaten country from the war. ..." (p. 459)
6. **salient** A portion of a battle line that extends forward into enemy territory. "... nine American divisions ... joined four French divisions to push the Germans from the St. Mihiel salient. ..." (p. 460)

7. **parliamentary** Concerning political systems in which the government is constituted from the controlling party's members in the legislative assembly. "Unlike all the parliamentary statesmen at the table, [Wilson] did not command a legislative majority at home." (p. 462)

8. **trustee** A nation that holds the territory of a former colony as the conditional agent of an international body. "The victors received conquered territory only as trustees of the League of Nations." (p. 462)

9. **mandate** A specific commission from the League of Nations that authorized a trustee to administer a former colonial territory. "Japan was conceded the strategic Pacific islands under a League of Nations mandate. . . ." (p. 463)

10. **reservation** A portion of a deed, contract, or treaty that places conditions or restrictions on the general obligations. ". . . he came up with fourteen formal reservations. . . ." (p. 464)

PART II: Checking Your Progress

A. True-False

Where the statement is true, mark **T.** Where it is false, mark **F,** and correct it in the space immediately below.

____ 1. Germany responded to Wilson's call for "peace without victory" by proposing a temporary armistice.

____ 2. Wilson's promotion of the war as a crusade to end war and spread democracy inspired intense ideological enthusiasm among Americans.

____ 3. Among Wilson's Fourteen Points were freedom of the seas, national self-determination for minorities, and an international organization to secure peace.

____ 4. The Committee on Public Information relied on American patriotism more than formal laws and censorship to promote the war cause.

____ 5. The primary targets of prosecution under the Espionage and Sedition Acts were German agents in the United States.

____ 6. Even during the war mobilization, Americans were extremely reluctant to grant the federal government extensive powers over the economy.

____ 7. Herbert Hoover's methods of forcible mobilization and rationing enabled the United States to increase food production and supply the Allied war effort.

____ 8. The World War I conscription law enabled wealthier draft-age men to hire substitutes to serve in their place.

____ 9. Effective American fighting forces did not reach Europe until more than a year after America declared war.

____ 10. American weapons and equipment proved crucial to the Allied victory.

____ 11. Before he would negotiate an armistice, President Wilson insisted that the Germans overthrow Kaiser Wilhelm II.

Name _____ Section _____ Date _____

___ 12. Wilson's skillful handling of domestic politics strengthened his hand at the Paris Peace Conference.

___ 13. Allied leaders forced Wilson to make serious compromises in his Fourteen Points in order to keep the League of Nations in the Treaty of Versailles.

___ 14. Wilson's unwillingness to compromise on the League sent the whole treaty down to defeat.

___ 15. In the election of 1920, Republican Harding supported the League of Nations while Democrat Cox tried to evade the issue.

B. Multiple Choice

Select the best answer and put the proper letter in the space provided.

___ 1. The immediate cause of American entry into World War I was

   a. German support for a possible Mexican invasion of the southwestern United States.
   b. Germany's resumption of unrestricted submarine warfare.
   c. the German defeat of France.
   d. the desire of American munitions makers for larger profits.

___ 2. Wilson aroused the divided American people to fervent support of the war by

   a. seizing control of the media and demanding national unity.
   b. declaring the German people to be immoral Huns and barbarians.
   c. proclaiming an ideological war to end war and make the world safe for democracy.
   d. proclaiming the war a religious crusade against a new form of paganism.

___ 3. The capstone "Fourteenth Point" of Wilson's declaration of war aims called for

   a. the establishment of parliamentary democracies throughout Europe.
   b. guarantees of the human rights of minorities and political dissenters.
   c. an international organization to guarantee collective security.
   d. freedom of international travel without restrictions.

___ 4. Among the primary victims of the prowar propaganda campaign to enforce loyalty were

   a. German-Americans and socialists.
   b. Russian-Americans and communists.
   c. Mexican-Americans and immigrants.
   d. African-Americans and feminists.

___ 5. Among the legal changes the war helped bring about was

   a. a constitutional amendment granting women the right to vote.
   b. a law granting labor unions the right to strike.
   c. a constitutional amendment guaranteeing African-Americans the right to integrated schools.
   d. a constitutional amendment prohibiting child labor.

6. American economic mobilization for the war was characterized by

    a. a reliance on strict rationing and federal takeover of the economy.
    b. a reliance on grants and loans from Britain and France.
    c. a reliance on voluntary compliance and a patriotic citizen participation.
    d. a reliance on industry-organized agencies to finance the war and discipline labor.

7. American soldiers were especially needed in France in the spring of 1918 because

    a. the Allied invasion of Germany was faltering short of its goal.
    b. Britain had moved many of its soldiers from the western front to Russia.
    c. a renewed German invasion was threatening Paris.
    d. the Russians had just entered the war on the Germans' side.

8. Wilson blundered when choosing the American peace delegation by failing to

    a. have a set of clear diplomatic plans.
    b. include any Republicans in the delegation.
    c. consult with the key Allies, Britain and France.
    d. become personally involved in the peace process.

9. The European powers and Japan weakened Wilson at the peace conference by

    a. refusing to support his proposed League of Nations.
    b. dealing with his Republican critics behind his back.
    c. rejecting any continuing American involvement in European affairs.
    d. forcing him to compromise his principles on matters of self-determination and punishment of Germany.

10. Wilson bore some responsibility for the failure of the United States to join the League of Nations because

    a. he finally withdrew his own support for the League.
    b. he ordered Democratic senators to defeat the pro-League treaty with the Lodge reservations.
    c. he failed to take the case for the League to the American public.
    d. he demanded that America pay too high a percentage of the cost of the League.

C. Identification

Supply the correct identification for each numbered description.

1. Wilson's appeal to all the belligerents in January 1917, just before the Germans resumed submarine warfare

2. The German proposal to Mexico for an anti-American alliance

3. Wilson's idealistic statement of American war aims in January 1918

4. American government propaganda agency that aroused zeal for Wilson's ideals and whipped up hatred for the kaiser

_____ 5. Radical antiwar labor union whose members were prosecuted under the Espionage and Sedition Act

_____ 6. Federal agency designed to organize and coordinate U.S. industrial production for the war effort

_____ 7. Constitutional revision, endorsed by Wilson as a war measure, whose ratification achieved a long-sought goal for American women

_____ 8. Treasury Department bond-selling drives that raised about $21 billion to finance the American war effort

_____ 9. Collective term for the nations that dominated the Paris Peace Conference—namely, Britain, France, Italy, and the United States

_____ 10. The proposed international body that, to Wilson, constituted the key provision of the Versailles Treaty

_____ 11. Controversial peace agreement that compromised many of Wilson's Fourteen Points but retained his League

_____ 12. Senatorial committee whose chairman vigorously opposed Wilson's treaty and League of Nations

_____ 13. A hard core of isolationist senators who bitterly opposed any sort of league; also called the "Battalion of Death"

_____ 14. Amendments to the proposed Treaty of Versailles, sponsored by Wilson's hated senatorial opponent, that attempted to guarantee America's sovereign rights in relation to the League of Nations

_____ 15. Wilson's view of what the presidential election of 1920 would be, if it were presented as a direct popular vote on the League

D. Matching People, Places, and Events

Match the person, place, or event in the left column with the proper description in the right column by inserting the correct letter on the blank line.

___ 1. George Creel

___ 2. Eugene V. Debs

___ 3. Bernard Baruch

___ 4. Herbert Hoover

A. Inspirational leader of the Western world in wartime who later stumbled as a peacemaker

B. Senatorial leader of the isolationist "irreconcilables," who absolutely opposed all American involvement in the League of Nations

C. Climactic battle of World War I

D. The "tiger" of France, whose drive for security forced Wilson to compromise at Versailles

___ 5. John J. Pershing

___ 6. Chateau-Thierry

___ 7. Meuse-Argonne

___ 8. Kaiser Wilhelm II

___ 9. Woodrow Wilson

___ 10. Henry Cabot Lodge

___ 11. Georges Clemenceau

___ 12. William Borah

___ 13. Saar Basin

___ 14. Pueblo, Colorado

___ 15. Warren G. Harding

E. Head of the American propaganda agency that mobilized public opinion for World War I

F. Folksy Ohio senator whose 1920 presidential victory ended the last hopes for U.S. participation in the League of Nations

G. Hated leader of America's enemy in World War I

H. Food Administration head who pioneered successful voluntary mobilization methods

I. Crucial battle of May 1918 in which American troops defended Paris in their first European engagement

J. Coal-rich valley that became the object of French-American dispute at the Paris Peace Conference

K. Commander of the American expeditionary force in France

L. Site of Wilson's collapse during his last-ditch trip to win public support for his League of Nations

M. Wilson's great senatorial antagonist, who succeeded in his goal of keeping America out of the League of Nations

N. Head of the War Industries Board, which attempted to impose some order on U.S. war production

O. Socialist leader who won nearly a million votes as a presidential candidate while in federal prison for antiwar activities

E. Putting Things in Order

Put the following events in correct order by numbering them from 1 to 5.

___ Germany's resumption of submarine warfare forces the United States into a declaration of war.

___ The Senate's final defeat of the Versailles Treaty and a Republican election victory end Wilson's last hopes for American entry into the League of Nations.

___ The United States takes the first hesitant steps toward preparedness in the event of war.

___ The effectiveness of American combat troops in crucial battles helps bring about an Allied victory in World War I.

___ Wilson struggles with other Allied leaders in Paris to hammer out a peace treaty and organize the postwar world.

PART III: Applying What You Have Learned

1. What caused American entry into World War I, and how did Wilson turn the war into an ideological crusade?
2. How did America demonstrate its traditional preference for voluntary methods in its war mobilization?
3. Were European leaders justified in their view that America's role in the peace conference was larger than its actual war effort? Why or why not?
4. How was Wilson forced to compromise during the peace negotiations, and why did America in the end refuse to ratify the treaty and join the League of Nations?
5. Given America's long history of isolation from European affairs, was the defeat of the treaty and U.S. refusal to join the League of Nations inevitable? Why or why not?

32
★★★★★★★★★

American Life in the "Roaring Twenties,"
1919–1929

PART I: Reviewing the Chapter

A. Checklist of Learning Objectives

After mastering this chapter, you should be able to

1. analyze the movement toward social conservatism following World War I.
2. describe the cultural conflicts over such issues as prohibition and evolution.
3. discuss the rise of the mass-consumption economy, led by the automobile industry.
4. describe the changes in American society brought about by radio, films, and new attitudes toward sexuality.
5. describe and explain the new cultural forces reflected in literature of the Jazz Age and the Harlem Renaissance.

B. Glossary

To build your social science vocabulary, familiarize yourself with the following terms.

1. **syndicalism** A theory or movement that advocates bringing all economic and political power into the hands of labor unions by means of strikes. ". . . a number of legislatures . . . passed criminal syndicalism laws." (p. 469)
2. **Bible Belt** The region of the American South, extending roughly from the Carolinas west to Oklahoma and Texas, where Protestant Fundamentalism and belief in literal interpretation of the Bible have been strongest. ". . . the Klan spread with astonishing rapidity, especially in . . . the 'Bible Belt' South." (p. 469)
3. **provincial** Narrow and limited; isolated from cosmopolitan influences. "Isolationist America of the 1920s, ingrown and provincial, had little use for . . . immigrants. . . ." (p. 470)
4. **racketeer** A person who obtains money illegally by fraud, bootlegging, gambling, or threats of violence. "Racketeers even invaded the ranks of local labor unions. . . ." (p. 471)
5. **underworld** Those who live outside society's laws, by vice or crime. ". . . the annual 'take' of the underworld was estimated to be from $12 billion to $18 billion. . . ." (pp. 471, 473)

6. **credit** In business, the arrangement of purchasing goods or services immediately but making the payment at a later date. "Buying on credit was another innovative feature of the postwar economy." (p. 475)

7. **repression** In psychology, the forcing of instincts or ideas painful to the conscious mind into the unconscious, where they continue to exercise influence. "[Freud] appeared to argue that sexual repression was responsible for a variety of nervous and emotional ills." (p. 477)

8. **impresario** The organizer or manager of a music or dance enterprise. "Caucasian impresarios cornered the profits. . . ." (p. 477)

9. **functionalism** The theory that a plan or design should be derived from practical purpose. "Architecture also married itself to the new materialism and functionalism." (p. 480)

10. **bull market** In stock trading, a market with rising prices. (A market with declining prices is a **bear market**.) ". . . an orgy of . . . trading pushed the bull market up to dizzy peaks." (p. 480)

11. **surtax** A special tax, usually involving a raised rate on an already existing tax. ". . . Congress . . . abolish[ed] the surtax, the income tax, and estate taxes." (p. 480)

PART II: Checking Your Progress

A. True-False

Where the statement is true, mark **T**. Where it is false, mark **F**, and correct it in the space immediately below.

____ 1. The "red scare" of 1919–1920 was focused on American attempts to suppress the new communist government in Russia.

____ 2. The Sacco-Vanzetti case aroused liberal and radical protest because of alleged prejudice by the judge and jury against the atheistic immigrant defendants.

____ 3. The Ku Klux Klan of the 1920s was strongest in the East and the West.

____ 4. The Immigration Act of 1924 reflected "nativist" prejudice against the New Immigration from southern and eastern Europe.

____ 5. The Eighteenth Amendment and the Volstead Act proved almost impossible to enforce.

____ 6. The Scopes trial verdict acquitted biology teacher Scopes and overturned the Tennessee law prohibiting the teaching of evolution in the schools.

____ 7. The 1920s saw a shift from heavy industrial production toward a mass-consumption economy.

____ 8. Henry Ford's great economic achievement was the production of a cheap, reliable, mass-produced automobile.

____ 9. The automobile strengthened such related areas of industrial production as the rubber, glass, and oil industries.

____ 10. The radio and film industries emphasized noncommercial and public-information uses of the mass media.

___ 11. The 1920s saw attempts to restore stricter standards of sexual behavior, especially for women.

___ 12. Jazz was initially pioneered by blacks but was eventually taken up and promoted by whites.

___ 13. The most prominent writers of the 1920s upheld the moral virtues of small-town American life against the critical attitudes and moral questioning of the big cities.

___ 14. The real estate and stock-market booms of the 1920s included large elements of speculation and excessive credit risk.

___ 15. Secretary of the Treasury Andrew Mellon made efforts to relieve the federal tax burden on the middle class.

B. Multiple Choice

Select the best answer and put the proper letter in the space provided.

___ 1. The "red scare" of the early 1920s was initially set off by

a. the Sacco-Vanzetti case.
b. the rise of the radical Industrial Workers of the World.
c. the Bolshevik revolution in Russia.
d. an influx of radical immigrants.

___ 2. The quota system established for immigration in the 1920s was based partly on the idea that

a. America could not accept all the refugees created by war and revolution in Europe.
b. immigrants from northern and western Europe were superior to those from southern and eastern Europe.
c. immigration from Europe should be largely replaced by immigration from Asia.
d. priority in immigration should be based on family relations, profession, and education.

___ 3. One result of prohibition was

a. a rise in criminal organizations that supplied illegal liquor.
b. an improvement in family relations and the general moral tone of society.
c. a turn from alcohol to other forms of substance abuse.
d. the rise of voluntary self-help organizations like Alcoholics Anonymous.

___ 4. The essential issue in the Scopes trial was whether

a. scientists ought to be allowed to investigate the biological origins of humanity.
b. the teachings of Darwin could be reconciled with those of religion.
c. Darwinian evolutionary science could be taught in the public schools.
d. Fundamentalist Protestantism could be taught in the public schools.

___ 5. The most highly acclaimed industrial innovator of the new mass-production economy was

    a. Babe Ruth.
    b. Charles Lindbergh.
    c. Ransom E. Olds.
    d. Henry Ford.

___ 6. One of the primary social effects of the new automobile age was

    a. a weakening of traditional family ties between parents and youth.
    b. a strengthening of intergenerational ties among parents, children, and grandchildren.
    c. a tightening of restrictions on women.
    d. a closing of the gap between the working class and the wealthy.

___ 7. Radio and the movies both had the cultural effect of

    a. increasing Americans' interest in history and literature.
    b. increasing mass standardization and weakening traditional forms of culture.
    c. undermining the tendency of industry toward big business and mass production.
    d. making Americans more aware of ethnic and racial diversity.

___ 8. In the 1920s, the major changes pursued by American women were

    a. voting rights and political equality.
    b. economic equality and equal pay for equal work.
    c. social reform and family welfare.
    d. personal freedom and expanded sexual freedom.

___ 9. In the 1920s, a prominent advocate of African-American self-reliance and migration to Africa was

    a. W. E. B. Du Bois.
    b. Marcus Garvey.
    c. Claude McKay.
    d. Louis Armstrong.

___ 10. Many of the noted new writers of the 1920s were

    a. fascinated by their own historical roots in New England.
    b. disgusted with European influences on American culture.
    c. interested especially in nature and social reform.
    d. highly critical of traditional American "puritanism" and small-town life.

C. Identification

Supply the correct identification for each numbered description.

_____ 1. The movement of 1919–1920, spawned by fear of the Bolshevik revolution, that resulted in the arrest and deportation of many political radicals

_____ 2. Hooded defenders of Anglo-Saxon and "Protestant" values against immigrants, Catholics, and Jews

_____ 3. Restrictive legislation that reduced the number of newcomers to the United States and discriminated against immigrants from southern and eastern Europe

_____ 4. New constitutional provision, popular in the Midwest and South, that encouraged lawbreaking and gangsterism in big cities of the East and North

_____ 5. Term for area of the South where traditional evangelical and Fundamentalist religion remained strong

_____ 6. Legal battle over teaching evolution that pitted modem science against Fundamentalist religion

_____ 7. New industry spawned by the mass-consumption economy that promoted still more consumption

_____ 8. Henry Ford's cheap, mass-produced automobile

_____ 9. Means of transportation invented in 1903 and first used primarily for stunts and mail carrying

_____ 10. One of the few new consumer products of the 1920s that encouraged people to stay at home

_____ 11. Marcus Garvey's organization that supported resettlement of blacks in Africa

_____ 12. The cause, promoted by feminist Margaret Sanger, that contributed to changing sexual standards, especially for women

_____ 13. The syncopated style of music, originally created by blacks, that attained national popularity in the 1920s

_____ 14. H. L. Mencken's monthly magazine, which led the literary attack on traditional moral values, the middle class, and "Puritanism"

_____ 15. The New York financial institution where rising prices and profits were fueled by speculation in the 1920s

D. Matching People, Places, and Events

Match the person, place, or event in the left column with the proper description in the right column by inserting the correct letter on the blank line.

____ 1. A. Mitchell Palmer

____ 2. Nicola Sacco and Bartolomeo Vanzetti

A. Site of the new motion picture industry and home of its "stars"

B. Writer whose novels reflected the disillusionment of many Americans with propaganda and patriotic idealism

___	3. Eugene O'Neill	**C.** Italian-American anarchists whose trial and execution aroused widespread protest
___	4. John Dewey	**D.** Mechanical genius and manufacturer of mass-produced automobiles
		E. Federal official who rounded up thousands of alleged Bolsheviks in the red scare of 1919–1920
___	5. William Jennings Bryan	**F.** Baltimore writer who criticized the supposedly narrow and hypocritical values of American society
___	6. Henry Ford	**G.** Leading American playwright of the 1920s
___	7. Bruce Barton	**H.** Former presidential candidate who led the fight against evolution at the 1925 Scopes trial
___	8. Langston Hughes	**I.** Federal official who attempted to promote business investment by reducing taxes on the rich
___	9. Charles A. Lindbergh	**J.** Founder of the advertising industry and author of a new interpretation of Christ in *The Man Nobody Knows*
___	10. Hollywood	**K.** Viennese psychoanalyst whose writings and therapies were interpreted by Americans as a call for sexual liberation and gratification
___	11. Sigmund Freud	**L.** Leading American philosopher and proponent of "progressive education"
___	12. H. L. Mencken	**M.** Humble aviation pioneer who became a cultural hero of the 1920s
___	13. F. Scott Fitzgerald	**N.** Minnesota-born writer whose daring novels were especially popular with young people in the 1920s
___	14. Ernest Hemingway	**O.** One of the prominent black writers of the Harlem Renaissance
___	15. Andrew Mellon	

E. Putting Things in Order

Put the following events in correct order by numbering them from 1 to 5.

___ The trial of a Tennessee high school biology teacher symbolizes a national conflict over values of religion and science.

___ Fear of the Bolshevik revolution sparks a crusade against radicals and communists in America.

___ A modest young man becomes a national hero by accomplishing a bold feat of aviation.

___ Two Italian immigrants are convicted of murder and robbery, provoking charges that the judge and jury were prejudiced.

___ A new immigration law tightens up earlier emergency restrictions and imposes discriminatory quotas against the New Immigrants.

PART III: Applying What You Have Learned

1. How and why did America turn toward domestic isolation and social conservatism in the 1920s?
2. How did some of the events of the 1920s reflect national conflicts over social, moral, and religious values?
3. How did the automobile and other new products create a mass-consumption economy in the 1920s?
4. Explain the large transformations that altered American music, movies, and literature in the 1920s. Why were the arts and culture so radically creative during a time of social and political conservatism?
5. In what ways were the 1920s a social and cultural reaction against the progressive idealism that held sway before and during World War I? (See Chapters 29, 30, and 31.)

33

★★★★★★★★

The Politics of Boom and Bust,

1920–1932

PART I: Reviewing the Chapter

A. Checklist of Learning Objectives

After mastering this chapter, you should be able to

1. analyze the political conservatism and economic prosperity of the 1920s.
2. explain the Republican administration's policies of isolationism, disarmament, and high-tariff protectionism.
3. describe the easygoing corruption of the Harding administration and the strait-laced uprightness of his successor Coolidge.
4. describe the international economic tangle of loans, war debts, and reparations and indicate how the United States attempted to solve it.
5. discuss how Hoover went from being a symbol of 1920s business success to a symbol of depression failure.
6. explain the roots of the Great Depression in the economy of the 1920s.
7. describe Hoover's responses to the Great Depression.

B. Glossary

To build your social science vocabulary, familiarize yourself with the following terms.

1. **dreadnought** A heavily armored battleship with large batteries of twelve-inch guns. ". . . Secretary Hughes startled the delegates with a comprehensive, concrete plan for . . . scrapping some of the huge dreadnoughts. . . ." (p. 485)
2. **accomplice** An associate or partner of a criminal who shares some degree of guilt. ". . . he and his accomplices looted the government to the tune of about $200 million. . . ." (p. 486)
3. **reparations** Compensation by a defeated nation for damage done to civilians and their property during a war. "Overshadowing all other foreign-policy problems . . . was . . . a complicated tangle of private loans, Allied war debts, and German reparations payments." (p. 486)
4. **pump-priming** Referring, in economics, to the spending or lending of a small amount of funds in order to stimulate a larger flow of economic activity. " 'Pump-priming' loans by the RFC were no doubt of widespread benefit. . . ." (p. 493)

PART II: Checking Your Progress

A. True-False

Where the statement is true, mark **T**. Where it is false, mark **F**, and correct it in the space immediately below.

___ 1. The corruption of the Harding administration involved U.S. officials taking bribes from foreign governments.

___ 2. The Republican administrations of the 1920s strictly enforced antitrust laws to maintain strong business competition.

___ 3. The Republican administrations of the 1920s guaranteed America's national security by maintaining U.S. forces in Europe.

___ 4. The high-tariff policies of the 1920s enhanced American prosperity but hindered Europe's economic recovery from World War I.

___ 5. Calvin Coolidge's image of honesty and thrift helped restore public confidence in the government after the Harding administration scandals.

___ 6. Farmers looked unsuccessfully to the federal government to help relieve their severe economic troubles in the 1920s.

___ 7. The main sources of support for liberal third-party presidential candidate Robert La Follette in 1924 were urban workers and reformers.

___ 8. The main exception to America's isolationist foreign policy in the 1920s was continuing U.S. armed intervention in Latin America.

___ 9. Britain and France were unable to repay their war debts to the United States until the Dawes Plan provided American loans to Germany.

___ 10. Democratic nominee Al Smith's urban, Catholic, and "wet" background cost him support in 1928 from traditionally Democratic southern voters.

___ 11. The Hawley-Smoot Tariff strengthened the trend toward expanded international trade and economic cooperation.

___ 12. The American economic collapse set off by the Great Depression was the most severe suffered by any major industrial nation in the 1930s.

___ 13. The depression was caused partly by overexpansion of credit and excessive consumer debt in the 1920s.

___ 14. Hoover consistently followed his belief that the federal government should play no role in providing economic relief and assisting the recovery from the depression.

____ 15. The Reconstruction Finance Corporation provided federal loans to business and governmental institutions but no aid to individuals.

B. Multiple Choice

Select the best answer and put the proper letter in the space provided.

____ 1. As president, Warren G. Harding proved to be

   a. thoughtful and ambitious but rather impractical.
   b. an able administrator and diplomat but a poor politician.
   c. politically competent and concerned for the welfare of ordinary people.
   d. weak-willed and tolerant of corruption among his friends.

____ 2. The general approach of the federal government toward industry in the early 1920s was

   a. a weakening of federal regulation and a lack of concern with social reform.
   b. an emphasis on federal regulation rather than state and local controls.
   c. an emphasis on vigorous antitrust enforcement rather than on regulation.
   d. a turn toward direct federal control of key industries like the railroads.

____ 3. The proposed ratio of "5-5-3" in the Washington Disarmament Conference of 1921–1922 referred to

   a. the allowable ratio of American, British, and Japanese troops in China.
   b. the number of votes Britain, France, and the United States would have in the League of Nations.
   c. the allowable ratio of battleships and carriers among the United States, Britain, and Japan.
   d. the number of nations that would sign each of the major treaties to emerge from the conference.

____ 4. The very high U.S. tariff rates of the 1920s had the economic effect of

   a. stimulating the formation of common markets among the major industrial nations.
   b. causing severe deflation in the United States and Europe.
   c. turning American trade away from Europe and toward Asia.
   d. causing the Europeans to erect their own tariff barriers and thus reduce international trade.

____ 5. The central scandal of Teapot Dome involved members of Harding's cabinet who

   a. sold spoiled foodstuffs to the army and navy.
   b. took bribes for leasing federal oil lands.
   c. undermined prohibition by tolerating gangster liquor operations.
   d. stuffed ballot boxes and played dirty tricks on campaign opponents.

____ 6. Besides deep divisions within the Democratic party, the election of 1924 revealed

   a. Coolidge's inability to attain Harding's level of popularity.
   b. the weakness of profarmer and prolabor progressivism.
   c. the turn of the solid South from the Democrats to the Republicans.
   d. the growth of liberalism within the Republican party.

7. The international economic crisis caused by unpaid war reparations and loans was partially resolved by
   a. private American bank loans to Germany.
   b. forgiving the loans and reparations.
   c. forming a new international economic agency under the League of Nations.
   d. the rise of Mussolini and Hitler.

8. Hoover's election victory over Smith in 1928 seemed to represent a victory of
   a. northern industrial values over southern agrarianism.
   b. small business over the ideas of big government and big business.
   c. ethnic and cultural diversity over traditional Anglo-Saxon values.
   d. big business and efficiency over big-city and Catholic values.

9. One important cause of the great stock-market crash of 1929 was
   a. overexpansion of production and credit beyond the ability to pay for them.
   b. a "tight" money policy that made it difficult to obtain loans.
   c. the lack of tariff protection for American markets from foreign competitors.
   d. excessive government regulation of business.

10. The federal agency Hoover established to provide "pump-priming" loans to business was the
   a. Tennessee Valley Authority.
   b. Bonus Expeditionary Force.
   c. Reconstruction Finance Corporation.
   d. Norris-LaGuardia Authority.

C. Identification

Supply the correct identification for each numbered description.

_____ 1. Poker-playing cronies from Harding's native state who contributed to the morally loose atmosphere in his administration

_____ 2. Supreme Court ruling invalidating a minimum-wage law for women

_____ 3. World War I veterans' group that promoted patriotism and economic benefits for former servicemen

_____ 4. Agreement emerging from the Washington Disarmament Conference that reduced naval strength and established a ratio of warships among the major shipbuilding powers

_____ 5. Toothless international agreement of 1928 that pledged nations to outlaw war

_____ 6. Naval oil reserve in Wyoming that gave its name to one of the major Harding administration scandals

_____ 7. Farm proposal of the 1920s, passed by Congress but vetoed by the president, that provided for the federal government to buy farm surpluses and sell them abroad

_____ 8. American-sponsored arrangement for rescheduling German reparations payments that only temporarily eased the international debt tangle of the 1920s

_____ 9. "Dry," Protestant southern Democrats who rebelled against their party's "wet" Catholic presidential nominee in 1928 and voted for the Republican candidate

_____ 10. Sky-high tariff bill of 1930 that deepened the depression and caused international financial chaos

_____ 11. October 29, 1929—the worst single day of the Wall Street stock-market crash

_____ 12. Depression shantytowns, named after the president whom many blamed for their financial distress

_____ 13. Hoover-sponsored federal agency that provided loans to hard-pressed banks and businesses after 1932

_____ 14. Encampment of unemployed veterans who were driven out of Washington by General Douglas MacArthur's forces in 1932

_____ 15. The Chinese province invaded and overrun by the Japanese army in 1931

D. Matching People, Places, and Events

Match the person, place, or event in the left column with the proper description in the right column by inserting the correct letter on the blank line.

___ 1. Warren G. Harding

___ 2. Charles Evans Hughes

___ 3. Chicago

___ 4. Washington, D.C.

___ 5. Fordney-McCumber Tariff

___ 6. Albert B. Fall

___ 7. Harry Daugherty

___ 8. Calvin Coolidge

A. The sudden collapse of stock values in October 1929 that set off the Great Depression
B. Arrangement for rescheduling German war reparations payments
C. The Democrats' "Happy Warrior" who attracted votes in the cities but lost them in the South
D. Harding's interior secretary, convicted of taking bribes for leases on federal oil reserves
E. High-tariff law that established the American economic isolationism of the 1920s
F. U.S. attorney general and a member of Harding's corrupt "Ohio Gang" who was forced to resign in administration scandals
G. Strong-minded leader of Harding's cabinet and initiator of major naval agreements
H. Site of large race riot in the summer of 1919
I. Weak-willed president whose easygoing ways opened the door to widespread corruption in his administration

_____ 9. Robert La Follette

_____ 10. Herbert Hoover

_____ 11. Al Smith

_____ 12. Great crash

_____ 13. Dawes Plan

_____ 14. Douglas MacArthur

_____ 15. Henry Stimson

J. Hoover's secretary of state, who sought sanctions against Japan for its aggression in Manchuria

K. Secretary of commerce through much of the 1920s whose reputation for economic genius became a casualty of the Great Depression

L. Leader of a liberal third-party insurgency who attracted little support outside the farm belt

M. Site of a major international conference that scaled back armaments and attempted to stabilize conditions in East Asia

N. Commander of the troops who forcefully ousted the "army" of unemployed veterans from Washington in 1932

O. Tight-lipped Vermonter who promoted frugality and probusiness policies during his presidency

E. Putting Things in Order

Put the following events in correct order by numbering them from 1 to 5.

_____ Amid economic collapse, Congress raises tariff barriers to new heights and thereby deepens the depression.

_____ An American-sponsored plan to ease German reparations payments provides a temporarily successful approach to the international war-debt tangle.

_____ An American-sponsored international conference surprisingly reduces naval armaments and stabilizes East Asian power relations.

_____ The prosperous economic bubble of the 1920s suddenly bursts, setting off a sustained period of hardship.

_____ A large number of corrupt dealings and scandals become public knowledge just as the president who presided over them is replaced by his impeccably honest successor.

PART III: Applying What You Have Learned

1. What basic economic and political policies were pursued by the conservative Republican administrations of the 1920s?
2. What were the effects of America's international economic and political isolationism in the 1920s?
3. What weaknesses existed beneath the surface of the general 1920s prosperity, and how did these weaknesses help cause the Great Depression?
4. What were the effects of the Great Depression on the American people, and how did President Hoover attempt to balance his belief in "rugged individualism" with the economic necessities of the time?
5. Is it fair to regard the politics of the 1920s as essentially subordinate to the interests of big business? Why or why not?

34
★★★★★★★★★

The Great Depression and the New Deal,

1933–1938

PART I: Reviewing the Chapter

A. Checklist of Learning Objectives

After mastering this chapter, you should be able to

1. describe the rise of Franklin Roosevelt to the presidency in 1932.
2. explain how the early New Deal pursued the "three Rs" of relief, recovery, and reform.
3. describe the New Deal's effect on labor and labor organizations.
4. discuss the early New Deal's efforts to organize business and agriculture in the NRA and the AAA.
5. describe the Supreme Court's hostility to many New Deal programs and explain why FDR's "court-packing" plan failed.
6. explain the political coalition that Roosevelt mobilized on behalf of the New Deal and the Democratic party.
7. analyze the arguments presented by both critics and defenders of the New Deal.

B. Glossary

To build your social science vocabulary, familiarize yourself with the following terms.

1. **dispossessed** The economically deprived. ". . . she . . . emerged as a champion of the dispossessed. . . ." (p. 497)
2. **rubber-stamp** To approve a plan or law quickly or routinely, without examination. "Measures pouring out of the White House were quickly rubber-stamped." (p. 498)
3. **blank-check** Referring to permission to use an unlimited amount of money or authority. ". . . laws gave the president extraordinary blank-check powers. . . ." (p. 498)
4. **foreign exchange** The transfer of credits or accounts between the citizens or financial institutions of different nations. "The new law invested the president with power to regulate banking transactions and foreign exchange. . . ." (p. 500)

5. **hoarding** Secretly storing up quantities of goods or money. "Roosevelt moved swiftly . . . to protect the melting gold reserve and to prevent panicky hoarding." (p. 500)

6. **boondoggling** Engaging in trivial or useless work; any enterprise characterized by such work. ". . . it was heavily criticized as 'boondoggling.'" (p. 501)

7. **Fascist** Referring to a political system or philosophy that advocates a mass-based party dictatorship, extreme nationalism, racism, and the glorification of war. "Fear of Long's becoming a Fascist dictator ended. . . ." (p. 501)

8. **parity** Equivalence in monetary value under different conditions; specifically, in the United States, the price for farm products that would give them the same purchasing power as in the period 1909–1914. ". . . this agency was to establish 'parity prices' for basic commodities." (p. 502)

9. **holding company** A company that owns, and usually controls, the stocks and securities of another company. "New Dealers likewise directed their fire at public utility holding companies. . . ." (p. 503)

10. **collective bargaining** Bargaining between an employer and his or her organized work force over hours, wages, and other conditions of employment. "The NRA Blue Eagles, with their call for collective bargaining, had been a godsend. . . ." (p. 505)

11. **checks and balances** In American politics, the interlocking system of divided and counterweighted authority among the executive, legislative, and judicial branches of government. ". . . Roosevelt was savagely condemned for attempting to break down the delicate checks and balances. . . ." (p. 509)

12. **pinko** Disparaging term for someone who is not a "red," or Communist, but is presumed to be sympathetic to communism. "Critics deplored the employment of . . . leftist 'pinkos.' . . ." (p. 510)

13. **deficit spending** The spending of public funds beyond the amount of income. ". . . better results would have been achieved by even greater deficit spending." (p. 510)

14. **left** (or **left-wing**) In politics, groups or parties that traditionally advocate greater economic and social equality and the welfare of the common worker. "He may even have headed off a more radical swing to the left. . . ." (p. 511)

PART II: Checking Your Progress

A. True-False

Where the statement is true, mark **T.** Where it is false, mark **F,** and correct it in the space immediately below.

____ 1. In the 1932 campaign, Roosevelt attacked Hoover's economic policies and promised to balance the federal budget.

____ 2. The economy was beginning to turn upward in the months immediately before Roosevelt's inauguration.

____ 3. The Hundred-Days Congress rushed to pass dozens of New Deal programs and granted large emergency powers to the president.

____ 4. Roosevelt's monetary reforms were designed to maintain the gold standard and protect the value of the dollar.

____ 5. The "Indian New Deal" ended the Dawes Act policy of assimilation and authorized tribal governments.

___ 6. Two early New Deal programs, the National Recovery Administration (NRA) and the Agricultural Adjustment Administration (AAA), were both declared unconstitutional by the Supreme Court.

___ 7. The primary agricultural problem of the Great Depression was declining farm production and soaring prices.

___ 8. The Securities and Exchange Commission and the Public Utilities Holding Company Act both imposed new federal controls to reform certain corrupt or deceptive business practices.

___ 9. The Tennessee Valley Authority (TVA) was designed primarily to aid in conserving water and soil resources in eroded hill areas of the South.

___ 10. The Committee for Industrial Organization (CIO) used sympathetic New Deal laws to unionize many unskilled workers previously ignored by the American Federation of Labor (A.F. of L.).

___ 11. Roosevelt's political coalition rested heavily on lower-income groups, including blacks and New Immigrants.

___ 12. The conservative Supreme Court continued to strike down New Deal legislation after Roosevelt's court-packing plan failed.

___ 13. After 1938 the New Deal lost momentum and ran into increasing opposition from an enlarged Republican bloc in Congress.

___ 14. The New Deal more than doubled the U.S. national debt through "deficit spending."

___ 15. By 1939 the New Deal had largely solved the major depression problem of unemployment.

B. Multiple Choice

Select the best answer and put the proper letter in the space provided.

___ 1. Franklin Roosevelt's presidential campaign in 1932

   a. called for large-scale federal spending to reduce unemployment and restore prosperity.
   b. focused primarily on issues of international trade.
   c. promised to aid the common man by balancing the federal budget and ending deficits.
   d. emphasized that there was no way out of the depression in the near future.

___ 2. Roosevelt's first bold action of the Hundred Days was

   a. taking the nation off the gold standard.
   b. declaring a national bank holiday.
   c. legalizing unions and farmers' cooperatives.
   d. expanding relief for the unemployed.

3. The *primary* purpose of the Civilian Conservation Corps (CCC) was

    a. to restore unproductive farmland to productive use.
    b. to protect wildlife and the environment.
    c. to provide better trained workers for industry.
    d. to provide jobs and experience for unemployed young people.

4. Strong political challenges to Roosevelt came from radical critics like

    a. Father Coughlin and Huey Long.
    b. Frances Perkins and Harry Hopkins.
    c. Harold Ickes and Frances Perkins.
    d. John Steinbeck and John Dewey.

5. Roosevelt's National Recovery Administration (NRA) ended when

    a. Dr. Francis Townsend attacked it as unfair to the elderly.
    b. Congress refused to provide further funding for it.
    c. it came to be considered too expensive for the results achieved.
    d. the Supreme Court declared it unconstitutional.

6. Roosevelt's Agricultural Adjustment Administration met sharp criticism because

    a. it failed to raise farm prices.
    b. it was overwhelmed by the extent of the Dust Bowl on the plains.
    c. it raised prices by paying farmers to slaughter animals and not grow crops.
    d. it relied too much on private bank loans to aid farmers.

7. The Social Security Act of 1935 provided for

    a. electricity and conservation for rural areas.
    b. pensions for older people, the blind, and other categories of citizens.
    c. assistance for low-income public housing and social services.
    d. unemployment and disability insurance for workers.

8. The new labor organization that flourished under depression conditions and New Deal sponsorship was

    a. the Knights of Labor.
    b. the American Federation of Labor.
    c. the National Labor Relations Board.
    d. the Congress of Industrial Organizations.

9. Among the groups that formed part of the powerful "Roosevelt coalition" in the election of 1936 were

    a. blacks, southerners, and Catholics.
    b. Republicans, New Englanders, and Old Immigrants.
    c. midwesterners, small-town residents, and Presbyterians.
    d. businessmen, prohibitionists, and Coughlinites.

___ 10. Roosevelt's attempt to "pack" the Supreme Court proved extremely costly because

    a. the Court members he appointed still failed to support the New Deal.

    b. Congress began proceedings to impeach him.

    c. he lost much of the political momentum for the New Deal.

    d. many of his New Deal supporters turned to back Huey Long.

C. Identification

Supply the correct identification for each numbered description.

_____ 1. Shorthand term for the entire Roosevelt program, first used in a 1932 campaign speech

_____ 2. FDR's reform-minded intellectual advisers, who conceived much of the New Deal legislation

_____ 3. The special session of Congress in early 1933 that passed vast quantities of Roosevelt-initiated legislation

_____ 4. The early New Deal agency that worked to solve the problems of unemployment and conservation by employing youth in reforestation and other tasks

_____ 5. Large federal employment program, established in 1935 under Harry Hopkins, that provided jobs in areas from road building to art

_____ 6. Widely displayed symbol of the National Recovery Administration (NRA), which attempted to reorganize and reform U.S. industry

_____ 7. New Deal farm agency that attempted to raise prices by paying farmers to reduce their production of crops and animals

_____ 8. The dry, windblown plains areas from which hundreds of thousands of "Okies" were driven during the Great Depression

_____ 9. New Deal agency that aroused strong conservative criticism for producing low-cost electrical power in competition with private utilities

_____ 10. New Deal program that financed old-age pensions and other forms of income assistance through a special payroll tax on employers and employees

_____ 11. The new union group that organized large numbers of unskilled workers with the help of the Wagner Act and the National Labor Relations Board

_____ 12. New Deal agency established to provide a public watchdog against deception and fraud in stock trading

_____ 13. Organization of wealthy Republicans and conservative Democrats whose attacks on the New Deal caused Roosevelt to denounce them as "economic royalists"

_____ 14. Sharp economic downturn of 1937–1938 that New Deal critics blamed on the president

_____ 15. Law of 1939 that prevented federal officials from engaging in campaign activities or using federal relief funds for political purposes

D. Matching People, Places, and Events

Match the person, place, or event in the left column with the proper description in the right column by inserting the correct letter on the blank line.

___ 1. Franklin D. Roosevelt

___ 2. Eleanor Roosevelt

___ 3. Banking holiday

___ 4. Harry Hopkins

___ 5. Father Coughlin

___ 6. Huey ("Kingfish") Long

___ 7. *Schechter* case

___ 8. Harold Ickes

___ 9. John Steinbeck

___ 10. John L. Lewis

___ 11. General Motors sit-down strike

___ 12. Alfred M. Landon

___ 13. John Collier

___ 14. Court-packing plan

___ 15. John Maynard Keynes

A. Republican who carried only two states against "The Champ" in 1936

B. The "microphone messiah" of Michigan whose mass radio appeals turned anti–New Deal and anti-Semitic

C. Writer whose best-selling novel portrayed the suffering of Dust Bowl "Okies" in the thirties

D. British economist whose theories justified FDR's deficit-spending policies

E. First Lady who became an effective lobbyist for the poor during the New Deal

F. Louisiana senator and popular mass agitator who promised to make "every man a king" at the expense of the wealthy

G. Former New York governor who roused the nation to action against the depression with his appeal to the "forgotten man"

H. Dramatic CIO labor action in 1936 that forced the auto industry to recognize unions

I. FDR's Commissioner of Indian Affairs who promoted an "Indian New Deal"

J. Former New York social worker who became an influential FDR adviser and head of several New Deal agencies

K. Former bull moose progressive who spent billions of dollars on public building projects while carefully guarding against waste

L. Roosevelt-declared closing of all U.S. financial institutions on March 6–10, 1933, in order to stop panic and prepare reforms

M. Controversial Roosevelt proposal to add one new justice to the Supreme Court for every justice over age seventy

N. Supreme Court ruling of 1935 that struck down a major New Deal industry-and-labor agency

O. Domineering boss of the mine workers' union who launched the CIO

E. Putting Things in Order

Put the following events in correct order by numbering them from 1 to 5.

____   FDR devalues the dollar to about sixty cents in gold in an attempt to raise domestic prices.

____   Congress passes numerous far-reaching laws under the pressure of a national crisis and strong presidential leadership.

____   Republican attempts to attack the New Deal fall flat, and FDR wins reelection in a landslide.

____   FDR's frustration at the conservative Supreme Court's overturning of New Deal legislation leads him to make a drastic proposal.

____   Passage of new federal prolabor legislation opens the way for a new union group and successful mass labor organizing.

PART III: Applying What You Have Learned

1. What qualities did FDR bring to the presidency, and how did he display them during the New Deal years?
2. How did the early New Deal legislation attempt to achieve the three goals of relief, recovery, and reform?
3. How did Roosevelt's programs develop such a strong appeal for the "forgotten man," and why did the New Deal arouse such opposition from conservatives, including those on the Supreme Court?
4. Did the New Deal lose momentum in the late 1930s because it had successfully achieved its goals, or because it had begun to lose political support among the public?
5. What were the New Deal's most important and enduring achievements? What were its greatest weaknesses or failures?

35

★★★★★★★★

Franklin D. Roosevelt and the Shadow of War,

1933–1941

PART I: Reviewing the Chapter

A. Checklist of Learning Objectives

After mastering this chapter, you should be able to

1. indicate how domestic concerns influenced FDR's early foreign-policy measures.
2. describe U.S. isolationism in the mid-1930s and explain its effects.
3. explain how America began to respond to the threat from totalitarian aggression while still trying to stay neutral.
4. describe Roosevelt's increasingly bold moves toward aiding Britain in the fight against Hitler and the sharp disagreements these efforts caused at home.
5. discuss the events and issues in the Japanese-American conflict that led up to Pearl Harbor.

B. Glossary

To build your social science vocabulary, familiarize yourself with the following terms.

1. **totalitarianism** A political system of absolute control, in which all social, moral, and religious values and institutions are put in direct service of the state. ". . . chaos in Europe . . . fostered the ominous concept of totalitarianism." (p. 515)
2. **quarantine** In politics, isolating a nation by refusing to have economic or diplomatic dealings with it. ". . . they feared that a moral quarantine would lead to a shooting quarantine." (p. 516)
3. **convoy** To escort militarily, for purposes of protection. "The fateful decision to convoy was taken in July 1941." (p. 522)
4. **warlord** A leader or ruler who maintains power by continually waging war, often against other similar rulers or local military leaders. ". . . Roosevelt had resolutely held off an embargo, lest he goad the Tokyo warlords. . . ." (p. 522)
5. **hara-kiri** Traditional Japanese ritual suicide. "Japan's *hara-kiri* gamble in Hawaii paid off only in the short run. . . ." (p. 523)

PART II: Checking Your Progress

A. True-False

Where the statement is true, mark **T**. Where it is false, mark **F**, and correct it in the space immediately below.

_____ 1. Roosevelt's approach to the 1933 London Economic Conference showed his concern for establishing a stable international economic order.

_____ 2. Roosevelt adhered to his Good Neighbor principle of nonintervention in Latin America even when Mexico seized American oil companies in 1938.

_____ 3. American isolationism was caused partly by disillusionment with U.S. participation in World War I.

_____ 4. The Neutrality Acts of the mid-1930s prevented Americans from lending money or selling weapons to warring nations, and from sailing on belligerent ships.

_____ 5. Despite the neutrality laws, the United States aided the Spanish Loyalist government in its civil war with the fascistic General Franco.

_____ 6. The United States reacted strongly when Japan sank the American gunboat *Panay* in Chinese waters.

_____ 7. The "appeasement" of Hitler by the Western democracies failed to stop his territorial demands.

_____ 8. The "cash-and-carry" Neutrality Act of 1939 allowed America to aid the Allies without making loans or transporting weapons on U.S. ships.

_____ 9. The fall of France to Hitler in 1940 strengthened U.S. determination to stay neutral.

_____ 10. Isolationists argued that economic and military aid to Britain would inevitably lead to U.S. involvement in the European war.

_____ 11. Republican presidential nominee Willkie led the isolationist attack on Roosevelt's pro-Britain policy in the 1940 campaign.

_____ 12. The 1941 Lend-Lease Act marked the effective abandonment of U.S. neutrality and the beginning of naval clashes with Germany.

_____ 13. The Atlantic Charter was an agreement on future war aims signed by Great Britain, the United States, and the Soviet Union.

_____ 14. U.S. warships were already being damaged and sunk in clashes with the German navy before Pearl Harbor.

_____ 15. The focal point of conflict between the United States and Japan in the pre–Pearl Harbor negotiations was Japan's refusal to withdraw from the Dutch East Indies.

B. Multiple Choice

Select the best answer and put the proper letter in the space provided.

____ 1. Roosevelt torpedoed the London Economic Conference of 1933 because

    a. he wanted to concentrate primarily on the recovery of the American domestic economy.
    b. he saw the hand of Hitler and Mussolini behind the conference's proposals.
    c. he was firmly committed to the gold standard.
    d. he was afraid of being drawn into European political conflicts.

____ 2. Roosevelt's Good Neighbor policy toward Latin America included

    a. a substantial program of American economic aid for Latin American countries.
    b. a renunciation of American intervention in Mexico or elsewhere in the region.
    c. American military intervention to block German influence in Argentina and Brazil.
    d. American acceptance of radical governments in Cuba and Panama.

____ 3. The immediate response of most Americans to the rise of the Fascist dictators Mussolini and Hitler was

    a. a call for a new military alliance to contain aggression.
    b. a focus on political cooperation with Britain and the Soviet Union.
    c. support for the Spanish government against its own Fascist rebels.
    d. a deeper commitment to remain isolated from European problems.

____ 4. The Neutrality Acts of 1935, 1936, and 1937 provided that

    a. the United States would remain neutral in a war between Britain and Germany.
    b. no American could sail on a belligerent ship, sell munitions, or make loans to a belligerent.
    c. no belligerent could conduct propaganda campaigns, sell goods, or make loans within the United States.
    d. the United States would support neutral efforts to end the wars in China and Ethiopia.

____ 5. The "cash-and-carry" Neutrality Act of 1939 was designed to

    a. guarantee that the United States would not sympathize with either side in World War II.
    b. enable American merchants to provide loans and shipping to the Allies.
    c. prepare America for involvement in the war.
    d. help Britain and France by letting them buy supplies and munitions in the United States.

____ 6. The "destroyers-for-bases" deal of 1940 provided that

    a. the United States would give Britain fifty American destroyers in exchange for eight British bases.
    b. the United States would give Britain bases in North America in exchange for fifty British destroyers.
    c. if America entered the war it would receive eight destroyer bases in Britain.
    d. the British would transfer captured French destroyers to the United States in exchange for the use of American bases in East Asia.

7. In the campaign of 1940, the Republican Willkie essentially agreed with Roosevelt on the issue of

    a. the New Deal.
    b. the third term.
    c. Roosevelt's use of power in office.
    d. foreign policy.

8. The Lend-Lease Act clearly indicated

    a. the end of isolationist opposition to Roosevelt's foreign policy.
    b. an end to the pretense of American neutrality in the conflict between Britain and Germany.
    c. Roosevelt's intention of drawing the United States into war with Japan.
    d. a lack of involvement by Congress in Roosevelt's foreign policy.

9. By the fall of 1940, American warships were being attacked by German destroyers near the coast of

    a. Spain.
    b. Ireland.
    c. Iceland.
    d. Canada.

10. The key issue in the failed negotiations with Japan just before Pearl Harbor was

    a. the strength of the Japanese navy.
    b. Japanese demands for a base in Vietnam.
    c. the Japanese refusal to withdraw from China.
    d. the Japanese refusal to guarantee the security of the Philippines.

C. Identification

Supply the correct identification for each numbered description.

1. International economic conference on stabilizing currency that was sabotaged by FDR

2. FDR's policy that declared his intention to work cooperatively with Latin American nations

3. Arrangements to lower tariffs with individual countries on a case-by-case basis, avidly pursued by Secretary of State Hull

4. A series of laws enacted by Congress in the mid-1930s that attempted to prevent any American involvement in future overseas wars

5. Conflict between the rebel Fascist forces of General Franco and the Loyalist government that proved a major test of U.S. neutrality legislation

6. Roosevelt's 1937 speech that proposed strong U.S. measures against overseas aggressors, thereby arousing a storm of protest

_____ 7. U.S. gunboat sunk by Japan in 1937

_____ 8. European diplomatic conference in 1938 where Britain and France practiced unsuccessful "appeasement" of Hitler

_____ 9. Leading U.S. group advocating American support for Britain in the fight against Hitler

_____ 10. Leading isolationist group, which advocated that America concentrate on continental defense and avoid involvement with Britain

_____ 11. Controversial 1941 law that made America the "arsenal of democracy" by providing supposedly temporary assistance to Britain

_____ 12. Communist nation invaded by Hitler in June 1941 and aided by American lend-lease

_____ 13. U.S.-British agreement of August 1941 to promote democracy and establish a new international organization for peace

_____ 14. U.S. destroyer sunk by German submarines off the coast of Iceland in October 1941, with the loss of over a hundred men

_____ 15. Major American Pacific naval base attacked by Japan in December 1941

D. Matching People, Places, and Events

Match the person, place, or event in the left column with the proper description in the right column by inserting the correct letter on the blank line.

____ 1. Cordell Hull

____ 2. Adolf Hitler

____ 3. Benito Mussolini

____ 4. Senator Gerald Nye

____ 5. Francisco Franco

____ 6. Rhineland

____ 7. Czechoslovakia

____ 8. Poland

____ 9. France

A. Courageous British prime minister who led Britain's lonely resistance to Hitler

B. Leader of the "America First" organization and chief spokesman for U.S. isolationism

C. Territory demilitarized under the Versailles Treaty, occupied by Hitler in 1936 in his first blatant act of aggression

D. Dynamic but politically inexperienced Republican presidential nominee who avoided criticizing FDR's foreign policy

E. Fanatical Fascist leader of Germany whose acts of aggression forced the United States to abandon its neutrality

F. Instigator of 1934 Senate hearings that castigated World War I munitions manufacturers as "merchants of death"

G. Nation whose sudden fall to Hitler in 1940 pushed the United States to provide aid to Britain

H. Site of a naval base where Japan launched a devastating surprise attack, plunging the United States into World War II

I. North Atlantic island near whose waters U.S. destroyers came under Nazi submarine attack

___ 10. Charles A. Lindbergh   **J.** Small East European democracy betrayed into Hitler's hands at Munich

___ 11. Wendell Willkie   **K.** The lesser partner of the Rome-Berlin Axis, who invaded Ethiopia and joined Hitler's war against France and Britain

___ 12. Winston Churchill   **L.** FDR's secretary of state, who promoted reciprocal trade agreements, especially with Latin America

___ 13. Joseph Stalin   **M.** Soviet dictator who first helped Hitler conquer Poland, then himself became a victim of Nazi aggression in 1941

___ 14. Iceland   **N.** East European nation whose invasion by Hitler in 1939 set off World War II in Europe

___ 15. Hawaii   **O.** Fascist leader who rebelled against the Loyalist government in the Spanish Civil War

E. Putting Things in Order

Put the following events in correct order by numbering them from 1 to 5.

___   FDR puts domestic recovery ahead of international economics, torpedoing a major monetary conference.

___   Western democracies try to appease Hitler by sacrificing Czechoslovakia, but his appetite for conquest remains undiminished.

___   Already engaged against Hitler in the Atlantic, the United States is plunged into World War II by a surprise attack in the Pacific.

___   The fall of France pushes FDR into providing increasingly open aid to Britain.

___   Japan invades China and attacks an American vessel, but the United States sticks to its neutrality principles.

PART III: Applying What You Have Learned

1. How and why did the United States attempt to isolate itself from foreign troubles in the early and mid-1930s?
2. How did the Fascist dictators' continually expanding aggression gradually erode the U.S. commitment to neutrality and isolationism?
3. How did Roosevelt manage to move the United States toward providing effective aid to Britain while slowly undercutting isolationist opposition?
4. Explain the causes of the growing conflict between the United States and Japan in the 1930s. Was war between the two countries inevitable? Why or why not?
5. In retrospect the policy of "appeasing" Hitler and other dictators seems disastrous. Why were Americans in the 1930s so committed to neutrality and isolationism? How did the "lessons" of World War I affect their outlook?

36

★★★★★★★★★

America in World War II,

1941–1945

PART I: Reviewing the Chapter

A. Checklist of Learning Objectives

After mastering this chapter, you should be able to

1. describe how America reacted to Pearl Harbor and prepared to wage war against both Germany and Japan.
2. describe the effects of World War II on American society.
3. explain the early Japanese successes in Asia and the Pacific and the American strategy for countering them.
4. describe the early Allied efforts against the Axis powers in North Africa and Italy.
5. discuss FDR's 1944 fourth-term election victory.
6. explain the final military efforts that brought Allied victory in Europe and Asia and discuss the significance of the atomic bomb.

B. Glossary

To build your social science vocabulary, familiarize yourself with the following terms.

1. **concentration camp** A place of confinement for prisoners or others a government considers dangerous or undesirable. "The Washington top command . . . forcibly herded them together in concentration camps. . . ." (p. 527)
2. *bracero* A Mexican farm laborer temporarily brought into the United States. "The *bracero* program outlived the war by some twenty years. . . ." (p. 529)
3. **U-boat** A German submarine. "Not until the spring of 1943 did the Allies . . . have the upper hand against the U- boat." (p. 535)
4. **beachhead** The first position on a beach secured by an invading force and used to land further troops and supplies. "The Allied beachhead, at first clung to with fingertips, was gradually enlarged. . . ." (p. 538)
5. **underground** A secret movement organized in a country to resist or overthrow the government. "With the assistance of the French 'underground,' Paris was liberated. . . ." (p. 538)
6. **acclamation** The general and unanimous action of a large public body, without a vote. "Roosevelt was nominated by acclamation for a fourth term." (p. 538)

7. **bastion** A fortified stronghold, often including earthworks or stoneworks, that guards against enemy attack. ". . . the 101st Airborne Division had stood firm at the vital bastion of Bastogne." (p. 538)

8. **genocide** The systematic liquidation or killing of an entire people. "The Washington government had long been informed about Hitler's campaign of genocide against the Jews. . . ." (p. 539)

PART II: Checking Your Progress

A. True-False

Where the statement is true, mark **T.** Where it is false, mark **F,** and correct it in the space immediately below.

___ 1. America's major strategic decision in World War II was to fight Japan first and then attack Hitler.

___ 2. Most American women worked in factories during World War II.

___ 3. The major civil liberties violation during World War II was the internment of Japanese-Americans.

___ 4. Imported Mexican labor helped overcome the human-resources shortage in agriculture during World War II.

___ 5. World War II stimulated black migration to the North and West and encouraged black demands for greater equality.

___ 6. In the early months of the war, Japan conquered the Dutch East Indies, the Philippines, and much of East Asia.

___ 7. American citizens at home had to endure serious economic deprivations during World War II.

___ 8. The Japanese navy established its domination of the Pacific sea-lanes at the 1942 Battles of Coral Sea and Midway.

___ 9. The American strategy in the Pacific was to encircle Japan by flank movements from Burma and Alaska.

___ 10. In the first years of the war in Europe, Britain and France bore the heaviest burden of Allied ground fighting against Hitler.

___ 11. Prior to D-Day, the primary British-American ground fighting took place in North Africa and Italy.

___ 12. At the Teheran Conference in 1943, Stalin, Churchill, and Roosevelt planned the D-Day invasion and the final strategy for winning the war.

___ 13. Liberal Democrats rallied to dump Vice President Henry Wallace from FDR's ticket in 1944 and replace him with Senator Harry Truman.

___ 14. The commander of the American navy in the Pacific war was General Douglas MacArthur.

___ 15. The United States modified its demand for "unconditional surrender" by allowing Japan to keep its emperor, Hirohito.

B. Multiple Choice

Select the best answer and put the proper letter in the space provided.

___ 1. The fundamental American strategic decision of World War II was

    a. to attack Germany and Japan simultaneously with equal force.
    b. to concentrate naval forces in the Pacific and ground forces in Europe.
    c. to attack Germany first while using just enough strength to hold off Japan.
    d. to attack Germany and Japan from the "back door" routes of North Africa and China.

___ 2. The major exception to the relatively good American civil liberties record during World War II was the treatment of

    a. communists.
    b. Japanese-Americans.
    c. Mexican-Americans.
    d. German-Americans.

___ 3. Compared with British and Soviet women during World War II, more American women

    a. did not work for wages in the wartime economy.
    b. worked in heavy-industry war plants.
    c. served in the armed forces.
    d. worked in agriculture.

___ 4. The Fair Employment Practices Commission was designed to

    a. prevent discrimination against blacks in wartime industries.
    b. guarantee all regions of the country an opportunity to compete for defense contracts.
    c. prevent discrimination in employment against women.
    d. guarantee that those who had been unemployed longest would be the first hired.

___ 5. The Japanese advance in the Pacific was finally halted at the Battles of

    a. Guadalcanal and Tarawa.
    b. Bataan and Corregidor.
    c. Guam and Wake Island.
    d. Coral Sea and Midway.

___ 6. The essential American strategy in the Pacific called for

    a. attacking the Japanese home islands as soon as possible from Chinese bases.
    b. carrying the war into Southeast Asia from India and the Philippines.
    c. advancing on as broad a front as possible all across the Pacific.
    d. "island hopping" by capturing only the most strategic Japanese bases and bypassing the rest.

_____ 7. The country *least* eager to establish a "second front" against Hitler in the west was

    a. the Soviet Union.
    b. the United States.
    c. Great Britain.
    d. France.

_____ 8. When U.S. troops entered Germany in 1945, they were shocked to discover

    a. that most German civilians still backed Hitler.
    b. the destruction caused by Allied bombing.
    c. the full dimensions of the Holocaust against the Jews.
    d. that the Soviets were already preparing to impose communism in East Germany.

_____ 9. Hitler's last-ditch effort to stop the British and American advance in the west occurred at

    a. the Battle of Normandy.
    b. the Battle of Château-Thierry.
    c. the Battle of Rome.
    d. the Battle of the Bulge.

_____ 10. The *second* American atomic bomb was dropped on the Japanese city of

    a. Nagasaki.
    b. Hiroshima.
    c. Tokyo.
    d. Kyoto.

C. Identification

Supply the correct identification for each numbered description.

_____ 1. A U.S. minority that was forced into concentration camps during World War II

_____ 2. A federal agency that coordinated U.S. industry and successfully mobilized the economy to produce vast quantities of military supplies

_____ 3. Women's units of the army and navy during World War II

_____ 4. Mexican-American workers brought into the United States to provide an agricultural labor supply

_____ 5. Symbolic personification of female laborers who took factory jobs in order to sustain U.S. production during World War II

_____ 6. The federal agency established to guarantee opportunities for black employment in World War II industries

_____ 7. U.S.-owned Pacific archipelago seized by Japan in the early months of World War II

_____ 8. Crucial naval battle of June 1942, in which U.S. Admiral Chester Nimitz blocked the Japanese attempt to conquer a strategic island near Hawaii

_____ 9. Major Pacific island near Australia conquered by General Douglas MacArthur in August 1944

_____ 10. Site of 1943 Roosevelt-Churchill conference in North Africa, at which the Big Two planned the invasion of Italy and further steps in the Pacific war

_____ 11. Iranian capital where Roosevelt, Churchill, and Stalin met to plan D-Day in coordination with Russian strategy against Hitler in the East

_____ 12. The Allied invasion of France in June 1944, which opened the long-awaited "second front" against Hitler

_____ 13. The December 1944 German offensive that marked Hitler's last chance to stop the Allied advance

_____ 14. The last two heavily defended Japanese islands conquered by the United States in 1945, at a high cost in casualties

_____ 15. The devastating new weapon used by the United States against Japan in August 1945

D. Matching People, Places, and Events

Match the person, place, or event in the left column with the proper description in the right column by inserting the correct letter on the blank line.

____ 1. Erwin Rommel

____ 2. Okinawa

____ 3. A. Philip Randolph

____ 4. Detroit

____ 5. Marianas

____ 6. Douglas MacArthur

____ 7. Chester Nimitz

____ 8. Dwight D. Eisenhower

____ 9. Winston Churchill

A. Commander of the Allied military assault against Hitler in North Africa and France

B. City where a single U.S. bomb caused 180,000 casualties and forced Japan's surrender

C. FDR's liberal vice president during most of World War II, who was dumped from the ticket in 1944

D. The Allied leader who constantly pressured the United States and Britain to open a "second front" against Hitler

E. Site of a serious racial disturbance during World War II

F. The German "Desert Fox" who battled the Allies for control of North Africa

G. Commander of the U.S. Army in the Pacific during World War II, who fulfilled his promise to return to the Philippines

H. Inconspicuous senator from Missouri who was suddenly catapulted to national and world leadership on April 12, 1945

I. Site of last large-scale ground battle in the war against Japan

_____ 10. Joseph Stalin

_____ 11. Thomas Dewey

_____ 12. Henry Wallace

_____ 13. Harry S Truman

_____ 14. Normandy

_____ 15. Hiroshima

J. Commander of the U.S. naval forces in the Pacific and brilliant strategist of the "island-hopping" campaign

K. Allied leader who met with FDR to plan strategy at Casablanca and Teheran

L. Site of Allied invasion of Europe on D-Day, 1944

M. Republican presidential nominee in 1944 who found little support for his effort to deny FDR a fourth term

N. Head of the Brotherhood of Sleeping Car Porters whose threatened march on Washington opened job opportunities for blacks during World War II

O. Key island group from which the United States began bombing Japan in 1944

E. Putting Things in Order

Put the following events in correct order by numbering them from 1 to 4.

_____ The United States and Britain invade Italy and topple Mussolini from power.

_____ Japan surrenders after two atomic bombs are dropped.

_____ The United States enters World War II and begins to "fight Hitler first."

_____ The United States stops the Japanese advance in the Pacific and attacks Germany in North Africa.

PART III: Applying What You Have Learned

1. How did World War II affect American society at home?
2. What strategies did the United States use to stop and then reverse the Japanese advance in the Pacific?
3. How did the United States and its Allies develop and carry out their strategy for defeating Italy and Germany?
4. Discuss U.S. relations with its Allies during World War II. What were their major points of agreement and disagreement during the war?
5. Compare and contrast America's role in World War I—domestically, militarily, and diplomatically—with its role in World War II. (See Chapter 31.)

37

★★★★★★★★★

The Cold War Begins,

1945–1952

PART I: Reviewing the Chapter

A. Checklist of Learning Objectives

After mastering this chapter, you should be able to

1. describe the economic transformation of the immediate post–World War II era.
2. describe the postwar migrations to the Sunbelt and the suburbs.
3. explain changes in postwar American society brought about by the baby boom.
4. explain the growth of tensions between the United States and the Soviet Union after Roosevelt's death and Germany's defeat.
5. describe the early Cold War conflicts over Germany and Eastern Europe.
6. discuss American efforts to "contain" the Soviets through the Truman Doctrine, the Marshall Plan, and NATO.
7. describe the expansion of the Cold War to Asia and the Korean War.
8. analyze the postwar domestic climate in America and explain the growing fear of internal communist subversion.

B. Glossary

To build your social science vocabulary, familiarize yourself with the following terms.

1. **gross national product** The total value of a nation's annual output of goods and services. "Real gross national product (GNP) slumped sickeningly in 1946 and 1947. . . ." (p. 546)
2. **population curve** The varying size and age structure of a given nation or other group, measured over time. "This boom-or-bust cycle of births begot a bulging wave along the American population curve." (p. 550)
3. **precinct** The smallest subdivision of a city, as it is organized for purposes of police administration, politics, voting, and so on. "He then tried his hand at precinct-level Missouri politics. . . ." (p. 551)
4. **protégé** Someone under the patronage, protection, or tutelage of another person or group. "Though a protégé of a notorious political machine in Kansas City, he had managed to keep his own hands clean." (p. 551)

5. **superpower** One of the two dominant international powers after World War II—the United States and the Soviet Union. "More specific understandings among the wartime allies—especially the two emerging superpowers, the United States and the Soviet Union—awaited the arrival of peace." (p. 552)

6. **underdeveloped** Economically and industrially deficient. ". . . the Western Allies established . . . the International Bank for Reconstruction and Development . . . to promote economic growth in war-ravaged and underdeveloped areas." (p. 553)

7. **military occupation** The holding and control of a territory and its citizenry by the conquering forces of another nation. ". . . Germany had been divided at war's end into four military occupation zones. . . . (p. 553)

8. **containment** In international affairs, the blocking of another nation's expansion through the application of military and political pressure short of war. "Truman's piecemeal responses . . . took on intellectual coherence in 1947, with the formulation of the 'containment doctrine.'" (p. 554)

9. **communist-fronter** One who belongs to an ostensibly independent political, economic, or social organization that is secretly controlled by the Communist party. ". . . he was nominated . . . by . . . a bizarre collection of disgruntled former New Dealers . . . and communist-fronters." (p. 557)

10. **Politburo** The small ruling group that controlled the Central Committee of the Soviet Communist party and hence dictated the political policies of the Soviet Union. "This so-called Pied Piper of the Politburo took an apparently pro- Soviet line. . . ." (p. 558)

11. **perimeter** The outer boundary of a defined territory. ". . . Korea was outside the essential United States defense perimeter in the Pacific." (p. 558)

PART II: Checking Your Progress

A. True-False

Where the statement is true, mark **T.** Where it is false, mark **F,** and correct it in the space immediately below.

____ 1. Americans were confident that there would be economic prosperity once World War II was ended.

____ 2. The postwar economic boom was fueled especially by military spending and cheap energy.

____ 3. The 40 million new jobs created after World War II in the United States came largely in agribusiness and blue-collar industries.

____ 4. The economic and population growth of the Sunbelt occurred because the South relied less than the North did on federal government spending for its economic well-being.

____ 5. After World War II, American big cities became heavily populated with minorities, while most whites lived in the suburbs.

____ 6. The postwar baby boom created an emphasis on childhood and youth culture in the 1950s and 1960s.

____ 7. The growing Cold War broke down the strong bonds of trust and common ideals that America and the Soviet Union had shared as World War II allies.

____ 8. The Western Allies pushed to establish a separate nation of West Germany, while the Soviets wanted to restore a unified German state.

___ 9. The Berlin crisis and airlift were important as a symbolic test of Allied will to resist growing Soviet power in Europe.

___ 10. The Truman Doctrine was initiated in response to threatened Soviet gains in Iran and Czechoslovakia.

___ 11. The Marshall Plan was developed as a response to the possible Soviet military invasion of Western Europe.

___ 12. Postwar American foreign policy achieved greater success in Japan than in China.

___ 13. The postwar hunt for communist subversion concentrated on rooting out American communists from positions in government and teaching, where they had allegedly served as spies or pro-Soviet agents.

___ 14. Truman defeated Dewey in 1948 partly because of the deep splits within the Republican party that year.

___ 15. Truman fired General MacArthur because MacArthur wanted to expand the Korean War to China.

B. Multiple Choice

Select the best answer and put the proper letter in the space provided.

___ 1. Besides giving educational benefits to returning veterans, the Servicemen's Readjustment Act of 1944 (the GI Bill of Rights) was intended to

   a. prevent returning soldiers from flooding the job market.
   b. provide the colleges with a new source of income.
   c. keep the GIs' military skills in high readiness for the Cold War.
   d. help to slow down the inflation that developed at the end of World War II.

___ 2. The economic boom of the postwar era lasted from approximately

   a. 1945 to 1950.
   b. 1950 to 1960.
   c. 1945 to 1990.
   d. 1950 to 1970.

___ 3. Among the principal causes of the long postwar economic expansion were

   a. foreign investment and international trade.
   b. military spending and cheap energy.
   c. labor's wage restraint and the growing number of small businesses.
   d. government economic planning and investment.

4. The regions that gained most in population and new industry in the postwar economic expansion were

    a. the Northeast and West.
    b. the Northeast and South.
    c. the Midwest and West.
    d. the South and West.

5. The postwar population expansion, called the "baby boom," helped cause

    a. the rise of elementary school enrollments in the 1970s.
    b. the strains on the Social Security system in the 1950s.
    c. the popular "youth culture" of the 1960s.
    d. the expanding job opportunities of the 1980s.

6. The primary reason that Franklin Roosevelt made concessions to Stalin at the Yalta Conference was that

    a. he sympathized with the Soviet need to dominate Eastern Europe.
    b. he wanted the Soviet Union to enter the war against Japan.
    c. he wanted the Soviets to agree to American domination of Central America and the Caribbean.
    d. he was afraid of a postwar confrontation with the Soviet Union over China.

7. The Berlin crisis of 1948–1949 occurred when

    a. the Soviet Union refused to accept the Western Allies' control of western Germany.
    b. the Soviet Army attacked West Berlin.
    c. the people of East Berlin rioted against communist rule.
    d. Soviet forces blocked the Western Allies' rail and highway access to West Berlin.

8. The Truman Doctrine originally developed because of the Communist threat to

    a. Turkey and Greece.
    b. France and West Germany.
    c. Iran and Afghanistan.
    d. Poland and Hungary.

9. The crusade of Senator Joseph McCarthy was primarily directed against

    a. the Soviet Union.
    b. potential communist revolutions in France and Italy.
    c. alleged American communist influence inside the United States.
    d. alleged Soviet spies inside the United States.

10. The Korean War broke out in 1950 when

    a. Chinese communists invaded Korea.
    b. the Soviet Union invaded South Korea.
    c. South Korea invaded North Korea.
    d. North Korea invaded South Korea.

Name _____ Section _____ Date _____

C. Identification

Supply the correct identification for each numbered description.

_____ 1. Popular name for the Servicemen's Readjustment Act, which provided assistance to former soldiers

_____ 2. The rate of worker output per hour, which grew in the United States from 1950 to 1970 and then stagnated

_____ 3. Term for the dramatic increase in the birth rate from 1945 to about 1960

_____ 4. Term for the region from Virginia to California that experienced booming population growth after World War II

_____ 5. Big Three wartime conference that later became the focus of charges that Roosevelt had "sold out" Eastern Europe to the Soviet Communists

_____ 6. The extended post–World War II confrontation between the United States and the Soviet Union that stopped just short of a shooting war

_____ 7. The *two* international economic agencies established at the Bretton Woods conference in 1944

_____ 8. New international organization that experienced some early successes in diplomatic and cultural areas but failed in areas like atomic arms control

_____ 9. Term for the line that Stalin used to block off Soviet-dominated nations of Eastern Europe from the West

_____ 10. American-sponsored effort to provide funds for the economic relief and recovery in Europe

_____ 11. The new anti-Soviet military alliance uniting the United States and western European nations

_____ 12. Jiang Jieshi's (Chiang Kai-shek's) pro-American forces, which lost the Chinese civil war to Mao Zedong's (Mao Tse- tung's) communists in 1949

_____ 13. Devastating new weapon added to the arms race by the United States in 1952 and matched by the Russians in 1953

_____ 14. U.S. House of Representatives committee that took the lead in investigating alleged procommunist agents such as Alger Hiss

_____ 15. The dividing line between North and South Korea, across which the fighting between communists and United Nations forces ebbed and flowed during the Korean War

D. Matching People, Places, and Events

Match the person, place, or event in the left column with the proper description in the right column by inserting the correct letter on the blank line.

_____ 1. Baby boom

_____ 2. Sunbelt

_____ 3. Joseph Stalin

_____ 4. Berlin

_____ 5. Iran

_____ 6. George F. Kennan

_____ 7. Greece

_____ 8. George C. Marshall

_____ 9. Japan

_____ 10. Nuremberg

_____ 11. Richard Nixon

_____ 12. Joseph McCarthy

_____ 13. Henry A. Wallace

_____ 14. Yalu River

_____ 15. Douglas MacArthur

A. The states of the South and West that became the focus of the economic boom after 1950

B. Popular term for the dramatic population increase of the 1940s and 1950s

C. Young California congressman whose investigation of Alger Hiss spurred fears of communist influence in America

D. Oil-rich Middle Eastern nation that became an early focal point of Soviet-American conflict

E. Originator of a massive program for the economic relief and recovery of devastated Europe

F. American military commander in Korea, fired by President Harry Truman

G. Former vice president of the United States whose 1948 campaign as a pro-Soviet liberal split the Democratic party

H. Site of a series of controversial war-crimes trials that led to the execution of twelve Nazi leaders

I. Wisconsin senator whose charges of communist infiltration of the U.S. government deepened the anti-red atmosphere of the early 1950s

J. Nation that was effectively converted from dictatorship to democracy by the strong leadership of General Douglas MacArthur

K. The tough leader whose insistence on establishing a sphere of influence in Eastern Europe helped launch the Cold War

L. Southern European nation whose threatened fall to communism in 1947 precipitated the Truman Doctrine

M. City deep inside the Soviet zone of Germany that became a focal point of Cold War confrontation

N. Boundary between Korea and China, where the approach of U.S. troops in 1950 brought the communist Chinese into the Korean War

O. Brilliant U.S. specialist on the Soviet Union and originator of the theory that U.S. policy should be to "contain" the Soviet Union

E. Putting Things in Order

Put the following events in correct order by numbering them from 1 to 5.

_____ The threatened communist takeover of Greece prompts a presidential request for aid and a worldwide effort to stop communism.

_____ The collapse of Jiang Jieshi's (Chiang Kai-shek's) corrupt government means victory for Mao Zedong's (Mao Tse-tung's) communists and a setback for U.S. policy in Asia.

_____ A new president takes charge of American foreign policy amid growing tension between America and its ally the Soviet Union.

_____   A "give-'em-hell" campaign by an underdog candidate overcomes a three-way split in his own party and defeats his overconfident opponent.

_____   Communists go on the offensive in a divided Asian nation, drawing the United States into a brutal and indecisive war.

PART III: Applying What You Have Learned

1. How and why did the American economy soar from 1950 to 1970?
2. How have economic and population changes shaped American society since World War II?
3. What were the immediate conflicts and deeper causes that led the United States and the Soviet Union to go from being allies to bitter Cold War rivals?
4. What role did the NATO military alliance and the Marshall Plan each play in countering the Soviet threat? Which was most important, and why?
5. Was the Cold War necessary? Was the Soviet Union solely to blame for the conflict, or did American policies help cause it?

38
★★★★★★★★★

The Eisenhower Era,

1952–1960

PART I: Reviewing the Chapter

A. Checklist of Learning Objectives

After mastering this chapter, you should be able to

1. explain how "Ike's" leadership coincided with the American mood of the 1950s.
2. describe Eisenhower's reactions to McCarthyism and the early civil rights movement.
3. indicate the basic elements of Eisenhower's foreign policy in Vietnam, Europe, and the Middle East.
4. describe the vigorous challenges Eisenhower faced from the Soviet Union and indicate how he responded to them.
5. analyze the election of 1960 and explain why Kennedy won.
6. describe the changes in American popular culture in the 1950s.

B. Glossary

To build your social science vocabulary, familiarize yourself with the following terms.

1. **McCarthyism** The practice of making sweeping, unfounded charges against innocent people with consequent loss of reputation, job, and so on. "But 'McCarthyism' passed into the English language as a label for the dangerous forces of unfairness. . . ." (p. 565)
2. **thermonuclear** Concerning the heat released in nuclear fission; specifically, the use of that heat in hydrogen bombs. "Thermonuclear suicide seemed nearer in July 1958. . . ." (p. 571)
3. **confiscation** The seizure of property by a public authority, often as a penalty. "Castro retaliated with further wholesale confiscations of Yankee property. . . ." (p. 572)
4. **hedonism (hedonistic)** The philosophy of pursuing pleasure as an end in itself. "The hedonistic 'consumer ethic' of modern capitalism . . . might undermine the older 'work ethic.' . . ." (p. 575)

PART II: Checking Your Progress

A. True-False

Where the statement is true, mark **T**. Where it is false, mark **F**, and correct it in the space immediately below.

____ 1. Eisenhower attempted to repeal most of the New Deal economic and social legislation.

____ 2. Eisenhower initially hesitated to oppose Senator Joseph McCarthy because of McCarthy's political popularity and power.

____ 3. McCarthy lost his power when he attacked alleged communist influence in the U.S. Army.

____ 4. The Supreme Court ruled in *Brown* v. *Board of Education* that schools could be segregated only if blacks were given facilities completely equal to those of whites.

____ 5. Eisenhower used his influence as president to support blacks' push for civil rights in the schools and elsewhere.

____ 6. Eisenhower sent federal troops to Little Rock, Arkansas, because the governor had used the National Guard to block court-ordered school integration.

____ 7. The roots of the civil rights movement were in northern colleges and universities.

____ 8. In the Hungarian crisis, the United States retreated from Secretary of State Dulles's talk of "rolling back" communism and liberating the "captive peoples" of Eastern Europe.

____ 9. Eisenhower began sending the first American troops to Vietnam in 1954 in order to prevent the communist Vietnamese from defeating the French.

____ 10. The Soviet *Sputnik* satellite raised American fears that the Soviet Union had forged ahead of the United States in rocketry, science, and education.

____ 11. In the 1950s Latin Americans sometimes demonstrated hostility toward the United States for supporting anticommunist dictators and ignoring Latin American interests.

____ 12. Senator Kennedy was able to successfully neutralize the issue of his Roman Catholicism during the 1960 campaign.

____ 13. In the 1950s the number of "white-collar" jobs surpassed the number of "blue-collar" jobs.

____ 14. Social critics and economists like J. K. Galbraith welcomed the growth of consumer culture in the 1950s.

____ 15. Post–World War II culture was marked by the rise of Jewish, black, and southern writers and artists.

B. Multiple Choice

Select the best answer and put the proper letter in the space provided.

____   1. The Korean War ended with

        a. an agreement to unify and neutralize Korea.

        b. a peace treaty that provided for withdrawal of American and Chinese forces from Korea.

        c. an American and South Korean military victory.

        d. a stalemated armistice and continued division of North and South Korea.

____   2. Senator Joseph McCarthy's anticommunist crusade finally collapsed when

        a. the Cold War wound down.

        b. Eisenhower publicly attacked him as a threat to the Republican party.

        c. McCarthy failed to force the alleged communists out of the federal government.

        d. McCarthy attacked the U.S. Army for alleged communist influence.

____   3. The precipitating event of Dr. Martin Luther King, Jr.'s civil rights movement was

        a. the lynching of Emmett Till.

        b. the Little Rock school crisis.

        c. the Montgomery bus boycott.

        d. the passage of the 1957 Civil Rights Act.

____   4. The primary governmental impetus for civil rights within the federal government came from

        a. the Supreme Court.

        b. Congress.

        c. President Eisenhower.

        d. the armed forces.

____   5. Martin Luther King, Jr.'s civil rights organization, the Southern Christian Leadership Conference, rested on the institutional foundation of

        a. black business.

        b. black churches.

        c. black colleges.

        d. labor unions.

____   6. Eisenhower's basic approach to domestic economic policy was

        a. to seek to overturn the Democratic New Deal.

        b. to propose major new federal social programs.

        c. to turn most New Deal programs over to the states.

        d. to trim back some New Deal programs but keep most in place.

___ 7. The United States first became involved in Vietnam by

a. providing economic aid to the democratic Vietnamese government of Ngo Dinh Diem.
b. providing economic aid to the French colonialists fighting Ho Chi Minh.
c. providing aid to Ho Chi Minh in his fight against the French colonialists.
d. sending American bombers to defend the French at Dien Bien Phu.

___ 8. The proposed 1960 summit between President Eisenhower and Soviet leader Khrushchev collapsed when

a. the communists seized power in Cuba.
b. the Soviets made renewed threats against Berlin.
c. the United States sent troops to aid the anticommunist government of Lebanon.
d. an American spy plane was shot down over the Soviet Union.

___ 9. Senator John F. Kennedy's main issue in the campaign of 1960 was that

a. as a Catholic he would better be able to deal with Catholic Latin America.
b. the United States should seek nuclear disarmament agreements with the Soviets.
c. the United States had fallen behind the Soviet Union in prestige and power.
d. the Eisenhower administration had failed to work hard enough for desegregation.

___ 10. Early television was most noted for

a. ignoring organized religion.
b. portraying diverse social roles of women.
c. promoting standardized mass culture and products.
d. replacing popular music as a source of teenage culture and role models.

C. Identification

Supply the correct identification for each numbered description.

_____ 1. Term for making ruthless and unfair charges against opponents, such as those leveled by a red-hunting Wisconsin senator in the 1950s

_____ 2. Supreme Court ruling that overturned the old *Plessy* v. *Ferguson* principle that black public facilities could be "separate but equal"

_____ 3. A French fortress whose 1954 collapse opened the way to a communist victory in Vietnam

_____ 4. An Asian alliance, set up by Secretary Dulles on the model of NATO, to help support the anticommunist regime in South Vietnam

_____ 5. The British-and-French-owned waterway whose nationalization by Egyptian President Nasser triggered a major Middle East crisis

_____ 6. A Soviet scientific achievement that set off a wave of American concern about Soviet superiority in science and education

_____ 7. The U.S. policy, developed after the Suez crisis, that authorized the president to use American troops to prevent communist advances in the Middle East

_____ 8. Latin American nation where a 1959 communist revolution ousted a U.S.-backed dictator

_____ 9. The religion of the 1960 Democratic candidate, which aroused strong Protestant fears but was finally neutralized as a campaign issue

_____ 10. Betty Friedan's 1963 best-seller that helped spark the revived women's movement

D. Matching People, Places, and Events

Match the person, place, or event in the left column with the proper description in the right column by inserting the correct letter on the blank line.

___ 1. Dwight D. Eisenhower

___ 2. Joseph R. McCarthy

___ 3. Earl Warren

___ 4. Martin Luther King, Jr.

___ 5. Ho Chi Minh

___ 6. Ngo Dinh Diem

___ 7. Gamal Abdel Nasser

___ 8. Adlai E. Stevenson

___ 9. Elvis Presley

___ 10. John Kenneth Galbraith

___ 11. West Berlin

___ 12. Nikita Khrushchev

___ 13. Fidel Castro

___ 14. Richard Nixon

___ 15. John F. Kennedy

A. Eloquent Democratic presidential candidate who was twice swamped by a popular Republican war hero

B. Anticommunist leader who set up a pro-American government to block Ho Chi Minh's expected takeover of all Vietnam

C. Latin American revolutionary who became economically and militarily dependent on the Soviet Union

D. The "bone in the throat" that Khrushchev tried to remove by staging a major East-West confrontation in 1959

E. Red-hunter turned world-traveling diplomat who narrowly missed becoming president in 1960

F. Black minister whose 1955 Montgomery bus boycott made him the leader of the civil rights movement

G. The soldier who kept the nation at peace for most of his two terms and ended up warning America about the "military-industrial complex"

H. Popular music hero who spread rock and roll to millions of young people

I. Youthful politician who combined television appeal with traditional big-city Democratic politics to squeak out a victory in 1960

J. Blustery Soviet leader who frequently challenged Eisenhower with both threats and diplomacy

K. Reckless and power-hungry anticommunist demagogue who intimidated even President Eisenhower before his bubble burst

L. A Vietnamese Nationalist and communist whose defeat of the French led to calls for American military intervention in Vietnam

M. Egyptian nationalist who seized the Suez Canal after the United States withdrew economic aid for building a dam

N. Harvard economist who criticized the U.S. economy's production of private wealth and public squalor

O. Controversial jurist who led the Supreme Court into previously off-limits social and racial issues

E. Putting Things in Order

Put the following events in correct order by numbering them from 1 to 5.

____ Major crises in Eastern Europe and the Middle East create severe challenges for Eisenhower's foreign policy.

____ An American plane is downed over the Soviet Union, disrupting a summit and rechilling the Cold War.

____ Eisenhower refuses to use American troops to prevent a communist victory over a colonial power in Asia.

____ Eisenhower orders federal troops to enforce a Supreme Court ruling over strong resistance from state officials.

____ Eisenhower's meeting with Soviet leader Khrushchev marks the first real sign of a thaw in the Cold War.

PART III: Applying What You Have Learned

1. What were the essential qualities of Eisenhower's leadership, and how did they appear in his handling of various issues?
2. How did Eisenhower balance assertiveness and restraint in his foreign policy in Vietnam, Europe, and the Middle East?
3. What were the dynamics of the Cold War with the Soviet Union in the 1950s, and how did Eisenhower and Khrushchev combine confrontation and conversation in their relationship?
4. How were the public policies of the Eisenhower era shaped by both mass consumer affluence and the Cold War?
5. How did America's role as the Cold War "leader of the free world" affect domestic culture and society in the 1950s? Would such phenomena as McCarthyism, the civil rights movement, and the criticism of "mass conformity" have developed without the global rivalry with communism?

39
★★★★★★★★

The Stormy Sixties,

1960–1968

PART I: Reviewing the Chapter

A. Checklist of Learning Objectives

After mastering this chapter, you should be able to

1. describe the high expectations Kennedy's New Frontier aroused and the political obstacles it encountered.
2. analyze the theory and practice of Kennedy's doctrine of "flexible response" in Asia and Latin America.
3. describe Johnson's succession to the presidency in 1963, his electoral landslide over Goldwater in 1964, and his Great Society successes of 1965.
4. discuss the course of the black movement of the 1960s, from civil rights to Black Power.
5. indicate how Johnson led the United States deeper into the Vietnam quagmire.
6. explain how the Vietnam War brought turmoil to American society and eventually drove Johnson and the divided Democrats from power in 1968.

B. Glossary

To build your social science vocabulary, familiarize yourself with the following terms.

1. **free world** The noncommunist democracies of the Western world, as opposed to the communist states. ". . . the 'Wall of Shame' looked to the free world like a gigantic enclosure around a concentration camp." (p. 580)
2. **exile** A person who has been banished or driven from her or his country by the authorities. "He had inherited . . . a CIA-backed scheme to topple Fidel Castro from power by invading Cuba with anticommunist exiles." (p. 582)
3. **peaceful coexistence** The principle or policy that communists and noncommunists—specifically, the United States and the Soviet Union—ought to live together without trying to dominate or destroy each other. "Kennedy thus tried to lay the foundations for a realistic policy of peaceful coexistence with the Soviet Union." (p. 583)
4. **détente** In international affairs, a period of relaxed agreement in areas of mutual interest. "Here were the modest origins of the policy that later came to be known as 'détente.'" (p. 583)

5. **sit-in** A demonstration in which people occupy a facility for a sustained period to achieve political or economic goals. "After the wave of sit-ins that surged across the South. . . ." (p. 584)

6. **establishment** The ruling inner circle of a nation and its principal institutions. "Goldwater's forces . . . [rode] roughshod over the moderate Republican 'eastern establishment.'" (p. 585)

7. **literacy test** A literacy examination that a person must pass before being allowed to vote. "Ballot-denying devices like the poll tax [and] literacy tests . . . still barred black people from the political process." (p. 586)

8. **ghetto** The district of a city where members of a religious or racial minority are forced to live, either by legal restriction or by informal social pressure. ". . . a bloody riot exploded in Watts, a black ghetto in Los Angeles." (p. 587)

9. **black separatism** The doctrine that blacks in the United States ought to separate themselves from whites, either in separate institutions or in a separate political territory. ". . . Malcolm X [was] a brilliant Black Muslim preacher who favored black separatism. . . ." (p. 587)

10. **hawk** During the Vietnam War, someone who favored vigorous prosecution or escalation of the conflict. "Hawkish illusions that the struggle was about to be won. . . ." (p. 589)

11. **dove** During the Vietnam War, someone who opposed the war and favored de-escalation or withdrawal by the United States. ". . . the murdered president's younger brother and now a 'dove' on Vietnam. . . ." (p. 589)

12. **dissident** Someone who dissents, especially from an established or normative institution or position. ". . . Spiro T. Agnew [was] noted for his tough stands against blacks and dissidents." (p. 590)

PART II: Checking Your Progress

A. True-False

Where the statement is true, mark **T.** Where it is false, mark **F,** and correct it in the space immediately below.

_____ 1. Kennedy's attempt to control rising steel prices met strong opposition from big business.

_____ 2. The Kennedy doctrine of "flexible response" was applied primarily to conflicts with Soviet communism in Europe.

_____ 3. The U.S.-supported coup against the corrupt Diem regime brought South Vietnam greater democracy and political stability.

_____ 4. The Kennedy administration financed and trained the Cuban rebels involved in the Bay of Pigs invasion but refused to intervene directly with American troops or planes.

_____ 5. The Cuban missile crisis ended in a humiliating defeat for Khrushchev and the Soviet Union.

_____ 6. The Kennedy administration pushed the civil rights movement to become more active in its opposition to segregation and discrimination.

_____ 7. Johnson won a narrow victory over Republican Barry Goldwater in the election of 1964.

_____ 8. The Gulf of Tonkin Resolution authorized the president to defend American forces against immediate attack but kept the power to make war in Vietnam firmly in the hands of Congress.

____ 9. Johnson's Great Society programs attempted to balance the federal budget and return power to the states.

____ 10. Martin Luther King, Jr.'s nonviolent civil rights movement achieved great victories in integration and voting rights for blacks in 1964 and 1965.

____ 11. The urban riots of the late 1960s showed that America's racial problems were most serious in the South.

____ 12. Despite sending half a million troops to Vietnam and conducting massive bombing raids, Johnson was unable to defeat the Viet Cong and the North Vietnamese.

____ 13. Domestic critics of the Vietnam War were reluctant to weaken a Democratic president because of his stand on civil rights.

____ 14. Political opposition from Senators McCarthy and Kennedy helped force Johnson to withdraw as a presidential candidate and de-escalate the Vietnam War.

____ 15. The youthful political activism of the 1960s helped produce a skepticism about all institutions and authorities.

B. Multiple Choice

Select the best answer and put the proper letter in the space provided.

____ 1. The industry that provoked a bitter conflict with President Kennedy over price increases was

   a. the aircraft industry.
   b. the meat industry.
   c. the steel industry.
   d. the oil industry.

____ 2. The fundamental military doctrine of the Kennedy administration involved

   a. a focus on a "flexible response" to "brushfire wars" in the Third World.
   b. a focus on massive nuclear retaliation against communist advances.
   c. a heavy buildup of conventional armed forces in Western Europe.
   d. a focus on precision air strikes against key communist installations.

____ 3. The Cuban missile crisis ended when

   a. the American-backed Cuban invaders were defeated at the Bay of Pigs.
   b. the United States agreed to allow Soviet missiles in Cuba as long as they were not armed with nuclear weapons.
   c. the Soviets agreed to pull all missiles out of Cuba and the United States agreed not to invade Cuba.
   d. the United States and the Soviet Union agreed that Cuba should become neutral in the Cold War.

_____ 4. The Kennedy administration was pushed into a stronger stand on civil rights by

    a. the civil rights movement led by the Freedom Riders and Martin Luther King, Jr.
    b. the political advantages of backing civil rights.
    c. the pressure from foreign governments and the United Nations.
    d. the threat of violence in northern cities.

_____ 5. President Johnson was more successful in pushing economic and civil rights measures through Congress than President Kennedy because

    a. he was better at explaining the purposes of the laws in his speeches.
    b. the Democrats gained overwhelming control of Congress in the landslide of 1964.
    c. Republicans were more willing to cooperate with Johnson than with Kennedy.
    d. Johnson was better able to swing southern Democrats behind his proposals.

_____ 6. The Civil Rights Act of 1965 was designed to guarantee

    a. desegregation in interstate transportation.
    b. job opportunities for African-Americans.
    c. desegregation of high schools and colleges.
    d. voting rights for African-Americans.

_____ 7. Escalation of the aerial bombardment in Vietnam

    a. bolstered the stability of the South Vietnamese government.
    b. forced the Viet Cong and North Vietnamese to turn to conventional warfare.
    c. strengthened the Viet Cong and North Vietnamese will to resist.
    d. enabled the United States to limit the use of ground forces in Vietnam.

_____ 8. Opposition to the Vietnam War in Congress centered in

    a. the House Foreign Affairs Committee.
    b. the Senate Armed Services Committee.
    c. the House Ways and Means Committee.
    d. the Senate Foreign Relations Committee.

_____ 9. The antiwar presidential candidates whose political showing forced Johnson to withdraw from the race were

    a. Richard Nixon and Spiro Agnew.
    b. Eugene McCarthy and Robert Kennedy.
    c. Hubert Humphrey and Richard Daley.
    d. George Wallace and Curtis LeMay.

_____ 10. Vietnam was not a major issue in the presidential election of 1968 partly because

    a. Humphrey and Nixon had few important differences on the war.
    b. the war had been drastically de-escalated.
    c. Nixon enjoyed overwhelming popular support for his position on the war.
    d. the public had lost interest in finding a way out of the war.

Name _____ Section _____ Date _____

C. Identification

Supply the correct identification for each numbered description.

_____ 1. Kennedy administration program that sent youthful American volunteers to work in underdeveloped countries

_____ 2. High barrier between East and West erected during the 1961 Berlin crisis

_____ 3. Elite antiguerrilla military units expanded by Kennedy as part of his doctrine of "flexible response"

_____ 4. An attempt to provide American aid for democratic reform in Latin America that met with much disappointment and frustration

_____ 5. Site where anti-Castro guerrilla forces failed in their U.S.-sponsored invasion

_____ 6. Tense confrontation between Kennedy and Khrushchev that nearly led to nuclear war in October 1962

_____ 7. New civil rights technique developed in the 1960s to desegregate lunch counters and other public facilities in the South

_____ 8. LBJ's broad program of welfare legislation and social reform that swept through Congress in 1965

_____ 9. The hastily passed 1964 congressional authorization that became a "blank check" for the Vietnam War

_____ 10. Law, spurred by Martin Luther King, Jr.'s march from Selma to Montgomery, that guaranteed rights originally given blacks under the Fifteenth Amendment

_____ 11. The ambiguous racial slogan that signaled a growing challenge to King's nonviolent civil rights movement by militant younger blacks

_____ 12. The communist guerrillas in South Vietnam who, along with the North Vietnamese, successfully matched the American escalation in Vietnam

_____ 13. The Vietnamese New Year celebration, during which the communists launched a heavy offensive against the United States in 1968

_____ 14. Site of the bitterly divided 1968 Democratic convention, where police clashed with antiwar demonstrators

_____ 15. Term for the opposition to traditional American values and lifestyles that became widespread in the 1960s

D. Matching People, Places, and Events

Match the person, place, or event in the left column with the proper description in the right column by inserting the correct letter on the blank line.

____ 1. John F. Kennedy

____ 2. Berlin

____ 3. Charles de Gaulle

____ 4. Laos

____ 5. Robert S. McNamara

____ 6. Nikita Khrushchev

____ 7. Martin Luther King, Jr.

____ 8. Lyndon B. Johnson

____ 9. Barry M. Goldwater

____ 10. James Meredith

____ 11. Eugene J. McCarthy

____ 12. Robert F. Kennedy

____ 13. Richard M. Nixon

____ 14. George C. Wallace

____ 15. Hubert Humphrey

A. First black student admitted to the University of Mississippi, shot during a civil rights march in 1966

B. Defense secretary who promoted "flexible response" but came to doubt the wisdom of the Vietnam War he had presided over

C. New York senator whose antiwar campaign for the presidency was ended by an assassin's bullet in June 1968

D. Former vice president who staged a remarkable political comeback to win the presidential election in 1968

E. Asian country where a civil war was halted by a Geneva conference in 1962

F. Minnesota senator whose antiwar "Children's Crusade" helped force Johnson to alter his Vietnam policies

G. Focal point of East-West conflict in Europe, divided by physical as well as political barriers after 1961

H. Nonviolent black leader whose advocacy of peaceful change came under attack from militants after 1965

I. Vice president whose loyalty to LBJ's Vietnam policies sent him down to defeat in the 1968 presidential election

J. Charismatic president whose brief administration experienced domestic stalemate and foreign confrontations with communism

K. Third-party candidate whose conservative, hawkish 1968 campaign won 9 million votes and carried five states

L. Aggressive Soviet leader whose failed gamble of putting missiles in Cuba cost him his job

M. Haughty French leader who opposed American domination of Western Europe and led his country out of the NATO military alliance

N. Conservative Republican candidate whose crushing defeat in 1964 opened the way for the liberal Great Society programs

O. Brilliant legislative operator whose domestic achievements in social welfare and civil rights fell under the shadow of his Vietnam disaster

E. Putting Things in Order

Put the following events in correct order by numbering them from 1 to 5.

____ A southern Texas populist replaces a Harvard-educated Irish-American in the White House.

____ An American-sponsored anticommunist invasion of Cuba fails.

____ Kennedy successfully risks nuclear confrontation to thwart Khrushchev's placement of Russian missiles in Cuba.

____ A candidate running on a "peace" platform obtains a congressional "blank check" for subsequent expanded military actions against the communist Vietnamese.

_____ Communist military assaults, political divisions between hawks and doves, and assassinations of national leaders form the backdrop for a turbulent election year.

PART III: Applying What You Have Learned

1. What successes and failures did Kennedy's New Frontier experience at home and abroad?
2. How did the civil rights movement progress from difficult beginnings to great successes in 1964–1965 and then encounter increasing opposition from both black militants and "white backlash" after 1965?
3. What role did the large population of young people play in the racial, political, and cultural upheavals of the 1960s?
4. How did the Vietnam War, and the domestic opposition to it, come to dominate American politics in the 1960s?
5. Was the increasing divisiveness and "backlash" in the late sixties primarily a response to the Vietnam War, or was it in part an inevitable letdown from the high hopes generated by Kennedy's "New Frontier" and Johnson's "Great Society"?

40
★★★★★★★★★

The Stalemated Seventies,

1968–1980

PART I: Reviewing the Chapter

A. Checklist of Learning Objectives

After mastering this chapter, you should be able to

1. describe Nixon's policies toward the war in Vietnam and Cambodia.
2. analyze Nixon's domestic policies and his appeal to the "silent majority."
3. describe the American withdrawal from Vietnam, the final communist victory there, and the "new isolationism" represented by the War Powers Act.
4. discuss the Watergate scandals and Nixon's resignation.
5. explain the related economic and energy crises of the 1970s and indicate how Nixon, Ford, and Carter attempted to deal with them.
6. analyze the successes and failures of the détente with Moscow and the opening to Beijing (Peking) pursued by the American administrations of the 1970s.
7. explain the connection between Middle East conflicts and the troubled American economy and describe the attempts of American administrations of the 1970s to solve both sets of problems.
8. discuss the Iranian crisis and its political consequences for Carter.

B. Glossary

To build your social science vocabulary, familiarize yourself with the following terms.

1. **moratorium** A period in which economic or social activity is suspended, often to achieve certain defined economic or political goals. "Antiwar protestors staged a massive national Vietnam moratorium in October 1969. . . ." (p. 598)
2. **antiballistic missile** A defensive missile designed to shoot down or otherwise protect against an offensive missile attack. ". . . the two superpowers agreed to an antiballistic missile (ABM) treaty. . . . (p. 599)
3. **audit** To examine accounts or records in order to determine their accuracy and legitimacy—a process performed by officials appointed for that purpose. "Even the Internal Revenue Service was called upon by Nixon's aides to audit or otherwise harass political opponents. . . ." (p. 601)

4. **echelon** An ordered subdivision of military troops or of a military or political headquarters. "John Dean III . . . testified glibly . . . as to the involvement of the top echelons in the White House. . . ." (p. 602)

5. **obstruction of justice** The crime of interfering with police, courts, or other officials to thwart the performance of their legal duties. "Dean in effect accused Nixon of the crime of obstructing justice." (p. 602)

6. **executive privilege** In American government, the claim that certain information known to the president or the executive branch of government should be unavailable to Congress or the courts because of the principle of separation of powers. "He took refuge behind various principles, including separation of powers and executive privilege. . . ." (p. 602)

7. **sheik** A traditional Arab clan chieftain or ruler. "The Middle Eastern sheiks had approximately quadrupled their price for crude oil. . . ." (p. 603)

8. **illegitimacy** The condition of being contrary to or outside of the law or formal rules. "The sour odor of illegitimacy hung about this president without precedent." (p. 606)

9. **born-again** The evangelical Christian belief in a spiritual renewal or rebirth, involving a personal experience of conversion and a commitment to moral transformation. ". . . this born-again Baptist touched many people with his down- home sincerity." (p. 607)

10. **recession** An economic downturn, less severe than a depression; defined by economists as two quarters (six months) of decline in gross domestic product. "A stinging recession in Gerald Ford's presidency had temporarily slowed inflation." (p. 608)

PART II: Checking Your Progress

A. True-False

Where the statement is true, mark **T**. Where it is false, mark **F**, and correct it in the space immediately below.

_____ 1. Nixon's "Vietnamization" policy sought to end the Vietnam War quickly.

_____ 2. Nixon's 1970 invasion of Cambodia provoked strong domestic protests and political clashes between "hawks" and "doves."

_____ 3. Nixon and Kissinger's diplomacy attempted to play the Soviet Union and China off against each other for America's benefit.

_____ 4. The Nixon-Kissinger moves toward improved relations with China resulted in increased tensions between the United States and the Soviet Union.

_____ 5. Nixon agreed with critics who believed that the Warren Supreme Court had gone too far toward judicial activism.

_____ 6. The basic issue in the 1972 Nixon-McGovern campaign was inflation and the management of the economy.

_____ 7. The 1973 Paris agreement on Vietnam provided for a cease-fire and American withdrawal but did not really end the civil war among the Vietnamese.

_____ 8. In the Watergate scandals, Nixon was accused of using the Central Intelligence Agency and the Federal Bureau of Investigation to harass citizens and obstruct justice.

___ 9. The disclosure of the secret bombing of Cambodia was accepted by Congress as necessary for national security.

___ 10. The 1973 Arab-Israeli War and oil embargo added to the inflation that began in the wake of the Vietnam War.

___ 11. The public continued to support Nixon even after Congress forced him to resign.

___ 12. President Ford attempted to stop the final communist victory in Vietnam by attacking the captured ship *Mayaguez*.

___ 13. Carter effectively used his "outsider" status in Washington to push his economic and energy programs through Congress.

___ 14. The Camp David accords brought an end to the Middle East conflict and the oil crisis and thus substantially eased inflation in the United States.

___ 15. The Iranian revolution against the shah brought the United States into a confrontation with militant Muslim fundamentalists.

B. Multiple Choice

Select the best answer and put the proper letter in the space provided.

___ 1. A primary cause of the economic decline that began in the 1970s was

    a. an international trade war.
    b. a rise in the price of agricultural goods.
    c. the breakup of efficient American companies.
    d. a decline in worker productivity.

___ 2. President Nixon's Vietnamization policy provided that

    a. the United States would accept a unified but neutral Vietnam.
    b. the United States would escalate the war in Vietnam but withdraw from Cambodia and Laos.
    c. the United States would gradually withdraw ground troops while supporting the South Vietnamese war effort.
    d. the United States would seek a negotiated settlement of the war.

___ 3. Antiwar opposition escalated sharply in 1970 when

    a. the ineffectiveness of American bombing efforts became clear.
    b. Nixon ordered further bombing of North Vietnam.
    c. the communist Vietnamese staged their Tet Offensive against American forces.
    d. Nixon ordered an invasion of Cambodia.

____ 4. Nixon attempted to pressure the Soviet Union into making diplomatic deals with the United States by

    a. playing the "China card" to balance the Chinese against the Soviet Union.
    b. using American economic aid as an incentive for the Soviets.
    c. threatening to attack Soviet allies such as Cuba and Vietnam.
    d. drastically increasing spending on nuclear weapons and missiles.

____ 5. The Supreme Court came under sharp political attack especially because of its rulings on

    a. antitrust laws and labor rights.
    b. voting rights and election laws.
    c. criminal defendants' rights and prayer in public schools.
    d. environmental laws and immigrants' rights.

____ 6. The corrupt Nixon administration practices exposed by the Senate Watergate Committee included

    a. payments to foreign agents.
    b. bribes to congressmen and senators.
    c. the illegal use of the Federal Bureau of Investigation and the Central Intelligence Agency.
    d. the illegal use of the Environmental Protection Agency and the Treasury Department.

____ 7. The War Powers Act was passed by Congress in response to

    a. the Watergate scandal.
    b. President Nixon's secret bombing of Cambodia.
    c. the end of the war in Vietnam.
    d. the Arab oil embargo.

____ 8. Gerald Ford came to be president because

    a. he had been elected as Nixon's vice president in 1972.
    b. he was speaker of the House of Representatives and was next in line after Nixon resigned.
    c. he was elected in a special national election called after Nixon resigned.
    d. he had been appointed vice president by Nixon after Vice President Spiro Agnew had resigned.

____ 9. President Carter's greatest success in foreign policy was

    a. handling the Arab oil embargo and the energy crisis.
    b. negotiating successful new agreements with the Soviet Union.
    c. negotiating the Camp David peace treaty between Israel and Egypt.
    d. maintaining peace and stability in Central America.

____ 10. President Carter's greatest problem in foreign policy was

    a. the Panama Canal issue.
    b. the Soviet invasion of Afghanistan.
    c. the continuing Arab-Israeli confrontation.
    d. the Iranian seizure of American hostages.

Name _____ Section _____ Date _____

C. Identification

Supply the correct identification for each numbered description.

_____ 1. Nixon's policy of withdrawing American troops from Vietnam while providing aid for the South Vietnamese to fight the war

_____ 2. The Ohio university where four students were killed during protests against the 1970 invasion of Cambodia

_____ 3. Top-secret documents, published by *The New York Times* in 1971, that showed the blunders and deceptions that led the United States into the Vietnam War

_____ 4. The first major achievement of the Nixon-Kissinger détente with the Soviet Union, which led to restrictions on defensive missile systems

_____ 5. Nixon's plan to win reelection by curbing the Supreme Court's judicial activism and soft-pedaling civil rights

_____ 6. A Washington office complex that became a symbol of the widespread corruption of the Nixon administration

_____ 7. Nixon's firing of special prosecutor Cox and other officials, which aroused angry public demands that he release the Watergate tapes

_____ 8. The law, passed in reaction to the secret Cambodia bombings, that restricted presidential use of troops overseas without congressional authorization

_____ 9. Arab-sponsored restriction on energy exports after the 1973 Arab-Israeli war

_____ 10. Ford's presidential action that freed Nixon from prosecution for the Watergate crimes

_____ 11. International agreement of 1975, signed by President Ford, that settled postwar European boundaries and attempted to guarantee human rights in Eastern Europe

_____ 12. Nixon-Ford-Kissinger policy of seeking relaxed tensions with the Soviet Union through trade and arms limitation

_____ 13. Arms-limitation agreement with the Soviet Union that was signed by Carter in 1979 but blocked by the Senate after the Soviet invasion of Afghanistan

_____ 14. The Arab oil-producing organization that drove energy prices sky-high during the 1970s

_____ 15. Middle Eastern nation where American diplomats were taken hostage in 1979

D. Matching People, Places, and Events

Match the person, place, or event in the left column with the proper description in the right column by inserting the correct letter on the blank line.

___ 1. Richard Nixon	**A.** The Muslim religious leader who led the 1979 Iranian revolution
___ 2. Spiro Agnew	**B.** The first appointed vice president and first appointed president of the United States
___ 3. Cambodia	**C.** Supreme Court justice whose judicial activism came under increasing attack by conservatives
___ 4. Daniel Ellsberg	**D.** Nixon's tough-talking conservative vice president, who was forced to resign in 1973 for taking bribes and kickbacks
___ 5. Henry Kissinger	**E.** Talented diplomatic negotiator and leading architect of détente with the Soviet Union during the Nixon and Ford administrations
___ 6. Earl Warren	**F.** Site of the Carter-negotiated peace agreement between Israel and Egypt
___ 7. George McGovern	**G.** Remote Middle Eastern nation whose 1979 invasion by the Soviet Union led to a freeze in U.S.-Soviet relations
___ 8. Sam Ervin	**H.** Vietnam's neighbor nation, the 1970 American invasion of which caused widespread protests
___ 9. Gerald Ford	**I.** South Dakota senator whose antiwar campaign was swamped by Nixon
___ 10. John Dean	**J.** Former Georgia governor whose presidency was plagued by economic difficulties and a crisis in Iran
___ 11. James Earl Carter	**K.** Former Pentagon official who "leaked" the Pentagon Papers
___ 12. Camp David	**L.** Winner of an overwhelming electoral victory who was forced from office by the threat of impeachment
___ 13. Shah of Iran	**M.** White House lawyer whose dramatic charges against Nixon were validated by the Watergate tapes
___ 14. Ayatollah Ruhollah Khomeini	**N.** North Carolina senator who conducted the Watergate hearings
___ 15. Afghanistan	**O.** Repressive pro-Western ruler whose 1979 overthrow precipitated a crisis for the United States

E. Putting Things in Order

Put the following events in correct order by numbering them from 1 to 6.

___ The overthrow of a dictatorial shah leads to an economic and political crisis for President Carter and the United States.

___ An impeachment-threatened president resigns, and his appointed vice president takes over the White House.

___ A U.S. president travels to Beijing (Peking) and Moscow, opening a new era of improved diplomatic relations with the communist powers.

____   The American invasion of a communist stronghold near Vietnam creates domestic turmoil in the United States.

____   The signing of an agreement with North Vietnam leads to the final withdrawal of American troops from Vietnam.

____   A plainspoken former governor becomes president by campaigning against Washington corruption and for honesty in government.

PART III: Applying What You Have Learned

1. What policies did Nixon pursue in Vietnam and Cambodia, and what were the consequences of those policies?
2. How did the Nixon-Kissinger policy of détente flourish in the early seventies and then decline at the end of the decade?
3. How did Nixon fall from the political heights of 1972 to his forced resignation in 1974? What were the political consequences of Watergate?
4. How did the political conflicts in the Middle East affect America's domestic economy and foreign policy in the 1970s?
5. What were the causes of the political and economic stalemate of the 1970s? Did America's political and economic weakness cause a decline in leadership, or did the weakness of leadership (including Watergate) contribute to the political and economic crises?

41
★★★★★★★★★

The Resurgence of Conservatism
1980–1999

PART I: Reviewing the Chapter

A. Checklist of Learning Objectives

After mastering this chapter, you should be able to

1. describe the rise of Reagan and the "new right" in the 1980s.
2. explain the "Reagan revolution" in economic policy and indicate its immediate and long-term consequences.
3. describe the revival of the Cold War in Reagan's first term.
4. discuss the American entanglement in Central American and Middle Eastern troubles, including the Iran-contra affair.
5. describe the end of the Cold War and its aftermath.
6. describe the Bush administration's foreign policies, including the Persian Gulf War.
7. trace the rise of ideological conflict in the 1990s between congressional Republicans and the Clinton administration.

B. Glossary

To build your social science vocabulary, familiarize yourself with the following terms.

1. **estate tax** A tax levied against the property of a deceased person. ". . . Congress . . . virtually eliminated federal estate taxes. . . ." (p. 614)
2. **red ink** Referring to a deficit in a financial account, with expenditures or debts larger than income or assets. "Ironically, this conservative president thereby plunged the government into a red-ink bath of deficit spending. . . ." (p. 615)
3. **leveraged buy-out** The purchase of one company by another using money borrowed on the expectation of selling a portion of assets after the acquisition. "A wave of mergers, acquisitions, and leveraged buy-outs. . . . " (p. 619)
4. **militia** Traditionally, a civilian force trained for temporary emergency military duty. ". . . a secret underground of paramilitary private 'militias'. . . ." (p. 627)

PART II: Checking Your Progress

A. True-False

Where the statement is true, mark **T.** Where it is false, mark **F,** and correct it in the space immediately below.

____ 1. Carter's bid for reelection was weakened by opposition from liberals within his own Democratic party.

____ 2. Reagan's 1980 presidential candidacy drew strength from conservative "new right" groups such as the Moral Majority.

____ 3. Once in office, Reagan backed away from most of his ideologically conservative election promises and concentrated on practical management of the economy.

____ 4. Reagan failed to get his supply-side economic proposals through Congress.

____ 5. "Reaganomics" was successful in lowering interest rates and balancing the budget but had difficulty bringing down inflation and creating economic growth.

____ 6. The revival of the Cold War in the early 1980s caused rising military budgets and growing doubts about American policy in Western Europe.

____ 7. Reagan pursued a tough policy of military intervention and aid to oppose leftist governments in Central America and the Caribbean.

____ 8. The Strategic Defense Initiative (SDI) attempted to eliminate the "balance of terror" between the United States and the Soviet Union by reducing the number of nuclear weapons.

____ 9. Soviet leader Mikhail Gorbachev's policies of *glasnost* and *perestroika* helped reduce Soviet-American conflict in Reagan's second term.

____ 10. The Iran-contra affair involved the secret exchange of weapons for American hostages and the illegal transfer of funds to Nicaraguan rebels.

____ 11. The end of the Cold War and the collapse of the Soviet Union caused new ethnic conflicts and wars in Eastern Europe.

____ 12. The Persian Gulf War occurred as a response to Saddam Hussein's seizure of the oil-rich nation of Kuwait.

____ 13. President Bush's nomination of Clarence Thomas to the Supreme Court helped quiet the national controversy over affirmative action and other "social issues."

____ 14. President Clinton experienced his greatest early success in the area of health care reform.

____ 15. The impeachment of Clinton culminated years of investigation by congressional Republicans and an independent counsel (special prosecutor).

B. Multiple Choice

Select the best answer and put the proper letter in the space provided.

___ 1. In the election of 1980, Reagan appealed to "populist" sentiments by attacking especially

    a. the lack of opportunities for minorities and women.
    b. big business as the enemy of the "forgotten man."
    c. big government as the enemy of the ordinary citizen.
    d. the ethical corruption and scandals of the Carter administration.

___ 2. "Supply-side" refers to Reagan's economic theory that

    a. providing new supplies for the military would stimulate growth in defense-related industries.
    b. more social services should be supplied by state and local government rather than the federal government.
    c. the government should lower trade barriers in order to increase international commerce.
    d. cutting taxes and federal spending would stimulate the economy and help balance the federal budget.

___ 3. By expanding military spending and proposing his expensive "Star Wars" plan, President Reagan hoped to

    a. force the economically weak Soviets to make concessions and negotiate on American terms.
    b. maintain the "balance of terror" in the nuclear arms competition with the Soviets.
    c. reassure the Western European allies of America's determination to defend them against the Soviet threat.
    d. shift the focus of the Cold War from Europe to Latin America and the Middle East.

___ 4. A primary goal of Reagan's policy in Central America and the Caribbean was

    a. to aid the economic development of this poverty-stricken region.
    b. to establish American bases to protect the Panama Canal against attack.
    c. to oppose the spread of leftist movements and governments in the region.
    d. to stem the flow of illegal immigration into the United States from Latin America.

___ 5. Mikhail Gorbachev's policies of *glasnost* and *perestroika* were aimed at

    a. liberating Eastern Europe from communist control.
    b. eliminating political repression and reviving the Soviet economy through the use of free-market practices.
    c. developing improved relations between the Soviet Union and the United States.
    d. creating opportunities for Soviet economic investment in Western Europe.

___ 6. The Iran-contra affair violated laws against

    a. providing military aid to the contra rebels in Nicaragua.
    b. shipping weapons to the Khomeini government of Iran.
    c. negotiating with terrorists holding American hostages.
    d. aiding the government of Libya.

7. Reagan's federal deficits fulfilled his *political* objectives because

    a. they were highly popular with the public.
    b. they enabled him to promote conservative social policies.
    c. they made further expansion of federal spending and big government almost impossible.
    d. they increased the confidence of such foreign governments as Japan in the American system.

8. The Supreme Court decisions in *Ward's Cove Packing* v. *Antonia* and *Martin* v. *Wilks* made it easier for

    a. white males to argue that they were victims of "reverse discrimination."
    b. state legislatures to limit the right to abortion established in *Roe* v. *Wade*.
    c. women to obtain the same rights in the workplace as men.
    d. blacks and other minorities to guarantee their right to affirmative action.

9. A primary source of economic trouble in the late 1980s and early 1990s was

    a. high interest rates.
    b. drastically increased inflation.
    c. the collapse of financial institutions, especially savings and loan associations (S&Ls).
    d. the recession caused by the stock-market crash of 1987.

10. Mikhail Gorbachev's policies of *glasnost* and *perestroika* had their greatest international effects in

    a. causing heightened tension with orthodox Marxists in China.
    b. causing the fall of communist regimes in Eastern Europe and the reunification of Germany.
    c. causing the outbreak of war in the Persian Gulf.
    d. heightening tensions with the United States.

11. Rising budget deficits forced George Bush to back off on his campaign pledge to

    a. oppose affirmative action for minorities.
    b. pursue a free trade agreement with Canada and Mexico.
    c. refuse to raise taxes.
    d. pursue further arms limitation agreements with the Soviet Union.

12. The most successful result of the Allied victory in the Persian Gulf War was

    a. the liberation of oppressed minorities within Iraq.
    b. the liberation of Kuwait from Iraqi control.
    c. the restoration of democracy in Lebanon and Syria.
    d. the overthrow of Iraqi dictator Saddam Hussein.

13. In 1989–1991, communist governments were overthrown in all of these countries except

    a. East Germany.
    b. Poland.
    c. China.
    d. Russia.

___ 14. Bill Clinton defeated George Bush largely on the issue of

   a. the weak economy.
   b. gays in the military.
   c. America's foreign policy stumbles in Europe.
   d. social issues like abortion and affirmation action.

___ 15. A common issue that united mainstream political movements and more extremist elements in the 1990s was

   a. concern for the economic and social welfare of the average citizen.
   b. worry about the rise of communism and anti-Americanism in the Third World.
   c. hostility to free trade agreements with foreign nations.
   d. suspicion of government and disenchantment with conventional politics.

C. Identification

Supply the correct identification for each numbered description.

_____ 1. Outspoken conservative movement of the 1980s that emphasized such social issues as opposition to abortion, the Equal Rights Amendment, pornography, homosexuality, and affirmative action

_____ 2. The economic theory of "Reaganomics" that emphasized cutting taxes and government spending in order to stimulate investment, productivity, and economic growth by private enterprise

_____ 3. Conservative southern Democrats who supported Reagan's economic policies in Congress

_____ 4. Polish labor union that steadfastly opposed and eventually helped overthrow the communist government of Poland

_____ 5. The leftist revolutionary rulers of Nicaragua, strongly opposed by the Reagan administration

_____ 6. Popular name for Reagan's proposed space-based nuclear defense system, officially called the Strategic Defense Initiative

_____ 7. Russian term for Mikhail Gorbachev's policy of "openness"

_____ 8. Russian term for Gorbachev's policy of "restructuring"

_____ 9. Initials for the category of intermediate weapons eliminated by a Soviet-American treaty in 1987

_____ 10. The secret deal involving selling weapons to Iran and providing funds to Nicaraguan anticommunist rebels

_____ 11. Ugly symbol of the division of Europe whose fall in December 1989 signaled the end of the Cold War

_____ 12. Nation whose invasion by Iraq in 1990 led to the Persian Gulf War

_____ 13. Fundamentalist religious sect stormed by federal agents in 1993

_____ 14. Action voted against President Clinton by the House of Representatives in December 1998

_____ 15. The ten-point program that helped Republicans win the congressional elections of 1994

D. Matching People, Places, and Events

Match the person, place, or event in the left column with the proper description in the right column by inserting the correct letter on the blank line.

___ 1. Ronald Reagan

___ 2. Lebanon

___ 3. Nicaragua

___ 4. Grenada

___ 5. Clarence Thomas

___ 6. Sandra Day O'Connor

___ 7. Mikhail Gorbachev

___ 8. George Bush

___ 9. Saddam Hussein

___ 10. H. Norman Schwarzkopf

___ 11. Boris Yeltsin

___ 12. Bill Clinton

___ 13. Hillary Rodham Clinton

___ 14. H. Ross Perot

___ 15. Newt Gingrich

A. Caribbean island whose Marxist government was ousted by a 1983 American military invasion

B. The successful American commander of Operation Desert Storm

C. Soviet leader whose summit meetings with Reagan achieved an arms-control breakthrough in 1987

D. Turbulent Middle Eastern country where more than two hundred American marines lost their lives in 1983

E. Brilliant legal scholar appointed by Reagan as the first woman on the Supreme Court

F. Conservative African-American Supreme Court justice appointed by President Bush in 1991

G. Iraqi dictator defeated in the Persian Gulf War

H. First Lady assigned to design health-care reform in her husband's administration

I. Georgia congressman who became the Republican Speaker of the House in 1995

J. Former Arkansas governor who successfully campaigned as a "new" Democrat in the 1992 presidential election

K. A wealthy "populist" from Texas who drew substantial support from disaffected Republicans and Democrats in the 1992 presidential election

L. Long-time Republican political figure who defeated Michael Dukakis for the presidency in 1988

M. Central American country whose Sandinista government was strongly opposed by the Reagan administration

N. Russian leader who succeeded Gorbachev when the Soviet Union dissolved

O. Political darling of Republican conservatives who won two landslide election victories in the 1980s

E. Putting Things in Order

Put the following events in correct order by numbering them from 1 to 6.

____ Republicans win control of Congress for the first time in forty years.

____ Reagan easily wins reelection by overwhelming divided Democrats.

____ Communism collapses in Eastern Europe.

____ Reagan's supply-side economic programs pass through Congress, cutting taxes and federal spending.

____ President Clinton is impeached by U.S. House of Representatives and acquitted by the Senate.

____ The United States defeats Iraq in the Persian Gulf War.

PART III: Applying What You Have Learned

1. What caused the rise of Reagan and the "new right" in the eighties, and how did this conservative movement affect American politics?
2. What were the goals of Reagan's "supply-side" economic policies, and what were their short-term and long-term effects?
3. What led to the revival of the Cold War in the early 1980s and to its decline and disappearance by 1991?
4. Trace the role of the "social issues" like abortion, affirmative action, and "family values" in the politics and policies of the 1980s. How did these issues contribute to Republicans' political success in that decade?
5. Were the ideological conflicts between the Republican Congress and the Democratic president a result of fundamental philosophical disagreement over the role of the federal government, or a sign of general public disillusionment with government in the 1990s?

42

★★★★★★★★★

The American People
Face a New Century

PART I: Reviewing the Chapter

A. Checklist of Learning Objectives

After mastering this chapter, you should be able to

1. describe the changing shape of the American economy and work force and the new challenges facing the United States in an international economy.
2. explain the changing roles of women since the 1970s and the impact of those changes on American society.
3. analyze the difficulties affecting the American family.
4. describe the impact of the newest wave of immigration from Asia and Latin America and the growing voice of minorities in American society.
5. describe the changing condition of African-Americans in American politics and society.
6. describe the difficulties and challenges facing American cities, including poverty and drug abuse.
7. discuss the major developments in American culture and arts since the 1970s.

B. Glossary

To build your social science vocabulary, familiarize yourself with the following terms.

1. **median** In statistics, the number midway between all the numbers in a sequence (i.e., one-half above and one-half below). ". . . by 2050, as the median age rose toward forty." (p. 639)
2. **undocumented** Lacking official or legal registration and immigrant status. ". . . by penalizing employers of undocumented aliens. . . ." (p. 640)
3. **bilingual** Concerning the speaking or knowledge of two languages. ". . . another measure to end bilingual education in California schools." (p. 640)
4. **affirmative action** Referring to the policies of government or other institutions designed to provide jobs, education, and so on to members of groups that have been subject to discrimination. "This ringing victory for the foes of affirmative action. . . ." (p. 643)

PART II: Checking Your Progress

A. True-False

Where the statement is true, mark **T**. Where it is false, mark **F**, and correct it in the space immediately below.

___ 1. Two expanding areas of the American economy in the late twentieth century were electronics and biotechnology.

___ 2. One economic trend of the 1990s was a decline in the wealth gap between rich and poor.

___ 3. Changes in society and the economy made the American family increasingly vulnerable after 1970.

___ 4. After 1980, federal spending for senior citizens' retirement benefits began to decline.

___ 5. The influx of new immigrants in the 1980s and 1990s stirred opposition among some old-stock Americans.

___ 6. African-Americans and Hispanics made substantial political gains at the local level in the 1960s and after.

___ 7. By the 1990s, a majority of American women with young children worked for pay outside the home.

___ 8. Asian-Americans and Native Americans both experienced a reawakening of ethnic pride in the 1970s and after.

___ 9. The 1996 welfare reform bill was designed to limit "corporate welfare" to business.

___ 10. American literature in the post-1970 period was dominated by southern white male writers.

B. Multiple Choice

Select the best answer and put the proper letter in the space provided.

___ 1. The fastest growing sector of the American economy after the 1970s was

    a. the steel industry.
    b. the oil industry.
    c. the information sector.
    d. the agricultural industries.

___ 2. The greatest force driving the United States economy after the 1970s was

    a. the transformation of America from an importing to an exporting nation.
    b. the protection of the American domestic economy behind high tariff walls.
    c. scientific research and information technology.
    d. the growth in media and the arts.

____ 3. The most dramatic change in the patterns of women's employment from 1950 to the 1990s was

    a. the end of women's concentration in lower paying positions.
    b. the inability of women to break into fields like aviation and medicine.
    c. the growth of employment by older women over forty.
    d. the increase in the number of mothers with small children in the work force.

____ 4. A primary change in the structure of the American population as the 1990s began was the increasing

    a. percentage of the population between eighteen and thirty-five.
    b. percentage of the population over sixty-five.
    c. percentage of the population under eighteen.
    d. disproportion of males to females in the population over fifty years of age.

____ 5. The new wave of immigration to America from 1980 to 2000 came primarily from

    a. Europe and Canada.
    b. Asia and Latin America.
    c. Africa and the Caribbean.
    d. Eastern Europe and the Middle East.

____ 6. The growing Hispanic population was most heavily concentrated in

    a. the Southwest.
    b. the Midwest.
    c. the Northeast.
    d. the Pacific Northwest.

____ 7. One notable success achieved by African-Americans in the 1970s and after was

    a. a decline in poverty among urban residents.
    b. an end to residential segregation.
    c. an equalizing of black and white income levels.
    d. the growth of a large black middle class.

____ 8. The passage of Proposition 209 in California in 1996 was aimed at ending

    a. future immigration to the state.
    b. bilingual education.
    c. police mistreatment of minorities.
    d. affirmative action.

____ 9. The strong interest in authors like Amy Tan and Zora Neale Hurston demonstrated the new prominence in American literature of

    a. Jews and immigrants.
    b. minorities and women.
    c. Hispanics and Native Americans.
    d. southerners and expatriates.

_____ 10. The American city that became the art capital of the world after World War II was

      a. San Francisco.

      b. Chicago.

      c. New Orleans.

      d. New York.

C. Identification

Supply the correct identification for each numbered description.

_____ 1. Large computer software corporation that symbolized the "information age" of U.S. industry

_____ 2. Government provision of retirement benefits for older citizens that became a large portion of federal expenditures in the 1980s and 1990s

_____ 3. Ethnic group that retained close ties with its land of origin and settled primarily in the U.S. Southwest

_____ 4. Hispanic-led labor union that organized American agricultural workers in California and elsewhere

_____ 5. City rocked by racial conflicts in the 1990s

_____ 6. California initiative that aimed to end affirmative action in the state

_____ 7. Region that produced noted writers of the 1980s and 1990s like Annie Dillard, David Guterson, and Norman McLean

_____ 8. Artistic movement led by Jackson Pollock that opposed realism and promoted "action painting"

D. Matching People, Places, and Events

Match the person, place, or event in the left column with the proper description in the right column by inserting the correct letter on the blank line.

_____ 1. Carol Mosely Braun

_____ 2. Andy Warhol

_____ 3. Cesar Chavez

_____ 4. Toni Morrison

_____ 5. Amy Tan

_____ 6. David Mamet

A. Nobel Prize–winning author of *Beloved* and other novels

B. Hispanic leader of the United Farm Workers union

C. Asian-American writer who explored relations between immigrant parents and their children

D. Painting experimenter, creator of abstract expressionism

E. Black author of the 1930s whose work was rediscovered in the 1990s

F. Long-lived architect who designed the Guggenheim Museum and other noted buildings

G. Playwright whose *Angels in America* explored results of the AIDS epidemic

___   7. Jackson Pollock

H. First African-American woman elected to the U.S. Senate

I. "Pop" artist who created images of common objects like soup cans

___   8. Tony Kushner

J. Playwright who criticized American capitalism in works like *Glengarry Glen Ross*

___   9. Frank Lloyd Wright

___   10. Zora Neale Hurston

PART III: Applying What You Have Learned

1. How was the American economy transformed from the 1970s to the 1990s?
2. What new forces affected the American family in the late twentieth century?
3. What has been the changing role of women in recent decades?
4. How did the latest wave of immigration, especially from Asia and Latin America, affect U.S. society in the late twentieth century? Was this immigration fundamentally different from earlier waves of immigration, or essentially similar?
5. How have changes in American culture and art reflected trends in American society since the 1970s? In what ways might artists and writers have helped to promote social and cultural change?

Answer Key to the Guidebook

Chapter 1

II. A.

1. True
2. False. They walked across a land bridge from Siberia to Alaska.
3. False. They were built on the economic foundations of corn.
4. True
5. True
6. False. Vikings had visited North America around A.D. 1000.
7. True
8. False. African slavery existed before the discovery of the Americas.
9. False. Columbus thought he had discovered islands of the Indies off the coast of Asia.
10. False. The effect was a decline in population through disease and conquest.
11. True
12. False. They regularly intermarried with Native Americans.
13. False. It was first settled by Spanish colonizers from the south (Mexico).
14. True
15. True

II. B.

1. a
2. b
3. d
4. a
5. d
6. c
7. b
8. b
9. b
10. c

II. C.

1. Great Ice Age
2. Cahokia
3. Newfoundland
4. Portugal
5. Mali
6. Indies
7. horse

8. syphilis
9. Treaty of Tordesillas
10. Tenochtitlan
11. mestiozo
12. *Dia de la Raza*
13. Popé's Rebellion
14. Pueblos
15. Franciscans

II. D.

1. D
2. J
3. L
4. E
5. H
6. A
7. I
8. B
9. C
10. F
11. G
12. K

II. E.

3
2
1
5
4

Chapter 2

II. A.

1. True
2. False. England's first efforts were complete failures.
3. False. It enabled England to gain control of the seas; Spain's empire was not conquered.
4. True
5. True
6. False. The purpose was to make a profit for investors.
7. False. Rolfe enabled the colony to survive by developing tobacco growing.
8. False. It was established to provide religious freedom for Roman Catholics.
9. True

10. False. Tobacco was a poor man's crop; sugar was not.
11. True.
12. True
13. True
14. False. It valued Georgia primarily as a defensive buffer against the Spanish in Florida
15. True

II. B.

1. b
2. c
3. b
4. a
5. d
6. c
7. b
8. b
9. c
10. a
11. c

II. C.

1. Ireland
2. Roanoke
3. wool
4. joint-stock company
5. Anglo-Powhatan Wars
6. Barbados Slave Code
7. Royal charter
8. indentured servants
9. Act of Toleration
10. squatters
11. royal colony
12. tobacco
13. Georgia

II. D.

1. B
2. M
3. 1
4. L
5. K
6. A
7. C
8. D
9. H

10. O
11. F
12. E
13. N
14. G
15. J

II. E.

1
3
4
5
2

Chapter 3

II. A.

1. True
2. False. Most Puritans wanted to stay within the Church of England and purify it; only extreme Puritans, the Separatists, wanted to break away.
3. False. Plymouth was smaller and did not influence Massachusetts Bay.
4. True
5. False. They were banished for teaching religious and political heresy.
6. True
7. True
8. True
9. False. England's neglect of the colonies enabled them to develop considerable autonomy, and attempts to assert tighter control failed.
10. False. New York was the most aristocratic and economically unequal of the middle colonies.
11. True
12. False. Penn welcomed people of diverse religious views from the beginning.
13. True
14. True
15. False. The description applies to New England, not the middle colonies, which were socially and religiously diverse.

II. B.

1. b
2. d
3. a

4. a
5. c
6. d
7. a
8. c
9. b
10. d

II. C.

1. Protestant Reformation
2. Puritans
3. Separatists
4. Mayflower Compact
5. covenant
6. dismissal of Parliament
7. Protestant ethic
8. antinomianism
9. banishment or exile
10. Wampanoags
11. Glorious Revolution
12. New Sweden
13. Hudson
14. test oaths
15. New Jersey (East Jersey or West Jersey OK)

IL D.

1. G
2. L
3. M
4. D
5. N
6. J
7. C
8. I
9. A
10. H
11. E
12. O
13. F
14. K
15. B

II. E.

8
2
6
3

1
9
4
7
5
10

Chapter 4

IL A.

1. False. The life expectancy of Chesapeake settlers was under fifty. The statement is true of New Englanders.
2. True
3. True
4. False. Rising production depressed prices, and planters struggled to find a stable labor supply.
5. True
6. True
7. False. The rebels were whites only. They attacked and killed Indians as well as wealthy whites.
8. True
9. True
10. False. Between the planters and indentured servants were two other classes: small landowning farmers and landless but free (nonindentured) laborers.
11. True
12. False. New England settlement was carried out in an orderly fashion by town fathers, who obtained charters and distributed land for settlement and town purposes.
13. True
14. False. New England shipping was based on fishing, lumber, and other nonagricultural commodities. New England soil was poor and produced little agricultural surplus.
15. True

II. B.

1. b
2. a
3. c
4. a
5. c
6. c
7. d

8. b
9. a
10. b

II. C.

1. the family
2. disease
3. freedom dues
4. headright
5. hanging
6. middle passage
7. slave trade
8. Gullah
9. slave revolts
10. rice
11. proprietors
12. town meeting
13. Half-Way Covenant
14. Salem witch trials
15. fanning

II. D.

1. I
2. D
3. N
4. K
5. M
6. E
7. G
8. A
9. F
10. J
11. O
12. L
13. B
14. H
15. C

II. E.

5
2
3
4
I

Chapter 5

II. A.

1. False. Most of the increase was natural.
2. True
3. False. The colonies were becoming less equal in the eighteenth century.
4. True
5. True
6. False. The ministry was the most honored profession, while doctors and lawyers were not well regarded.
7. True
8. False. American merchants evaded British trade restrictions by smuggling.
9. False. Congregationalism was more influential than Anglicanism.
10. True
11. False. The Great Awakening used emotion to "revive" traditional ideas of conversion and salvation.
12. True
13. True
14. False. Most colonial achievement was in theology and political theory rather than literature and the arts.
15. True

II. B.

1. b
2. d
3. c
4. c
5. b
6. b
7. b
8. c
9. a
10. d

II. C.

1. Pennsylvania Dutch
2. frontier or West
3. war or military supply
4. "jayle birds"
5. plagues
6. law (lawyer)

7. triangular trade
8. taverns
9. established
10. Great Awakening
11. new lights
12. University of Pennsylvania
13. libel
14. council
15. property

II. D.

1. D
2. E
3. K
4. H
5. N
6. I
7. O
8. J
9. A
10. G
11. M
12. B
13. F
14. L
15. C

II. E.

6
1
9
10
2
4
8
7
3
5

Chapter 6

II. A.

1. True
2. False. Its economic foundation was the fur trade.
3. True
4. False. The colonies became directly involved in every one of Britain's wars with France.

5. False. It arose because of competition over land and the fur trade in the Ohio Valley, which was being fortified by France.
6. False. It was a temporary setback that sparked the Seven Years' War (French and Indian War).
7. True
8. True
9. False. Braddock's forces were also defeated by the French.
10. False. France lost all its North American possessions. It reacquired Louisiana after the American Revolution.
11. False. The war increased friction between British officers and American colonials.
12. False. Colonists often gave half-hearted support to Britain, and some even worked with the enemy.
13. True
14. True
15. True

II. B.

1. d
2. b
3. b
4. c
5. a
6. b
7. c
8. b
9. c
10. c

II. C.

1. Huguenots
2. New France or Canada
3. beaver
4. Jesuits
5. *coureurs des bois*
6. Jenkins' ear
7. Louisbourg
8. Ohio Valley
9. Germany
10. Albany Congress.
11. George Washington
12. Quebec
13. militia
14. Native Americans (Indians)
15. Seven Years' War

II. D.

1. H
2. N
3. L
4. D
5. J
6. K
7. A
8. G
9. O
10. 1
11. M
12. F
13. B
14. E
15. C

II. E.

6
8
1
2
10
4
9
5
7
3

Chapter 7

II. A.

1. True
2. True
3. False. European goods could be imported, but they first had to be landed and taxed in Britain.
4. True
5. True
6. False. The colonists accepted the right of Parliament to legislate but not to tax.
7. False. The colonies did not want representation in Parliament, where they could be outvoted; they wanted to be able to decide on their own taxes.
8. True
9. False. The protest was less organized and effective than the Stamp Act protest.
10. False. The Townshend Acts were repealed in 1770, except for the symbolic tea tax.
11. True
12. True
13. False. The Congress sought only an end to parliamentary taxation and a return to the earlier system, not independence.
14. False. Britain had the better trained regular army; America had only a militia.
15. False. The Americans only needed to fight to a draw; the British had to conquer all of America in order to defeat the Revolution.

II. B.

1. c
2. b
3. a
4. d
5. b
6. a
7. b
8. b
9. a
10. a

II. C.

1. mercantilism
2. Navigation Laws
3. enumerated
4. admiralty courts
5. virtual representation
6. nonimportation agreements
7. tea
8. Committees of Correspondence
9. Roman Catholicism
10. Whigs
11. Hessians
12. continentals
13. The Association
14. Minute Men
15. redcoats

II. D.

1. F
2. A
3. B
4. M
5. G

6. K
7. J
8. H
9. O
10. I
11. N
12. C
13. E
14. L
15. D

II. E.

3
9
6
10
5
2
7
4
8
1

Chapter 8

II. A.

1. False. He was chosen more for his personal and political abilities than for his military skill.
2. False. After Bunker Hill the king proclaimed the colonies in rebellion and slammed the door on reconciliation.
3. True
4. False. Paine's *Common Sense* encouraged them to declare independence. They were already in rebellion against the king.
5. True
6. True
7. True
8. False. The description fits the Loyalist centers of strength. The Patriots were strongest in New England.
9. False. Only a minority were driven out of the country, and almost none was killed.
10. True
11. True
12. True

13. False. Yorktown was successful because of French naval aid.
14. False. They gained both political independence and the western territorial concessions they wanted.
15. True

II. B.

1. b
2. d
3. a
4. c
5. b
6. a
7. d
8. a
9. c
10. a

II. C.

1. Continental Congress
2. Canada
3. *Common Sense*
4. Declaration of Independence
5. Patriots or Whigs
6. Loyalists
7. Anglican
8. Hudson Valley
9. Armed Neutrality
10. South
11. privateers
12. Whigs
13. Mississippi River
14. militia
15. Holland

II. D.

1. J
2. H
3. B
4. M
5. N
6. D
7. I
8. O
9. A
10. E
11. L

12. C
13. G
14. K
15. F

II. E.

5
2
3
6
1
4

Chapter 9

II. A.

1. True
2. True
3. False. They did abolish slavery in the North but made no effort to do so in the South.
4. True
5. False. The new state governments were more democratic and reflected the interests of western farmers.
6. True
7. False. Handling western lands was the greatest success of the national government under the Articles.
8. True
9. False. The ordinance set up an orderly process by which territories could become states, with a status equal to that of the original thirteen.
10. True
11. False. The delegates' original purpose was to amend the Articles.
12. False. The delegates were a propertied elite.
13. True
14. False. The antifederalists opposed the Constitution because they thought it gave too much power to the whole federal government and not enough to the states and to the people.
15. True

II. B.

1. c
2. c
3. a
4. b
5. c
6. b
7. d
8. d
9. c
10. b

II. C.

1. Protestant Episcopal church
2. New Jersey
3. Constitutional Convention
4. Articles of Confederation
5. Old Northwest
6. sections
7. territory
8. Shays's Rebellion
9. large-state plan
10. small-state plan
11. Three-fifths Compromise
12. antifederalists
13. *The Federalist*
14. president
15. Bill of Rights

II. D.

1. C
2. E
3. O
4. J
5. G
6. F
7. M
8. B
9. D
10. A
11. L
12. N
13. I
14. K
15. H

II. E.

4
2
1
5
3

Chapter 10

II. A.

1. True
2. False. It demonstrated the federalist concession to antifederalist fears that a powerful central government would trample individual rights.
3. True
4. True
5. True
6. False. Jefferson favored strict construction and Hamilton favored loose construction.
7. True
8. False. The Federalists opposed the French Revolution, especially in its radical phase.
9. False. They feared political parties as divisive and dangerous.
10. False. The British regularly violated American neutrality.
11. True
12. False. The public favored war, and Adams lost popularity by negotiating peace with France.
13. True
14. False. Jeffersonian Republicans believed that common people could be trusted.
15. False. Jeffersonian Republicans sympathized with France, and Hamiltonian Federalists with Britain.

II. B.

1. b
2. b
3. a
4. a
5. a
6. b
7. b
8. a
9. c
10. d

II. C.

1. Electoral College
2. vice president
3. secretary of the treasury
4. funding
5. assumption
6. the Bill of Rights
7. political parties
8. French Revolution
9. French-American Alliance
10. Neutrality Proclamation
11. Jay's Treaty
12. France
13. compact theory
14. nullification
15. Great Britain

II. D.

1. E
2. C
3. M
4. F
5. B
6. H
7. G
8. A
9. O
10. D
11. L
12. J
13. I
14. N
15. K

III. E.

4
5
1
2
3

Chapter 11

II. A.

1. False. Jefferson kept most Federalist officials in office and made only a few patronage appointments of Republicans.
2. True
3. True
4. False. They impeached Justice Samuel Chase, not Marshall.
5. False. It established judicial review, the right of the Supreme Court to declare legislation unconstitutional.

6. True
7. True
8. False. His deepest concern was that the purchase might be unconstitutional.
9. True
10. True
11. False. It hurt all sections.
12. True
13. False. The westerners took the lead on foreign policy issues.
14. True
15. False. They opposed the acquisition of more western territory, including Canada.

II. B.

1. c
2. b
3. a
4. b
5. c
6. a
7. a
8. d
9. c
10. a
11. b
12. b

II. C.

1. excise tax
2. pardon
3. midnight judges
4. *Marbury* v. *Madison*
5. judicial review
6. impeachment
7. navy
8. Santo Domingo
9. Oregon
10. Orders in Council
11. $15 million
12. *Chesapeake*
13. embargo
14. impressment
15. Non-Intercourse Act

II. D.

1. E

2. C
3. O
4. K
5. G
6. L
7. N
8. D
9. M
10. I
11. A
12. H
13. J
14. B
15. F

II. E.

4
1
2
3
5

Chapter 12

II. A.

1. False. The strategy was flawed from the start.
2. True
3. False. The British were strong and ready to invade the United States.
4. True
5. True
6. False. It favored only constitutional amendments.
7. True
8. False. They were vetoed by Republican presidents.
9. False. The Panic of 1819 interrupted prosperity with a severe economic downturn.
10. True
11. False. Missouri was admitted as a slave state in exchange for the admission of Maine as a free state.
12. True
13. True
14. False. It was Britain that initially proposed a joint declaration.
15. False. The Monroe Doctrine had no such effect on Latin America; it was mostly a paper document.

II. B.

1. c
2. c
3. d
4. c
5. c
6. c
7. a
8. b
9. c
10. d
11. c
12. b

II. C.

1. Lake Erie
2. "The Star-Spangled Banner"
3. The *U.S.S. Constitution*
4. Hartford Convention
5. North American Review
6. Bank of the United States
7. American System
8. internal improvements
9. Era of Good Feelings
10. Federalists
11. wildcat banks
12. Erie Canal
13. 36° 30′ (southern boundary of Missouri)
14. Oregon
15. Monroe Doctrine

II. D.

1. G
2. M
3. O
4. C
5. N
6. H
7. K
8. A
9. L
10. E
11. I
12. B
13. J
14. D
15. F

II. E.

2
6
8
3
7
5
4
1

Chapter 13

II. A.

1. True
2. False. Presidents were still chosen by the Electoral College, but the college was chosen by the people rather than by state legislatures.
3. False. National conventions replaced congressional caucuses.
4. True
5. False. Clay provoked the charges by accepting the position of secretary of state after backing Adams.
6. True
7. False. They favored it in 1816 but opposed it in 1828.
8. False. It was notable for mudslinging rather than issues.
9. True
10. False. Jackson distrusted the federal government as a bastion of privilege and believed only the states could act for the people.
11. True
12. True
13. False. Jackson had a weak cabinet and relied on his informal "Kitchen Cabinet" for political advice.
14. False. They both fed the growing spirit of sectionalism against nationalism.
15. True

II. B.

1. b
2. b
3. d
4. a
5. b
6. b

7. d
8. a
9. b
10. a

II. C.

1. New Democracy
2. property qualifications
3. congressional caucus
4. conventions
5. Anti-Masonic party
6. House of Representatives
7. corrupt bargain
8. secretary of state
9. Tariff of Abominations
10. slave rebellion
11. South Carolina Exposition
12. "Revolution of 1828"
13. spoils system
14. machines
15. "Kitchen Cabinet"

II. D.

1. F
2. K
3. C
4. J
5. D
6. G
7. E
8. O
9. A
10. M
11. L
12. N
13. H
14. B
15. I

II. E.

5
2
3
1
4

Chapter 14

II. A.

1. False. He ended it by political pressure, compromise, and the *threat* of military action.
2. False. None of the other southern states backed South Carolina.
3. True
4. True
5. False. He destroyed it by moving federal deposits to state banks; the independent treasury was not established until 1840.
6. True
7. False. The Seminoles and Black Hawk fought wars against the whites.
8. True
9. False. Jackson recognized Texas's independence but refused to support its entry into the Union.
10. True
11. False. Van Buren suffered the bad effects of the antibank battle, especially in the Panic of 1837.
12. False. Harrison did not come from a poor background; his family was wealthy.
13. True
14. False. The Whigs favored harmony and activism, the Democrats liberty and equality.
15. True

II. B.

1. b
2. a
3. d
4. c
5. c
6. b
7. a
8. d
9. b
10. c

II. C.

1. South Carolina
2. Tariff of 1833
3. force bill
4. Bank of the United States
5. Masons
6. evangelical Protestants

7. pet banks
8. Specie Circular
9. Sequoyah
10. Trail of Tears
11. Seminoles
12. Mexico
13. Whigs
14. independent treasury
15. log cabins and hard cider

II. D.

1. F
2. K
3. M
4. A
5. N
6. C
7. H
8. D
9. I
10. E
11. L
12. O
13. J
14. G
15. B

II. E.

2

4

5

1

3

Chapter 15

II. A.

1. True
2. False. It contributed to the rise of nativism and anti-Catholicism.
3. False. Most manufacturing was concentrated in New England.
4. True
5. False. Most early factory jobs involved long hours and low wages.
6. True
7. True

8. False. Most working women were unmarried.
9. True
10. False. The railroad met much early opposition, especially from canal interests.
11. True
12. True
13. False. The gap between rich and poor increased.
14. True
15. False. Only a small portion of the American economy depended on foreign trade.

II. B.

1. c
2. b
3. c
4. a
5. d
6. d
7. c
8. a
9. d
10. b

II. C.

1. Ireland
2. "ecological imperialism"
3. Forty-Eighters
4. Know-Nothings (nativists)
5. industrial revolution
6. cotton gin
7. limited liability
8. telegraph
9. women and children
10. labor unions
11. mechanical reaper
12. National Road (Cumberland Road)
13. steamboat
14. Erie Canal
15. clipper ships

II. D.

1. F
2. J
3. C
4. G
5. D
6. K

7. A
8. H
9. E
10. I
11. B

II. E.

4
1
5
3
2

Chapter 16

II. A.

1. True
2. False. They tended to increase sectional, denominational, and class division.
3. True
4. True
5. False. Most of higher education remained in ex-
   clusively male hands.
6. True
7. False. The temperance movement first relied on
   voluntary abstention, and only later turned to
   legal prohibition.
8. True
9. True
10. True
11. False. It came in the aftermath of the War of 1812.
12. True
13. False. Emerson emphasized self-improvement and
    scholarship; Thoreau emphasized simple living
    and nonviolence.
14. True
15. False. Most came from New England.

II. B.

1. c
2. d
3. b
4. c
5. a
6. c
7. a
8. b

9. c
10. a

II. C.

1. Deism
2. Second Great Awakening
3. Methodists, Baptists
4. Mormons
5. Seneca Falls Convention
6. New Harmony
7. Brook Farm
8. Monticello
9. Knickerbocker group
10. transcendentalism
11. civil disobedience
12. *Leaves of Grass*
13. *The Scarlet Letter*
14. *Moby Dick*
15. "Father of American History"

II. D.

1. J
2. C
3. L
4. O
5. K
6. D
7. G
8. A
9. F
10. M
11. N
12. H
13. B
14. I
15. E

II. E.

3
4
5
1
2

Chapter 17

II. A.

1. True
2. True
3. False. It was economically inefficient and agriculturally destructive of the soil.
4. False. Most slaveowners owned fewer than ten slaves.
5. True
6. True
7. True
8. False. Free blacks had an extremely vulnerable status and were generally poor.
9. True
10. False. The black family under slavery was generally strong, and most slave children were raised in two-parent homes.
11. True
12. False. Abolitionists were very unpopular in the North.
13. True
14. True
15. True

II. B.

1. d
2. b
3. c
4. c
5. b
6. a
7. c
8. d
9. c
10. a

II. C.

1. cotton kingdom
2. lords of the loom
3. "poor white trash"
4. free blacks
5. *American Slavery As It Is*
6. black belt
7. American Colonization Society
8. Lane Rebels
9. *The Liberator*
10. American Anti-Slavery Society
11. gag resolution
12. free-soilers

II. D.

1. H
2. F
3. B
4. L
5. O
6. A
7. C
8. E
9. N
10. D
11. I
12. M
13. G
14. J
15. K

II. E.

2
4
3
1
5

Chapter 18

II. A.

1. False. Tyler turned away from the Whig policies of Clay and Webster.
2. False. British-American hostility remained strong.
3. True
4. True
5. True
6. True
7. True
8. True
9. True
10. False. It was a dispute over the southern boundary of Texas.
11. True
12. True
13. False. It gave the United States large territorial gains.

14. True
15. False. It forced the slavery controversy to the center of national politics.

II. B.

1. b
2. c
3. c
4. d
5. a
6. c
7. b
8. d
9. c
10. b

II. C.

1. Tippecanoe
2. Maine
3. Britain
4. "Conscience Whigs"
5. joint resolution
6. 54° 40′
7. Oregon Trail
8. Manifest Destiny
9. Liberty party
10. 49° (49th parallel)
11. California
12. Nueces River
13. spot resolutions
14. Treaty of Guadalupe Hidalgo
15. Wilmot Proviso

II. D.

1. O
2. C
3. H
4. E
5. J
6. N
7. M
8. G
9. A
10. F
11. K
12. B
13. I

14. D
15. L

II. E.

3
1
5
4
2

Chapter 19

II. A.

1. True
2. False. The Free Soil party's primary goal was to stop the spread of slavery.
3. False. California was admitted as a free state in 1850.
4. True
5. False. Calhoun defended sectional (southern) interests and opposed compromise.
6. False. California was admitted as a free state. New Mexico and Utah were organized as territories left open to popular sovereignty concerning slavery.
7. True
8. False. The North was the winner.
9. True
10. True
11. False. It sharpened the debate over whether to build the railroad across the northern or southern route.
12. True
13. False. The southerners voted in favor of the plan and pushed it through Congress.
14. True
15. True

II. B.

1. c
2. c
3. a
4. c
5. b
6. a
7. c
8. a

9. c
10. c

II. C.

1. fire-eaters
2. popular sovereignty
3. Mason-Dixon line
4. Underground Railroad
5. higher law
6. Fugitive Slave Law
7. Free Soil party
8. Compromise of 1850
9. Whigs
10. Nicaragua
11. Ostend Manifesto
12. Gadsden Purchase
13. Missouri Compromise
14. Democratic party
15. Republican party

II. D.

1. B
2. H
3. O
4. J
5. D
6. N
7. L
8. M
9. C
10. G
11. F
12. A
13. 1
14. K
15. E

II. E.

3
1
2
5
4

Chapter 20

II. A.

1. True
2. False. Few proslavery people brought slaves with them to Kansas.
3. True
4. False. Douglas's opposition to the Lecompton Constitution divided the Democrats.
5. True
6. True
7. False. The Dred Scott decision held that slavery could not be prohibited in a territory because slaves were property protected by the Constitution.
8. True
9. False. Douglas adhered to popular sovereignty despite Lincoln's criticism.
10. True
11. False. It was southern delegates who walked out when northern Democrats nominated Douglas.
12. True
13. False. Lincoln obtained a minority of the popular vote but a majority of the Electoral College.
14. True
15. False. Lincoln rejected the Crittenden Compromise.

II. B.

1. a
2. d
3. d
4. c
5. c
6. a
7. b
8. b
9. a
10. b

II. C.

1. *Uncle Tom's Cabin*
2. *The Impending Crisis of the South*
3. Beecher's Bibles
4. "Bleeding Kansas"
5. Lecompton Constitution
6. Know-Nothing party

7. Dred Scott case
8. Panic of 1857
9. Lincoln-Douglas debates
10. Constitutional Union party
11. South Carolina
12. Confederate States of America
13. Crittenden Compromise
14. election of 1860
15. "lame duck" period

II. D.

1. E
2. G
3. O
4. F
5. N
6. K
7. A
8. J
9. C
10. L
11. B
12. H
13. M
14. I
15. D

II. E.

3
2
4
5
1
6

Chapter 21

II. A.

1. False. Four more states seceded after his inauguration.
2. True
3. True
4. False. The South had superior military leadership, while the North struggled to find commanders.
5. True
6. True
7. True

8. False. The British permitted the *Alabama* to leave their ports.
9. True
10. True
11. False. The Civil War draft was unfair to poor citizens, who could not afford substitutes.
12. True
13. True
14. False
15. True

II. B.

1. d
2. b
3. a
4. c
5. b
6. b
7. c
8. b
9. a
10. b

II. C.

1. border states
2. naval blockade
3. *Trent*
4. *Alabama*
5. Laird rams
6. draft
7. "bounty jumpers"
8. greenbacks
9. National Banking System
10. "shoddy millionaires"

II. D.

1. F
2. A
3. G
4. B
5. I
6. E
7. C
8. D
9. J
10. H

II. E.

4
5
1
2
3

Chapter 22

II. A.

1. False. Bull Run was an initial battle, not the turning point of the war.
2. True
3. False. The Union first succeeded in the West.
4. True
5. False. The turn to a war against slavery cost Lincoln popularity.
6. False. Black soldiers were militarily effective.
7. True
8. True
9. True
10. True
11. True
12. True
13. True
14. True
15. False. The war settled all those issues.

II. B.

1. b
2. a
3. d
4. b
5. a
6. c
7. a
8. a
9. b
10. d

II. C.

1. First Battle of Bull Run (Bull Run OK)
2. Peninsula campaign
3. Battle of Antietam
4. Emancipation Proclamation
5. "Unconditional Surrender"
6. Vicksburg

7. Gettysburg
8. Fort Pillow
9. Copperheads
10. War Democrats
11. Atlanta
12. Union party
13. Ford's Theater
14. Appomattox Court House
15. "The Lost Cause"

II. D.

1. O
2. N
3. F
4. H
5. A
6. B
7. K
8. E
9. D
10. C
11. M
12. I
13. G
14. L
15. J

II. E.

3
1
2
5
4

Chapter 23

II. A.

1. True
2. False. White southerners strongly rejected northern political domination.
3. True
4. False. Its greatest success was in education.
5. True
6. False. The conflict began while Lincoln was still president.
7. True
8. False. It weakened the moderates and strengthened the radicals.

9. True
10. False. Redistribution of land was opposed by moderates and never became part of Reconstruction policy.
11. False. Blacks controlled only one house of one state legislature—South Carolina.
12. True
13. False. The Klan did succeed in intimidating black voters.
14. True
15. False. Reconstruction failed to heal either racial or sectional bitterness.

II. B.

1. c
2. c
3. b
4. b
5. c
6. a
7. c
8. b
9. b
10. d

II. C.

1. freedmen
2. Freedmen's Bureau
3. 10 percent plan
4. Wade-Davis Bill
5. Thirteenth Amendment
6. Black Codes
7. Fourteenth Amendment
8. moderates
9. radicals
10. Joint Committee (on Reconstruction)
11. *Ex parte Milligan*
12. scalawags
13. carpetbaggers
14. the church
15. Alaska

II. D.

1. H
2. K
3. C
4. M

5. B
6. J
7. O
8. I
9. F
10. G
11. E
12. A
13. L
14. N
15. D

II. E.

4
1
5
3
2

Chapter 24

II. A.

1. False. Grant's lack of political experience made him an unsuccessful president.
2. True
3. False. The political mistakes of the Liberal Republicans caused them to fail.
4. True
5. False. The parties agreed on national issues; their disagreements were at the local level.
6. True
7. False. The Republicans got the presidency and the Democrats received other political and economic concessions.
8. True
9. True
10. False. Arthur had previously supported the patronage system and opposed civil service.
11. True
12. False. The campaign was based on personal mudslinging rather than issues.
13. True
14. True
15. False. The federal government provided no aid to farmers and workers.

II. B.

1. c
2. b
3. c
4. a
5. d
6. c
7. a
8. d
9. b
10. c
11. b
12. d
13. b
14. a
15. c

II. C.

1. bloody shirt
2. Crédit Mobilier
3. Liberal Republican
4. silver
5. Greenback Labor party
6. "Gilded Age"
7. Grand Army of the Republic
8. Stalwarts
9. Half-Breeds
10. Compromise of 1877
11. Chinese
12. civil service
13. grandfather clause
14. *Plessy* v. *Ferguson*
15. Populists

II. D.

1. D
2. B
3. A
4. N
5. J
6. H
7. I
8. K
9. O
10. C
11. G
12. E

13. L
14. F
15. M

II. E.

4
1
5
3
2

Chapter 25

II. A.

1. False. The railroads received subsidies and land grants to build the rail lines.
2. True
3. True
4. False. Railroads were often unfair and corrupt in their dealings with shippers, the government, and the public.
5. True
6. False. The description applies to Carnegie's technique of "vertical integration." Rockefeller's "horizontal integration" meant consolidating with competitors in the same market.
7. True
8. True
9. False. The South remained poor and dependent, despite the "New South."
10. True
11. False. Industrialization gave the wage earner less control and status.
12. False. The public did not generally sympathize with unions.
13. True
14. True
15. True

II. B.

1. b
2. d
3. b
4. d
5. c
6. c
7. b

8. a
9. c
10. b

II. C.

1. land grants
2. Union Pacific Railroad
3. Central Pacific Railroad
4. Great Northern Railroad
5. stock watering
6. *Wabash* case
7. Interstate Commerce Commission
8. telephone
9. Standard Oil Company
10. United States Steel Corporation
11. "New South"
12. National Labor Union
13. Knights of Labor
14. craft unions
15. American Federation of Labor (or A.F. of L.)

II. D.

1. J
2. H
3. M
4. G
5. F
6. 0
7. A
8. 1
9. E
10. B
11. D
12. L
13. N
14. C
15. K

II. E.

5
4
3
2
1

Chapter 26

II. A.

1. True
2. False. They came from southern and eastern Europe.
3. False. Most were originally peasants driven from the countryside.
4. True
5. True
6. True
7. False. Darwinian science weakened the churches and religious belief.
8. False. Secondary education was increasingly carried out in public schools.
9. False. Washington did not advocate social equality.
10. True
11. True
12. False. They favored social realism in their fiction.
13. False. They disagreed sharply over sexual morality and the role of women.
14. True
15. True

II. B.

1. c
2. c
3. a
4. b
5. d
6. d
7. d
8. b
9. a
10. d

II. C.

1. dumbbell tenement
2. New Immigrants
3. birds of passage
4. social gospel
5. Hull House
6. social work
7. American Protective Association
8. Roman Catholicism
9. Christian Science
10. National Association for the Advancement of Colored People (or NAACP)

11. *Progress and Poverty*
12. Comstock Law
13. *Women and Economics*
14. National American Women's Suffrage Association (or NAWSA)
15. Women's Christian Temperance Union (or WCTU)

II. D.

1. M
2. E
3. J
4. N
5. D
6. F
7. L
8. G
9. A
10. O
11. B
12. H
13. K
14. I
15. C

II. E.

4
2
3
5
I

Chapter 27

II. A.

1. True
2. False. The Indians were defeated only slowly and with difficulty.
3. True
4. False. Humanitarian reformers did not respect the Indians' culture and tried to destroy their tribal way of life.
5. True
6. True
7. False. More families acquired land from the states and private owners than from the federal government under the Homestead Act.
8. True

9. True
10. True
11. False. The greatest problem was depression of prices they received for their products.
12. True
13. False. McKinley far outspent Bryan.
14. False. It marked the beginning of a Republican era.
15. True

II. B.

1. d
2. b
3. d
4. a
5. c
6. d
7. c
8. a
9. b
10. c
11. b
12. a
13. a
14. b
15. c

II. C.

1. Sioux
2. Apache
3. reservations
4. Ghost Dance
5. Dawes Severalty Act
6. Homestead Act
7. Oklahoma
8. safety valve
9. Grange
10. Greenback Labor party
11. Coxey's Army
12. Pullman strike
13. income tax
14. Coin's Financial School
15. Cross of Gold speech

II. D.

1. H
2. J
3. E
4. B

5. G

6. 1

7. F

8. K

9. L

10. A

11. N

12. D

13. C

14. M

15. O

II. E.

3

7

2

1

4

6

5

Chapter 28

II. A.

1. True

2. False. He argued that control of the sea was the key to history.

3. True

4. True

5. False. The Hearst press promoted war with Spain.

6. True

7. True

8. True

9. False. Americans were sharply divided over the Philippines.

10. False. The Court ruled that these constitutional rights did not apply in the colonies.

11. True

12. False. The Open Door notes called for free trade and no colonial acquisitions in China.

13. True

14. True

15. True

II. B.

1. b

2. d

3. a

4. c

5. b

6. b

7. d

8. c

9. a

10. d

11. c

12. c

13. b

14. d

15. b

II. C.

1. Monroe Doctrine

2. Pearl Harbor

3. yellow press or yellow journalism

4. *Maine*

5. Teller Amendment

6. Manila Bay

7. Rough Riders

8. Puerto Rico

9. Anti-Imperialist League

10. insular cases

11. Open Door notes

12. Boxer Rebellion

13. "big stick"

14. Hay-Bunau-Varilla Treaty

15. Roosevelt corollary

II. D.

1. F

2. D

3. N

4. C

5. H

6. L

7. G

8. E

9. B

10. I

11. O

12. K

13. M

14. A

15. J

II. E.

2
3
9
5
6
10
8
1
7
4

Chapter 29

II. A.

1. False. Progressives favored federal government involvement in the economy and society.
2. True
3. False. The Progressives arose mostly from the middle class.
4. True
5. False. He threatened the owners with federal intervention, saying he would seize their mines.
6. True
7. False. He believed that there were "good trusts" and "bad trusts," and that only the bad trusts should be broken up.
8. False. It was intended to focus attention on the plight of the meat-packing workers.
9. True
10. True
11. True
12. False. Taft's policies caused greater division among Republicans.
13. False. Taft actually broke more trusts than Roosevelt; their anger was over Taft's tariff and conservation policies.
14. True
15. True

II. B.

1. c
2. a
3. c
4. d
5. b
6. c
7. d

8. a
9. c
10. c

II. C.

1. progressivism
2. muckrakers
3. initiative
4. recall
5. Square Deal
6. Hepburn Act
7. Northern Securities Company
8. *The Jungle*
9. Roosevelt panic
10. dollar diplomacy
11. Standard Oil Company
12. New Nationalism

II. D.

1. E
2. I
3. F
4. K
5. D
6. C
7. H
8. J
9. B
10. A
11. L
12. G

II. E.

5
1
4
2
3

Chapter 30

II. A.

1. True
2. False. Wilson's New Freedom favored small enterprise and antitrust activities; Roosevelt's New Nationalism favored federal regulation and social activism.
3. True

4. True
5. False. Wilson's policies were unfavorable to blacks.
6. True
7. False. Wilson sent troops to Haiti and Santo Domingo.
8. True
9. True
10. False. It was sent in response to Villa's raids into New Mexico and the killing of U.S. citizens.
11. False. Most Americans sympathized with Britain from the beginning.
12. True
13. False. The East was ready to go to war; the Midwest and West favored attempts at negotiation.
14. True
15. True

II. B.

1. c
2. b
3. c
4. c
5. b
6. a
7. d
8. c
9. d
10. d

II. C.

1. bull moose
2. New Freedom
3. Underwood Tariff
4. Federal Reserve Board
5. Federal Trade Commission
6. Clayton Anti-Trust Act
7. Federal Farm Loan Act
8. Haiti and Dominican Republic
9. ABC Powers
10. Central Powers
11. Allies
12. submarine
13. *Lusitania*
14. *Sussex* pledge
15. California

II. D.

1. H
2. K
3. L
4. I
5. D
6. O
7. M
8. C
9. B
10. G
11. F
12. A
13. N
14. J
15. E

II. E.

5
2
1
4
3

Chapter 31

II. A.

1. False. Germany responded by resuming unrestricted submarine warfare.
2. True
3. True
4. True
5. False. The primary targets were antiwar Socialists and members of the Industrial Workers of the World (IWW).
6. True
7. False. Hoover achieved those goals by *voluntary* methods.
8. False. There was no provision for hiring substitutes, as in the Civil War draft.
9. True
10. False. America supplied relatively small amounts of weapons and supplies.
11. True
12. False. His poor handling of domestic politics weakened his hand in Paris.
13. True

14. True
15. False. Cox supported the League, while Harding tried to evade the issue.

II. B.

1. b
2. c
3. c
4. a
5. a
6. c
7. c
8. b
9. d
10. b

II. C.

1. "peace without victory"
2. Zimmerman note
3. Fourteen Points
4. Committee on Public Information
5. Industrial Workers of the World (IWW)
6. War Industries Board
7. Nineteenth Amendment
8. Liberty Loans
9. Big Four
10. League of Nations
11. Treaty of Versailles
12. Foreign Relations Committee
13. irreconcilables
14. Lodge reservations
15. "solemn referendum"

II. D.

1. E
2. O
3. N
4. H
5. K
6. I
7. C
8. G
9. A
10. M
11. D
12. B
13. J

14. L
15. F

II. E.

2
5
1
3
4

Chapter 32

II. A.

1. False. It focused on alleged communist sub-version *inside* the United States.
2. True
3. False. It was strongest in the Midwest and South.
4. True
5. True
6. False. Scopes was found guilty, and the law was upheld.
7. True
8. True
9. True
10. False. They emphasized entertainment and com-mercial advertising from the beginning.
11. False. The decade saw further changes of sexual behavior, especially among women.
12. True
13. False. They attacked small-town values and reflected the more critical values of the cities.
14. True
15. False. He increased the burden on the middle class but reduced the burden on the wealthy.

II. B.

1. c
2. b
3. a
4. c
5. d
6. a
7. b
8. d
9. b
10. d

II. C.

1. red scare
2. Ku Klux Klan
3. Immigration Act of 1924
4. Eighteenth Amendment
5. Bible Belt
6. Scopes trial ("monkey trial")
7. advertising
8. Model T
9. airplane
10. radio
11. United Negro Improvement Association (UNIA)
12. birth control
13. jazz
14. *American Mercury*
15. stock market

II. D.

1. E
2. C
3. G
4. L
5. H
6. D
7. J
8. 0
9. M
10. A
11. K
12. F
13. N
14. B
15. 1

II. E.

4
1
5
2
3

Chapter 33

II. A.

1. False. The corruption involved bribes and theft within the U.S. government.

2. False. The antitrust laws were generally not enforced.
3. False. There were no U.S. forces in Europe.
4. True
5. True
6. True
7. False. The main source of La Follette's support was farmers.
8. True
9. True
10. True
11. False. The Hawley-Smoot Tariff represented a policy of economic isolationism and helped undercut international trade.
12. True
13. True
14. False. He modified his policies somewhat and provided some federal funds for relief and recovery.
15. True

II. B.

1. d
2. a
3. c
4. d
5. b
6. b
7. a
8. d
9. a
10. c

II. C.

1. Ohio gang
2. *Adkins* v. *Children's Hospital*
3. American Legion
4. Five-Power Naval Treaty
5. Kellogg-Briand Pact
6. Teapot Dome
7. McNary-Haugen bill
8. Dawes Plan
9. Hoovercrats
10. Hawley-Smoot Tariff
11. Black Tuesday
12. Hoovervilles
13. Reconstruction Finance Corporation

14. Bonus Army (Bonus Expeditionary Force)
15. Manchuria

II. D.

1. I
2. G
3. H
4. M
5. E
6. D
7. F
8. O
9. L
10. K
11. C
12. A
13. B
14. N
15. J

II. E.

5
2
1
4
3

Chapter 34

II. A.

1. True
2. False. The economy was turning downward.
3. True
4. False. FDR took the United States off the gold standard and devalued the dollar.
5. True
6. True
7. False. It was excessive farm production and falling prices.
8. True
9. False. It was also designed to provide jobs, electricity, and low-income housing to residents of the area.
10. True
11. True
12. False. The Supreme Court "switched" and began approving New Deal measures.

13. True
14. True
15. False. Unemployment remained high despite the New Deal.

II. B.

1. c
2. b
3. d
4. a
5. d
6. c
7. b
8. d
9. a
10. c

II. C.

1. New Deal
2. Brain Trust
3. Hundred Days
4. Civilian Conservation Corps
5. Works Progress Administration (WPA)
6. blue eagle
7. Agricultural Adjustment Administration (AAA)
8. Dust Bowl
9. Tennessee Valley Authority (TVA)
10. Social Security
11. Committee for Industrial Organization (CIO)
12. Securities and Exchange Commission (SEC)
13. American Liberty League
14. "Roosevelt depression"
15. Hatch Act

II. D.

1. G
2. E
3. L
4. J
5. B
6. F
7. N
8. K
9. C
10. O
11. H
12. A

13. I
14. M
15. D

II. E.

2
1
4
5
3

Chapter 35

II. A.

1. False. It showed that he put domestic recovery ahead of establishing a stable international economic order.
2. True
3. True
4. True
5. False. The United States adhered to its neutrality laws and refused to help the Loyalist government.
6. False. The United States reacted mildly to the Japanese attack.
7. True
8. True
9. False. It strengthened the movement to give aid to Britain.
10. True
11. False. Willkie agreed with Roosevelt's pro-British stance and did not attack him on foreign policy.
12. True
13. False. It was an agreement between Britain and the United States.
14. True
15. False. The point of conflict was Japan's refusal to withdraw from China.

II. B.

1. a
2. b
3. d
4. b
5. d
6. a
7. d
8. b

9. c
10. c

II. C.

1. London Conference
2. Good Neighbor policy
3. reciprocal trade agreements
4. Neutrality Acts
5. Spanish Civil War
6. "Quarantine Speech"
7. *Panay*
8. Munich
9. Committee to Defend America by Aiding the Allies
10. America First
11. lend-lease
12. Soviet Union
13. Atlantic Charter
14. *Reuben James*
15. Pearl Harbor

II. D.

1. L
2. E
3. K
4. F
5. O
6. C
7. J
8. N
9. G
10. B
11. D
12. A
13. M
14. I
15. H

II. E.

1
2
5
4
3

Chapter 36

II. A.

1. False. The decision was to fight Hitler first and then Japan.
2. False. Only a minority of U.S. women engaged in war work.
3. True
4. True
5. True
6. True
7. False. Americans enjoyed economic prosperity during World War 11.
8. False. The Battles of Coral Sea and Midway enabled the United States to block Japanese domination of the Pacific sea- lanes.
9. False. The plan was to "island-hop" directly toward Japan.
10. False. The Soviet Union bore the heaviest burden of the ground fighting.
11. True
12. True
13. False. It was conservative Democrats who dumped Wallace for Truman.
14. False. The U.S. naval commander was Chester Nimitz.
15. True

II. B.

1. c
2. b
3. a
4. a
5. d
6. d
7. c
8. c
9. d
10. a

II. C.

1. Japanese-Americans
2. War Production Board
3. WAACS and WAVES
4. *braceros*
5. "Rosie the Riveter"
6. Fair Employment Practices Commission (FEPC)
7. Philippines
8. Battle of Midway
9. New Guinea
10. Casablanca
11. Teheran
12. D-Day
13. Battle of the Bulge
14. Iwo Jima and Okinawa
15. atomic bomb

II. D.

1. F
2. I
3. N
4. E
5. O
6. G
7. J
8. A
9. K
10. D
11. M
12. C
13. H
14. L
15. B

II. E.

3
4
1
2

Chapter 37

II. A.

1. False. There was widespread concern that the depression would return.
2. True
3. False. Most new jobs came in the white-collar and service sectors.
4. False. The Sunbelt relied more than the North on federal spending.
5. True
6. True
7. False. The United States and the Soviet Union had allied to defeat Germany, not out of common ideals.

8. False. The Soviets wanted to break Germany apart.
9. True
10. False. The threat was to Greece and Turkey.
11. False. It was developed in response to the economic weakness and threat of domestic communism in Western Europe.
12. True
13. True
14. False. Truman defeated Dewey despite splits in his own Democratic party.
15. True

II. B.

1. a
2. d
3. b
4. d
5. c
6. b
7. d
8. a
9. c
10. d

II. C.

1. GI Bill of Rights
2. productivity
3. baby boom
4. Sunbelt
5. Yalta
6. Cold War
7. World Bank and International Monetary Fund (IMF)
8. United Nations
9. iron curtain
10. Marshall Plan
11. North Atlantic Treaty Organization (NATO)
12. Nationalists
13. hydrogen bomb
14. House Un-American Activities Committee (HUAC)
15. 38th parallel

II. D.

1. B
2. A

3. K
4. M
5. D
6. O
7. L
8. E
9. J
10. H
11. C
12. I
13. G
14. N
15. F

II. E.

2
4
1
3
5

Chapter 38

II. A.

1. False. He left most New Deal legislation in place.
2. True
3. True
4. False. It held that segregation was inherently unequal, overturning the old "separate but equal" doctrine of *Plessy* v. *Ferguson*.
5. False. Eisenhower refrained from using his personal or presidential influence on behalf of civil rights.
6. True
7. False. The roots of the civil rights movement were among southern blacks.
8. True
9. False. Eisenhower refused to send U.S. troops to aid the French in Vietnam.
10. True
11. True
12. True
13. True
14. False
15. True

II. B.

1. d
2. d
3. c
4. a
5. b
6. d
7. b
8. d
9. c
10. c

II. C.

1. McCarthyism
2. *Brown* v. *Board of Education*
3. Dien Bien Phu
4. SEATO
5. Suez Canal
6. *Sputnik*
7. Eisenhower Doctrine
8. Cuba
9. Roman Catholicism
10. *The Feminine Mystique*

II. D.

1. G
2. K
3. O
4. F
5. L
6. B
7. M
8. A
9. H
10. N
11. D
12. J
13. C
14. E
15. I

II. E.

3
5
1
4
2

Chapter 39

II. A.

1. True
2. False. It was applied mostly to struggles with communism in the underdeveloped world—Asia and Latin America.
3. False. The coup brought military dictatorships and political instability.
4. True
5. True
6. False. The civil rights movement encouraged Kennedy to become more outspoken.
7. False. Johnson won a landslide victory.
8. False. The Gulf of Tonkin Resolution gave the president a blank check for the whole war in Vietnam.
9. False. The Great Society authorized deficit spending and gave more power to the federal government.
10. True
11. False. The riots showed that race was a northern as well as a southern problem.
12. True
13. False. Antiwar activists opposed Johnson despite his civil rights stand.
14. True
15. True

II. B.

1. c
2. a
3. c
4. a
5. b
6. d
7. c
8. b
9. b
10. d

II. C.

1. Peace Corps
2. Berlin Wall
3. Special Forces or Green Berets
4. Alliance for Progress
5. Bay of Pigs

6. Cuban missile crisis

7. sit-in

8. Great Society

9. Gulf of Tonkin Resolution

10. Voting Rights Act of 1965

11. Black Power

12. Viet Cong

13. Tet

14. Chicago

15. "counterculture"

II. D.

1. J
2. G
3. M
4. E
5. B
6. L
7. H
8. O
9. N
10. A
11. F
12. C
13. D
14. K
15. I

II. E.

3
1
2
4
5

Chapter 40

II. A.

1. False. It sought to transfer the burden of the war to the South Vietnamese while Americans withdrew.

2. True

3. True

4. False. Relations with the Soviet Union improved at the same time.

5. True

6. False. The basic issue was Vietnam.

7. True

8. True

9. False. Congress strongly opposed the bombing.

10. True

11. False. The public largely welcomed Nixon's resignation.

12. False. The attack on the *Mayaguez* came after the communist victory in Vietnam, which the United States did not attempt to stop.

13. False. Carter's "outsider" status made it difficult for him to get his programs through Congress.

14. False. The Camp David agreement brought peace between Egypt and Israel but did nothing to alleviate American energy and economic difficulties.

15. True

II. B.

1. d
2. c
3. d
4. a
5. c
6. c
7. b
8. d
9. c
10. d

II. C.

1. Vietnamization

2. Kent State

3. Pentagon Papers

4. ABM (Anti-Ballistic Missile) treaty

5. southern strategy

6. Watergate

7. Saturday Night Massacre

8. War Powers Act

9. oil embargo

10. pardon

11. Helsinki accords

12. détente

13. SALT II

14. OPEC (Organization of Petroleum Exporting Countries)

15. SALT I and SALT II

II. D.

1. L

2. D
3. H
4. K
5. E
6. C
7. I
8. N
9. B
10. M
11. J
12. F
13. O
14. A
15. G

II. E.

6
4
2
I
3
5

Chapter 41

II. A.

1. True
2. True
3. False. Reagan carried out his conservative campaign promises.
4. False. Reagan successfully passed his economic program.
5. False. It was successful in bringing down inflation and creating economic growth but had difficulty lowering interest rates and balancing the budget.
6. True
7. True
8. False. It attempted to eliminate the balance of terror by building a space-based defense against nuclear weapons.
9. True
10. True
11. True
12. True
13. False. The Thomas nomination increased national conflict over "social issues."

14. False. Clinton emphasized the economy and domestic policy.
15. True

II. B.

1. c
2. d
3. a
4. c
5. b
6. a
7. c
8. a
9. c
10. b
11. c
12. b
13. c
14. a
15. d

II. C.

1. "new right"
2. supply-side
3. boll weevils
4. Solidarity
5. Sandinistas
6. "Star Wars"
7. *glasnost*
8. *perestroika*
9. INF
10. Iran-contra affair
11. Berlin Wall
12. Kuwait
13. Branch Davidians
14. Impeachment
15. Contract with America

II. D.

1. O
2. D
3. M
4. A
5. F
6. E
7. C
8. L

9. G
10. B
11. N
12. J
13. H
14. K
15. I

II. E.

6
2
3
1
5
4

Chapter 42

II. A.

1. True
2. False. The gap in wealth increased.
3. True
4. False. Federal spending on senior citizens continued to rise.
5. True
6. True
7. True
8. True
9. False. It was designed to move welfare recipients
   into the work force.
10. False. It was dominated by new racial, ethnic, and
    gender voices.

II. B.

1. c
2. c
3. d
4. b
5. b
6. a
7. d
8. d
9. b
10. d

II. C.

1. Microsoft Corporation
2. Social Security
3. Mexican-Americans
4. United Farm Workers
5. Los Angeles
6. Proposition 209
7. Pacific Northwest
8. abstract expressionism

II. D.

1. H
2. I
3. B
4. A
5. C
6. J
7. D
8. G
9. F
10. E